French
phrase book

Berlitz Publishing Company, Inc.
Princeton   Mexico City   London   Eschborn   Singapore

HOW TO USE THIS BOOK

We suggest that you start with the Pronunciation section (pp. 6-9), then turn to Basic Expressions (pp. 10-19). These sections give you some useful words, phrases, and short dialogs and help you get used to pronouncing and using the language.

Consult the Contents pages (pp. 2-5) for the section you need. In each chapter you'll find travel facts, hints, and useful information. Sample phrases are followed by translations and pronunciation.

Look for special YOU MAY HEAR and YOU MAY SEE boxes that highlight phrases that someone may say to you or signs you may see during your travels.

Read along with the dialog boxes (e.g. IN A CAFÉ) that present short, useful conversations. An audio recording of the dialogs in this book can be heard in the Cassette Pack and CD Pack versions.

If you want to know the meaning of a word, your fastest look-up is via the Dictionary section (pp. 168-214).

If you wish to learn about constructing sentences, check the Grammar in the Reference section (pp. 215-223).

Note the color margins are indexed to help you quickly locate the section you need.

If you have difficulty speaking and understanding the language, you can hand the phrase book to the French speaker to encourage pointing to the appropriate sentence.

Layout: Media Content Marketing, Inc.

ISBN 2-8315-7842-6
Printed in Spain
010/201 REV

TABLE OF CONTENTS

PRONUNCIATION

This section is designed to make you familiar with the sounds of French. You'll find the pronunciation of the French letters and sounds explained below, together with their "imitated" equivalents. Simply read the pronunciation as if it were English, noting any special rules below.

THE FRENCH LANGUAGE

Here are the countries where you can expect to hear French spoken (figures are approximate):

La France   France
French is spoken by the whole population (56 million). Other languages occasionally heard: Provençal (southeast France), Breton (Brittany), Alsacien (German dialect in Alsace and Lorraine), Corse (an Italian dialect in Corsica), and Catalan and Basque (along the border with Spain).

La Belgique   Belgium
French is one of the official languages; it is understood everywhere and has 3.5 million native speakers. Other languages: Flemish (4.5 million native speakers) with 1 million bilingual.

Le Luxembourg   Luxembourg
French is the official language. Other languages: German and occasionally Luxembourgian.

La Suisse   Switzerland
French is one of the national languages; native tongue of 20% of the population. Other languages: German in the north and east, Italian in the south, and the much rarer Romansh.

Le Canada   Canada
French is one of the official languages, together with English. 7 million speakers, mainly in Quebec.

L'Afrique   Africa
French is the official language (or one of them) in: Benin, Burkina Faso, Burundi, Cameroon, Central African Republic, Chad, Congo, Gabon, Guinea, Ivory Coast, Madagascar, Niger, Rwanda, Senegal, Togo and Zaïre. It is spoken to varying degrees, alongside native languages. Also heard in Algeria, Morocco and Tunisia.

Les Antilles françaises   French West Indies
Consisting of the Caribbean islands of Guadeloupe and Martinique. Other languages: French creole, English. French is also the official language in Haïti.

The French alphabet is the same as English, although the letter **w** appears only in foreign words. It also uses several accents: grave (`), acute (´), circumflex (^) and the cedilla (**ç** - only on the letter **c**).

Historical interaction between France and England has meant that many French words will be comprehensible to the English speaker.

But watch out for the "false friends" that don't mean what you might think: **la cave** (cellar, basement), **la conférence** (lecture), **la librairie** (bookstore), **le magasin** (store), **le médecin** (doctor), **la monnaie** (change/coins), **une prune** (plum), **un raisin** (grape), **sale** (dirty), etc.

CONSONANTS

Letter	Approximate pronunciation	Symbol	Example	Pronunciation
ch	like *sh* in *sh*ut	sh	**chercher**	shehrshay
ç	like *s* in *s*it	s	**ça**	sa
g	1)before **e, i, y,** like *s* in plea*s*ure	zh	**manger**	mangzhay
	2)before **a, o, u,** like *g* in *g*o	g	**garçon**	garsawng
gn	like *ni* in o*ni*on	ñ	**ligne**	leeñ
h	always silent		**homme**	om
j	like *s* in plea*s*ure	zh	**jamais**	zhamay
qu	like *k* in *k*ill	k	**qui**	kee
r	rolled in the back of the mouth, rather like gargling	r	**rouge**	roozh
w	usually like *v* in *v*oice	v	**wagon**	vagawng

VOWELS

a, à or â	between the *a* in h*a*t and the *a* in f*a*ther	a/ah	**mari**	maree
é or ez	like *a* in l*a*te	ay	**été**	aytay
è, ê, e	like *e* in g*e*t	e/eh	**même**	mem
e	sometimes like *er* in oth*er*	er	**je**	zher
i	like *ee* in m*ee*t	ee	**il**	eel
o	generally like *o* in h*o*t but	o/	**donner**	donnay
	sometimes like *oa* in s*oa*r	oa	**rose**	roaz
ô	like *oa* in s*oa*r	oa	**Rhône**	roan
u	like *ew* in d*ew*	ew	**cru**	krew

Letters **b, c, d, f, k, l, m, n, p, s, t, v, x** and **z** are pronounced as in English.

SOUNDS SPELLED WITH TWO OR MORE LETTERS

ai, ay,	can be pronounced	*ay*	**j'ai**	*zhay*	
aient, ais,	like *a* in late or		**vais**	*vay*	
ait, aî, ei	like *e* in g*e*t	*e/eh*	**chaîne**	*shen*	
			peine	*pen*	
(e)au	similar to *oa* in s*oa*r	*oa*	**chaud**	*shoa*	
eu, eû,	like *ur* in f*ur*, but with	*ur*	**peu**	*pur*	
œu	lips rounded, not spread				
euil, euille	like *uh* in h*uh*, but without pronouncing the *h* and with a *y* sound added	*uhy*	**feuille**	*fuhy*	
ail, aille	like *ie* in t*ie*	*ie*	**taille**	*tie*	
oi, oy	like *w* followed by the *a* in h*a*t	*wa*	**moi**	*mwa*	
ou, oû	like *o* in m*o*ve or *oo* in h*oo*t	*oo*	**nouveau**	*noovoa*	
ui	approximately like *wee* in betw*ee*n	*wee*	**traduire**	*tradweer*	

NASAL SOUNDS

French contains nasal vowels, which are transcribed with a vowel symbol plus *ng*. This *ng* should not be pronounced strongly but is included to show the nasal quality of the previous vowel. A nasal vowel is pronounced simultaneously through the mouth and the nose.

am, an	something like *arn* in t*arn*ish	*ahng*	**tante**	*tahngt*	
em, en	generally like the previous sound	*ahng*	**entrée**	*ahngtray*	
ien	sounds like *yan* in *yan*k	*yang*	**bien**	*byang*	
im, in, aim, ain, eim, ein	approximately like *ang* in r*ang*	*ang*	**instant**	*angstahng*	
om, on	approximately like *ong* in s*ong*	*awng*	**maison**	*mayzawng*	
um, un	approximately like *ang* in r*ang*	*ang*	**brun**	*brang*	

LIAISON

Normally, final consonants of words are not pronounced in French. However, when a word ending in a consonant is followed by one beginning with a vowel, they are often run together, and the consonant is pronounced as if it began the following word. Examples:

nous	*noo*
nous avons un enfant	*noo zavawng zang nahngfahng*
comment	*komahng*
comment allez-vous?	*komahng talay voo*

STRESS

All syllables in French are pronounced with more or less the same degree of stress (loudness). So stress has not been indicated in the phonetic transcription and each syllable should be pronounced with equal stress.

PRONUNCIATION OF THE FRENCH ALPHABET

A	*ah*	**J**	*zhee*	**S**	*ess*
B	*bay*	**K**	*kah*	**T**	*tay*
C	*say*	**L**	*el*	**U**	*ew*
D	*day*	**M**	*em*	**V**	*vay*
E	*er*	**N**	*en*	**W**	*dooblervay*
F	*ef*	**O**	*oa*	**X**	*eex*
G	*zhay*	**P**	*pay*	**Y**	*ee grek*
H	*ahsh*	**Q**	*kew*	**Z**	*zed*
I	*ee*	**R**	*ehr*		

BASIC EXPRESSIONS

GREETINGS/APOLOGIES

ESSENTIAL	
Yes.	**Oui.** *wee*
No.	**Non.** *nawng*
Okay.	**D'accord.** *dakor*
Very good.	**Très bien.** *treh byang*
Please.	**S'il vous plaît.** *seel voo pleh*
Thank you (very much.)	**Merci (beaucoup).** *mehrsee (boakoo)*
You're welcome.	**De rien.** *de reeang*

Hello!/Hi!	**Bonjour!/Salut!** *bawngzhoor/salew*
Good morning/afternoon.	**Bonjour.** *bawngzhoor*
Good evening.	**Bonsoir.** *bawngswar*
Good night.	**Bonne nuit.** *bon nwee*
Good-bye.	**Au revoir.** *oa rervwar*
Excuse me! *(getting attention)*	**Excusez-moi, (s'il vous plaît)!** *exkewzay mwa (seel voo pleh)*
Excuse me. *(may I get past?)*	**Excusez-moi!/Pardon!** *exkewzay mwa/pardawng*
Excuse me!/Sorry!	**Pardon!/Désolé(e)!** *pardawng/dayzolay*
It was an accident.	**Je ne l'ai pas fait exprès.** *zher ner lay pa feh expreh*
Don't mention it.	**Je vous en prie.** *zher voo zahng pree*
Never mind.	**Ça ne fait rien.** *sa ner feh ryang*

COMMUNICATION DIFFICULTIES

Do you speak English?	**Parlez-vous anglais?** *parlay voo ahnggleh*
Does anyone here speak English?	**Y a-t-il quelqu'un ici qui parle anglais?** *ee ateel kelkang eessee kee parl ahnggleh*
Could you speak more slowly?	**Pourriez-vous parler plus lentement?** *pooryay voo parlay plew lahngtmahng*
Could you repeat that?	**Pourriez-vous répéter ça?** *pooryay voo raypaytay sa*
Pardon?/What was that?	**Pardon?/Qu'avez-vous dit?** *pardawng/kavay voo dee*
Could you spell it?	**Pourriez-vous l'épeler?** *pooryay voo layplay*
Please write it down.	**Pourriez-vous l'écrire, s'il vous plaît?** *pooryay voo laykreer seel voo pleh*
Can you translate this for me?	**Pourriez-vous me traduire ça?** *pooryay voo mer tradweer sa*
What does this/that mean?	**Qu'est-ce que ça veut dire?** *kess ker sa vuh deer*
Please point to the phrase in the book.	**Pourriez-vous me montrer l'expression dans le livre?** *pooryay voo mer mawng tray lexpressyawng dahng ler leevr*
I (don't) understand.	**Je (ne) comprends (pas).** *zher ner kawngprahng pa*
Do you understand?	**(Est-ce que) vous comprenez?** *(ess ker) voo kawngprernay*

ON THE STREET

Bonjour! Ça va? *bawngzhoor sa va* *(Hi. How are you?)*
Très bien, merci. Et vous? *treh byang mehrsee eh voo*
(Fine., thanks. And you?)
Très bien, merci. *treh byang mehrsee (Fine . Thanks.)*

Where?

Where is it?	**Où est-ce?** *oo ess*
Where are you going?	**Où allez-vous?** *oo alay voo*
to the meeting place [point]	**au point de rendez-vous** *oa pwang der rahngday voo*
across the market	**en face du marché** *ahng fas dew marshay*
away from me	**loin de moi** *lwang der mwa*
downstairs	**en bas** *ahng ba*
from the U.S.	**des États-Unis** *day zayta zewnee*
here (to here)	**ici** *eessee*
in the car	**dans la voiture** *dahng la vwatewr*
in France	**en France** *ahng frahngs*
inside	**à l'intérieur** *a langtayryurr*
near the bank	**près de la banque** *preh der la bahngk*
next to the apples	**à côté des pommes** *a koatay day pom*
on the left/right	**à gauche/à droite** *a goash/a drwat*
there	**là-bas** *la ba*
to the hotel	**à l'hôtel** *a loatel*
toward Paris	**vers Paris** *ver paree*
outside the café	**devant le café** *devahng ler kafay*
up to the traffic light	**jusqu'aux feux** *zhewskoa fur*
upstairs	**en haut** *ahng oa*

When ...?

When does the museum open?	**Quand le musée est-il ouvert?** *kahng ler mewzay ehteel oovehr*
When does the train arrive?	**À quelle heure arrive le train?** *a kel urr areev ler trang*
after lunch	**après le déjeuner** *apreh ler dayzhurnay*
always	**toujours** *toozhoor*
around midnight	**vers minuit** *vehr meenwee*
at 7 o'clock	**à sept heures** *a set urr*
before Friday	**avant vendredi** *avahng vahngdrerdee*
by tomorrow	**pour demain** *poor dermang*
early	**tôt/de bonne heure** *toa/der bon urr*
every week	**chaque semaine** *shak sermayn*
for 2 hours	**pendant deux heures** *pahngdahng dur zurr*
from 9 a.m. to 6 p.m.	**de neuf heures à dix-huit heures** *der nurf urr a deezweet urr*
immediately	**tout de suite** *too der sweet*
in 20 minutes	**dans vingt minutes** *dahng vang meenewt*
never	**jamais** *zhameh*
not yet	**pas encore** *pa zahngkor*
now	**maintenant** *mangtnahng*
often	**souvent** *soovahng*
on March 8	**le huit mars** *ler wee mars*
on weekdays	**pendant la semaine** *pahngdahng la sermayn*
sometimes	**quelquefois** *kelkefwa*
soon	**bientôt** *byangtoa*
then	**alors/ensuite/puis** *alor/ahngsweet/pwee*
within 2 days	**en deux jours** *ahng dur zhoor*
10 minutes ago	**il y a dix minutes** *eel ee a dee meenewt*

What kind of …?

I'd like	**Je voudrais quelque chose de** …
something …	*zher voodrey kelker shoaz der*
It's …	**C'est** … *seh*
beautiful/ugly	**beau (belle)/laid(e)**
	boa (bel)/lay(d)
better/worse	**mieux/pire** *myur/peer*
big/small	**grand(e)/petit(e)** *grahng(d)/pertee(t)*
cheap/expensive	**bon marché/cher**
	bawng marshay/shehr
clean/dirty	**propre/sale** *propr/sal*
dark/light	**foncé/clair(e)** *fongsay/klehr*
delicious/revolting	**délicieux(-ieuse)/dégoûtant(e)**
	dayleesyur(z)/daygootahng(t)
easy/difficult	**facile/difficile** *fasseel/deefeesseel*
empty/full	**vide/plein** *veed/plang*
good/bad	**bon(ne)/mauvais(e)**
	bawng (bon)/moavay(z)
heavy/light	**lourd(e)/léger(-ère)**
	loor(d)/layzhay (layzhehr)
hot, warm/cold	**chaud(e)/froid(e)** *shoa(d)/frwa(d)*
modern/old-fashioned	**moderne/démodé(e)**
	modern/daymoday
narrow/wide	**étroit(e)/large** *aytrwa(t)/larzh*
old/new	**vieux (vieille)/neuf (neuve)**
	vyur (vyay)/nurf (nurv)
open/shut	**ouvert(e)/fermé(e)**
	oovehr(t)/fehrmay
pleasant, nice/unpleasant	**agréable, beau (belle)/désagréable**
	agrayabl, boa (bel)/dayzagrayabl
quick/slow	**rapide/lent(e)** *rapeed/lahng(t)*
quiet/noisy	**silencieux(-ieuse)/bruyant(e)**
	seelahngsyur(z)/brewyahng(t)

right/wrong	**juste/faux (fausse)** *zhewst/foa(ss)*
large/small	**grand(e)/petit(e)** *grahng(d)/pertee(t)*
vacant/occupied	**libre/occupé(e)** *leebr/okkewpay*
young/old	**jeune/vieux (vieille)** *zhurn/vyur (vyay)*

How much/many?

How much is that?	**C'est combien?** *seh kawnbyang*
How many are there?	**Combien y en a-t-il?** *kawnbyang ee ahng na teel*
1/2/3	**un/deux/trois** *ang/dur/trwa*
4/5	**quatre/cinq** *katr/sangk*
none	**aucun(e)** *oakang(-kewn)*
about 100 francs	**environ cent francs** *ahngveerawng sahng frahng*
a little	**un peu** *ang pur*
a lot of traffic	**beaucoup de circulation** *boakoo der seerkewlasyawng*
enough	**assez** *assay*
few/a few of them	**quelques/quelques-un(e)s** *kelker/kelker zung (zewn)*
more than that	**plus que ça** *plew ker sa*
less than that	**moins que ça** *mwang ker sa*
much more	**beaucoup plus** *boakoo plews*
nothing else	**rien d'autre** *ryang doatr*
too much	**trop** *tro*

Why?

Why is that?	**Pourquoi?** *poorkwa*
Why not?	**Pourquoi pas?** *poorkwa pa*
because of the weather	**à cause du temps** *a koaz dew tahng*
because I'm in a hurry	**parce que je suis pressé(e)** *pars ker zher swee pressay*
I don't know why.	**Je ne sais pas pourquoi.** *zher ner say pa poorkwa*

How?

How would you like to pay?	**Comment voulez-vous payer?** *kommahng voolay voo payay*
How are you getting here?	**Comment y allez-vous?** *kommahng ee alay voo*
by car	**en voiture** *ahng vwatewr*
by credit card	**avec une carte de crédit** *avek ewn kart der kraydee*
by chance	**par hasard** *pa razar*
equally	**également** *aygalmahng*
extremely	**extrêmement** *extremmahng*
on foot	**à pied** *a pyay*
quickly	**vite/rapidement** *veet/rapeedmahng*
slowly	**lentement** *lahngtmahng*
too fast	**trop vite** *tro veet*
totally	**totalement** *totalmahng*
very	**très** *treh*
with a friend	**avec un(e) ami(e)** *avek ang (ew) namee*
without a passport	**sans passeport** *sahng passpor*

Is it …?/Are there …?

Is it …?	**(Est-ce que) c'est …?** *(ess ker) seh*
Is it free?	**C'est libre?** *seh leebr*
It isn't ready.	**Ce n'est pas prêt.** *ser neh pa preh*
Is/Are there …?	**Y a-t-il …?** *ee a teel*
Are there buses going into town?	**Y a-t-il des bus pour aller en ville?** *ee a teel day bews poor alay ahng veel*
Here it is/they are.	**Le/Les voici.** *ler/ley vwasee*
There it is/they are.	**Le/Les voilà.** *ler/ley vwala*

Can …?

Can I have …?	**Est-ce que je peux avoir …?** *ess ker zher pur zavwar*
Can we have …?	**Est-ce que nous pouvons avoir …?** *ess ker noo poovawng zavwar*

Can you tell me …?	**Pouvez-vous me dire …?** *poovay voo mer deer*
Can you help me?	**Pouvez-vous m'aider?** *poovay voo mayday*
Can I help you?	**Est-ce que je peux vous aider?** *ess ker zher pur voo zayday*
Can you direct me to …?	**Pouvez-vous m'indiquer le chemin** **pour …?** *poovay voo mangdeekay* *ler shermang poor*
I can't.	**Je ne peux pas.** *zher ner pur pa*

What would you like?

I'd like …	**Je voudrais …** *zher voodray*
Could I have …?	**Est-ce que je pourrais avoir …?** *ess ker zher pooray zavwar*
We'd like …	**Nous voudrions …** *noo voodryawng*
Give me …	**Donnez-moi …** *donay mwa*
I'm looking for …	**Je cherche …** *zher shehrsh*
I need to …	**Je dois …** *zher dwa*
go …	**aller …** *alay*
find …	**trouver …** *troovay*
see …	**voir …** *vwar*
speak to …	**parler à …** *parlay a*

AT THE STORE

Comment voulez-vous payer? *kommahng voolay voo payay*
(How would you like to pay?)
En liquide, s'il vous plaît. *ahng leekeed seel voo pleh*
(Cash, please.)

17

Who?/Which?

Who's there?	**Qui est là?**	*kee eh la*
It's me!	**C'est moi!**	*seh mwa*
It's us!	**C'est nous!**	*seh noo*
someone	**quelqu'un**	*kelkang*
no one	**personne**	*pehrson*
Which one do you want?	**Lequel voulez-vous?** *lerkel voolay voo*	
one like that	**un(e) comme ceci** *ang (ewn) kom sersee*	
that one/this one	**celui-là/celui-ci** *serlwee la/serlwee see*	
not that one	**pas celui-là** *pa serlwee la*	
something	**quelque chose**	*kelker shoaz*
nothing	**rien**	*ryang*
none	**aucun**	*oakang*

Whose?

Whose ... is that?	**À qui est-ce?**	*a kee ess*
It's ...	**C'est ...**	*seh*
mine/ours/yours	**à moi /à nous/à vous** *a mwa/a noo/a voo*	
his/hers/theirs	**à lui/à elle/à eux** *a lwee/a ell/a ur*	
It's ... turn.	**C'est ... tour.**	*seh ... toor*
my/our/your	**mon/notre/votre** *mawng/notr/votr*	
his/her/their	**son/son/leur**	*sawng/ lurr*

AT THE STORE

Quand les magasins sont-ils ouvert? *kahng lay magazang sonteel oovehr* (When are the stores open?)
À neuf heures. *a nurf urr* (At 9 o'clock.)
Merci. *mehrsee* (Thanks.)

OTHER USEFUL WORDS

fortunately	**heureusement** *urrurzmahng*
hopefully	**en espérant ...** *ahng espehrahng*
of course	**bien sûr** *byang sewr*
perhaps/possibly	**peut-être** *pur tetr*
probably	**probablement** *probablurmahng*
unfortunately	**malheureusement** *malurrurzmahng*

EXCLAMATIONS

At last!	**Enfin!** *ahngfang*
Carry on.	**Continuez.** *kawngteeneway*
Damn!	**Zut!** *zewt*
Good God!	**Mon Dieu!** *mawng dyur*
I don't mind.	**Ça ne me fait rien.** *sa ner mer feh ryang*
No way!	**Pas question!/Pas possible!** *pa kestyawng/pa posseebl*
Really?	**Ah bon?/Vraiment?** *a bawng/vremahng*
Nonsense.	**Quelle bêtise!** *kel beteez*
That's enough.	**Ça suffit!** *sa sewfee*
That's true.	**C'est vrai.** *seh vreh*
How are things?	**Comment ça va?** *kommahng sa va*
Fine, thank you.	**Bien, merci.** *byang mehrsee*
great/brilliant	**super** *sewpehr*
great	**formidable** *formeedabl*
fine	**très bien** *treh byang*
not bad	**pas mal** *pa mal*
okay	**ça va** *sa va*
not good	**pas bien** *pa byang*
fairly bad	**plutôt mal** *plewtoa mal*
terrible	**(ça ne va) pas du tout** *(sa ner va) pa dew too*

Accommodations

All types of accommodations, from hotels to campsites, can be found through the tourist information center (**Office du Tourisme** or **Syndicat d'initiative**).

Hôtels *oatel*

Usually called **hôtels** or **hôtels de tourisme**, hotels in France are officially classified into four categories, ranging from basic one-star accommodations to luxury four-star establishments. Room prices, fixed according to amenities, size and to the hotel's star rating, must be posted visibly at the reception desk or in the window and behind each room door. Most hotels offer breakfast (which is rarely included in the total price, unless specified) but not all will have a restaurant. **Hôtel garni** means bed and breakfast.

Châteaux-Hôtels de France *chatoa zoatel der frahngss*

Hotels belonging to this association are four-star establishments, usually converted **châteaux**. They tend to be expensive but offer very high quality service. They are listed in a directory available from tourist offices.

Logis de France *lozhee der frahngss*

This voluntary organization places the emphasis on a warm welcome, comfort, good regional cooking and the best value for money. These hotels are usually located outside towns and offer a relaxed atmosphere. They are classified into four levels, from one to four **cheminées** (chimneys). A directory can be obtained from the French national tourist office.

Auberges *oabehrzh*

These country inns tend to be small and offer simple, economical accommodations. Some have very good restaurants and they are often in pleasant locations.

Gîtes de France *zheet der frahngss*

Gîtes are furnished rented holiday cottages or apartments in rural areas.

Auberges de jeunesse *oaberzh der zhurness*

Youth hostels require you to show your membership card, but you'll usually be able to get one on the spot. Some local student associations operate dormitories during high season.

RESERVATIONS/BOOKING

Can you recommend a hotel in …?
Pouvez-vous me recommander un hôtel à …? *poovay voo mer rerkommahng day ang noatel a*

Is it near the center of town?
Est-ce près du centre-ville? *ess preh dew sahngter veel*

How much is it per night?
C'est combien par nuit? *seh kawnbyang par nwee*

Is there anything cheaper?
Y a-t-il quelque chose de moins cher? *ee ateel kelker shoaz der mwang shehr*

Could you reserve me a room there, please?
Pourriez-vous m'y réserver une chambre, s'il vous plaît? *pooryay voo mee rayzehrvay ewn shahngbrer seel voo pleh*

At the hotel

Do you have any vacancies?
Avez-vous des chambres libres? *avay voo day shahngbrer leebr*

I'm sorry, we're full.
Je regrette, l'hôtel est complet. *zher rergret loatel eh kawngpleh*

Is there another hotel nearby?
Y a-t-il un autre hôtel près d'ici? *ee ateel ang noatr oatel preh deessee*

I'd like a single/. double room
Je voudrais une chambre à un lit/chambre pour deux personnes. *zher voodray ewn shahngbr a ang lee/shahngbr poor dur person*

I'd like a room with …
Je voudrais une chambre avec … *zher voodray ewn shahngbr avek*

a bath/shower
salle de bains/douche *sal der bang/doosh*

AT THE HOTEL RECEPTION

Avez-vous des chambres libres? *avay voo day shahngbr leebr (Do you have any vacancies?)*

Je regrette. L'hôtel est complet. *zher rergret loatel eh kawngpleh (I'm sorry, we're full.)*

Merci, madame/monsieur. *mehrsee mahdahm/murssyew (Thank you, m'am/sir.)*

Reception

I have a reservation. My name is …	**J'ai réservé. Je m'appelle …** *zhay rayzehrvay. zher mapell*
We've reserved a double and a single room.	**Nous avons réservé une chambre pour deux personnes et une chambre à un lit.** *noo zavawng rayzervay ewn shahngbr poor dur person ay ewn shahngbr a ang lee*
I confirmed my reservation by mail.	**J'ai confirmé par lettre.** *zhay kawngfeermay par letr*
Could we have adjoining rooms?	**Pourrions-nous avoir des chambres côte à côte?** *poorryawng noo zavvar day shahngbr koat a koat*

Amenities and facilities

Is there … in the room?	**Y a-t-il … dans la chambre?** *ee ateel … dahng la shahngbr*
air conditioning	**la climatisation** *la kleemateezasyawng*
TV/telephone/fax	**la télévision/le téléphone/le fax** *la taylayveezyawng/ler taylayfon/ler fax*
Does the hotel have (a) …?	**Y a-t-il … à l'hôtel?** *ee ateel … a loatel*
cable TV	**la télévision par câble** *la taylayveezyawng par kabl*
laundry service	**un service de nettoyage** *ang sehrvees der nettwahyazh*
solarium	**un solarium** *ang solaryom*
swimming pool	**une piscine** *ewn peesseen*
Could you put … in the room?	**Pourriez-vous mettre … dans la chambre?** *pooryay voo metr … dahng la shahngbr*
an extra bed	**un lit supplémentaire** *ang lee sewplaymahngtehr*
a crib [cot]	**un lit d'enfant** *ang lee dahngfahng*
Do you have facilities for children/the disabled?	**Y a-t-il des aménagements pour enfants/handicapés?** *ee ateel day zamaynazhmahng poor ahngfahng/ahngdeekapay*

How long?

We'll be staying …	**Nous resterons …** *noo resterawng*
overnight only	**une nuit seulement** *ewn nwee surlmahng*
a few days	**quelques jours** *kelker zhoor*
a week (at least)	**une semaine (au moins)** *ewn sermayn (oa mwang)*
I'd like to stay an extra night.	**Je voudrais rester une nuit supplémentaire.** *zher voodray restay ewn nwee sewplaymahngtehr*

YOU MAY SEE

CHAMBRE SEULE … FF	room only FF…
PETIT DÉJEUNER COMPRIS	breakfast included
REPAS	meals available
NOM/PRÉNOM	name/first name
LIEU DE RÉSIDENCE/RUE/ NUMÉRO	home address/street/ number
NATIONALITÉ/PROFESSION	nationality/profession
DATE/LIEU DE NAISSANCE	date/place of birth
NUMÉRO DE PASSEPORT	passport number
NUMÉRO D'IMMATRICULATION DE LA VOITURE	license plate number
LIEU/DATE	place/date
SIGNATURE	signature

YOU MAY HEAR

Est-ce que je peux voir votre passeport, s'il vous plaît?	May I see your passport, please?
Pouvez-vous remplir cette fiche?	Please fill out this form.
Quel est votre numéro d'immatriculation?	What is your license plate number?

23

Price

How much is it …?	**Combien coûte …?** *kawngbeeahn koot*
per night/week	**par nuit/semaine** *par nwee/sermayn*
for bed and breakfast	**pour la chambre et le petit déjeuner** *poor la shahngbr ay ler pertee dayzhurnay*
excluding meals	**sans les repas** *sahng lay repa*
for American Plan (A.P.) [full board]	**pour la pension complète** *poor la pahngsyawng kawngplet*
for Modified American Plan (M.A.P.) [half board]	**pour la demi-pension** *poor la dermee pahngsyawng*
Does the price include …?	**Est-ce-que cela comprend …?** *ess ker serla kawngprahng*
breakfast	**le petit déjeuner** *ler pertee dayzhurnay*
sales tax [VAT]	**la T.V.A.** *la tay vay ah*
Do I have to pay a deposit?	**Dois-je verser des arrhes?** *dwazh vehrsay day zar*
Is there a discount for children?	**Y a-t-il une réduction pour enfants?** *ee ateel ewn raydewksyawng poor ahngfahng*

Decision

May I see the room?	**Puis-je voir la chambre?** *pweezh vwar la shahngbr*
That's fine. I'll take it.	**C'est bien. Je la prends.** *seh byang. zher la prahng*
It's too …	**Elle est trop …** *eleh tro*
dark/small	**sombre/petite** *sawngbr/perteet*
noisy	**bruyante** *brewyahngt*
Do you have anything …?	**Avez-vous quelque chose de …?** *avay voo kelker shoaz der*
bigger/cheaper	**plus grand/moins cher** *plew grahng/mwang sher*
quieter/warmer	**plus calme/plus chaud** *plew kalm/plew shoa*
No, I won't take it.	**Non, je ne la prends pas.** *nawng zher ner la prahng pa*

Problems

The … doesn't work.	**… ne marche pas.** *ner marsh pa*
air conditioning	**La climatisation** *la kleemateezassyawng*
fan	**Le ventilateur** *ler vahngteelaturr*
heat [heating]	**Le chauffage** *ler shoafazh*
light	**La lumière** *la lewmyehr*
I can't turn the heat [heating] on/off.	**Je ne peux pas allumer/éteindre le chauffage.** *zher ner pur pa alewmay/aytangdr ler shoafazh*
There is no hot water/ toilet paper.	**Il n'y a pas d'eau chaude/de papier toilette.** *eel nee a pa doa shoad/der papyay twalett*
The faucet [tap] is dripping.	**Le robinet fuit.** *ler robeeneh fwee*
The sink/toilet is clogged.	**Le lavabo est bouché./Les toilettes sont bouchées.** *ler lavaboa eh booshay/lay twalett sawng booshay*
The window/door is jammed.	**La fenêtre/porte est coincée.** *la fernetr port eh kwangsay*
My room has not been made up.	**Ma chambre n'a pas été faite.** *ma shahngbr na pa zaytay fet*
The … is broken.	**… est cassé(e).** *eh kassay*
blind	**Le store** *ler stor*
lock	**La serrure** *la sehrewr*
There are insects in our room.	**Il y a des insectes dans notre chambre.** *eel ee a day zangsekt dahng notrer shahngbr*

Action

Could you have that taken care of?	**Pourriez-vous vous en occuper?** *pooray voo voo zahng nokewpay*
I'd like to move to another room.	**Je voudrais changer de chambre.** *zher voodray shahngzhay der shahngbr*
I'd like to speak to the manager.	**Je voudrais parler au directeur.** *zher voodray parlay oa deerekturr*

The 220-volt, 50-cycle AC is now almost universal in France, Belgium and Switzerland, although 110 volts may still be encountered, especially in older buildings.

If you bring your own electrical appliances, buy a Continental adapter plug (round pins, not square) before leaving home. You may also need a transformer appropriate to the wattage of the appliance.

About the hotel

Where's the ...?	**Où est ...?** *oo eh*
bar	**le bar** *ler bar*
parking lot [car park]	**le parking** *ler parking*
dining room	**la salle à manger** *la sala mahngzhay*
elevator [lift]	**l'ascenseur** *lassahngsurr*
shower	**la douche** *la doosh*
swimming pool	**la piscine** *la peesseen*
tour operator's bulletin board	**le tableau d'affichage de l'agence de voyages** *ler tabloa dafeeshazh der lazhahngs der vwahyazh*
Where is the restroom?	**Où sont lès toilettes?** *oo sawng lay twalett*
What time is the front door locked?	**À quelle heure fermez-vous la porte d'entrée?** *a kelurr fermay voo la port dahngtray*
What time is breakfast served?	**À quelle heure servez-vous le petit déjeuner?** *a kel urr servay voo ler pertee dayzhurnay*
Is there room service?	**Y a-t-il un service de chambre?** *ee ateel ang sehrvees der shahngbr*

YOU MAY SEE

COMPOSER LE ... POUR L'EXTÉRIEUR	dial ... for an outside line
NE PAS DÉRANGER	do not disturb
PORTE COUPE-FEU	fire door
PRISE POUR RASOIRS	shavers only
SORTIE DE SECOURS	emergency exit

The key to room …, please.	**La clé de la chambre …, s'il vous plaît.** *la klay der la shahngbr … seel voo pleh*
I've lost my key.	**J'ai perdu ma clé.** *zhay pehrdew ma klay*
I've locked myself out of my room.	**Je ne peux plus ouvrir la porte de ma chambre.** *zher ner pur plew oovreer la port der ma shahngbr*
Could you wake me at … please?	**Pourriez-vous me réveiller à …, s'il vous plaît?** *pooray voo mer rayvayay a … seel voo pleh*
I'd like breakfast in my room.	**Je voudrais le petit déjeuner dans ma chambre.** *zher voodray ler pertee dayzhurnay dahng ma shahngbr*
Can I leave this in the hotel safe?	**Puis-je laisser ceci dans le coffre-fort de l'hôtel?** *pweezh layssay sersee dahng ler kofrer for der loatel*
Could I have my things from the safe?	**Puis-je prendre mes affaires dans le coffre-fort?** *pweezh prahngdrer may zafer dahng ler kofrer for*
Where is our tour representative?	**Où est le représentant de notre voyage organisé?** *oo eh ler reprayzahngtanf der notrer vwahyazh orgahneezay*
the maid	**la femme de chambre** *la fam der shahngbr*
May I have a(n) (extra)…?	**Puis-je avoir …(supplémentaire)?** *pweezh avwar …(sewplaymahngtehr)*
bath towel	**une serviette de bain** *ewn servyett der bang*
blanket	**une couverture** *ewn koovehrtewr*
hangers	**des cintres** *day sangtr*
pillow	**un oreiller** *ang norayay*
soap	**du savon** *dew savawng*
Is there any mail for me?	**Y a-t-il du courrier pour moi?** *ee ateel dew kooryay poor mwa*
Are there any messages for me?	**Y a-t-il des messages pour moi?** *ee ateel day messazh poor mwa*

RENTING

We've reserved an apartment/house in the name of …	**Nous avons réservé un appartement/une maison au nom de** … *noo zavawng rayzervay ang napartermahng/ewn mayzawng oa nawng der*
Where do we pick up the keys?	**Où devons-nous prendre les clés?** *oo dervawng noo prahngdrer lay klay*
Where is the …?	**Où est …?** *oo eh*
electric meter	**le compteur électrique** *ler kawngturr aylektreek*
fuse box	**la boîte à fusibles** *la bwat a fewzeebl*
faucet [tap]	**le robinet d'arrêt** *ler robeeneh dareh*
water heater	**le chauffe-eau** *ler shoaf oa*
Are there any spare …?	**Y a-t-il des … de rechange?** *ee ateel day … der rershahngzh*
fuses	**fusibles** *fewzeebl*
gas bottles	**bouteilles de gaz** *bootayy der gaz*
sheets	**draps** *dra*
Which day does the housekeeper come?	**Quel jour vient la femme de ménage?** *kel zhoor vyang la fam der maynazh*
Where/When do I put out the trash [rubbish]?	**Où/Quand dois-je sortir les poubelles?** *oo/kahng dwazh sorteer lay poobell*

Problems?

Where can I contact you?	**Où est-ce que je peux vous contacter?** *oo ess ker zher pur voo kawngtaktay*
How does the water heater/ stove [cooker] work?	**Comment fonctionne le chauffe-eau/ la cuisinière?** *kommahng fawngksyon ler shoafoa/la kweezeenyehr*
The … is/are dirty.	**… est sale/sont sales.** *eh sal/sawng sal*
The … has broken down.	**… est cassé(e).** *eh kassay*
We have accidentally broken/lost …	**Nous avons cassé/perdu** … *noo zavawng kassay/pehrdew*
That was already damaged when we arrived.	**C'était déjà abîmé quand nous sommes arrivés.** *sayteh dayzha abeemay kahng noo som zareevay*

Useful terms

boiler	**la chaudière** *la shoadyehr*
freezer	**le congélateur** *ler kawngzhaylaturr*
frying pan	**la poêle** *la pwal*
kettle	**la bouilloire** *la booywar*
lamp	**la lampe** *la lahngp*
dishes [crockery]	**la vaisselle** *la vessell*
refrigerator	**le réfrigérateur/frigo** *ler rayfreezhayraturr/freego*
saucepan	**la casserole** *la kasrol*
stove [cooker]	**la cuisinière** *la kweezeenyehr*
toilet paper	**le papier toilette/hygiénique** *ler papyay twalett/eezhyayneek*
utensils [cutlery]	**les couverts** *lay koovehr*
washing machine	**la machine à laver** *la mashee na lavay*

Rooms

balcony	**le balcon** *ler balkawng*
bathroom	**la salle de bains** *la sal der bang*
bedroom	**la chambre** *la shahngbr*
dining room	**la salle à manger** *la sa la mahngzhay*
kitchen	**la cuisine** *la kweezeen*
living room	**la salle de séjour/le salon** *la sal der sayzhoor/ler salawng*
bathroom [toilets]	**les toilettes/les WC** *lay twalett/lay doobler-vay say*

YOUTH HOSTEL

Do you have any places left for tonight?	**Vous reste-t-il des places pour ce soir?** *voo rester teel day plass poor ser swar*
Do you rent bedding?	**Louez-vous des draps?** *looay voo day dra*
What time are the doors locked?	**À quelle heure les portes ferment-elles?** *a kel urr lay port fermer tell*
I have an International Student Card.	**J'ai une carte d'étudiant internationale.** *zhay ewn kart daytewdyahng angtehrnasyonal*

CAMPING

Camping is very well organized. A **camping municipal** (public campsite) can be found in most towns, while tourist areas will also have other privately owned campsites.

Checking in

Is there a camp site near here?	**Y a-t-il un camping près d'ici?** *ee ateel ang kahngpeeng preh deessee*
Do you have space for a tent/trailer [caravan]?	**Avez-vous de la place pour une tente/une caravane?** *avay voo der la plass poor ewn tahngt/ewn karavahn*
What is the charge …?	**Quel est le tarif …?** *kel eh ler tareef*
per day/week	**par jour/semaine** *par zhoor/sermayn*
for a tent/a car	**pour une tente/voiture** *poor ewn tahngt/vwatewr*
for a trailer/camper	**pour une caravane** *poo rewn karavahn*

Facilities

Are there cooking facilities on site?	**Est-il possible de faire la cuisine sur le terrain?** *eteel posseebl der fer la kweezeen sewr ler terang*
Are there any electric outlets [power points]?	**Y a-t-il des branchements électriques?** *ee ateel day brahngshmahng aylektreek*
Where is/are the …?	**Où est/sont …?** *oo eh/sawng*
drinking water	**l'eau potable** *loa potabl*
trashcans [dustbins]	**les poubelles** *lay poobell*
laundry facilities	**les bacs à linge/les machines à laver** *lay bak a langzh/lay masheen a lavay*
showers	**les douches** *lay doosh*
Where can I get some butane gas?	**Où puis-je trouver du gaz butane?** *oo pweezh troovay dew gaz bewtahn*

YOU MAY SEE

CAMPING INTERDIT	no camping
EAU POTABLE	drinking water
FEUX/BARBECUES INTERDITS	no fires/barbecues

Complaints

It's too sunny/shady/crowded here.	**Il y a trop de soleil/d'ombre/de gens ici.** *eel ee a tro der solayy/dawngbr/der zhahng eessee*
The ground's too hard/uneven.	**Le sol est trop dur/inégal.** *ler sol eh trop dewr/eenaygal*
Do you have a more level spot?	**Avez-vous un emplacement plus plat?** *avay voo ang nahngplasmahng plew pla*
You can't camp here.	**Vous ne pouvez pas camper ici.** *voo ner poovay pa kahngpay eessee*

Camping equipment

butane gas	**du gaz butane** *dew gaz bewtahn*
campbed	**un lit de camp** *ang lee der kahng*
charcoal	**du charbon** *dew sharbawng*
hammer	**un marteau** *ang martoa*
mallet	**un maillet** *ang mieyeh*
matches	**des allumettes** *day zalewmet*
(air) mattress	**un matelas (pneumatique)** *ang matla (pnurmateek)*
kerosene [primus] stove	**un réchaud (de camping)** *ang rayshoa (der kahngpeeng)*
knapsack	**un sac à dos** *ang sa ka doa*
rope	**une corde de tente** *ewn kord der tahngt*
sleeping bag	**un sac de couchage** *ang sak der kooshazh*
tarpaulin	**un tapis de sol** *ang tapee der sol*
tent	**une tente** *ewn tahngt*
tent pegs	**des piquets de tente** *day peekeh der tahngt*
tent pole	**un (grand) piquet de tente** *ang (grahng) peekeh der tahngt*
flashlight [torch]	**une lampe de poche/électrique** *ewn lahngp der posh/aylektreek*

Checking out

What time do we need to vacate the room?	**À quelle heure devons-nous libérer la chambre?** *a kel urr dervawng noo leebayray la shahngbr*
Could we leave our baggage here until … p.m.?	**Pourrions-nous laisser nos bagages ici jusqu'à … heures du soir?** *pooryawng noo layssay no baga zheessee zhewska … urr dew swar*
I'm leaving now.	**Je pars maintenant.** *zher par mangtnahng*
Could you call me a taxi, please?	**Pourriez-vous m'appeler un taxi, s'il vous plaît?** *pooryay voo maplay ang taxee seel voo pleh*
It's been a very enjoyable stay.	**J'ai passé un très bon séjour.** *zhay passay ang treh bawng sayzhoor*

Paying

May I have my bill, please?	**Puis-je avoir ma note, s'il vous plaît?** *pweezh avwar ma not seel voo pleh*
I think there's a mistake in this bill.	**Je crois qu'il y a une erreur sur cette note.** *zher krwa keel ee a ewn erurr sewr set not*
I've made … telephone calls.	**J'ai passé … coups de téléphone.** *zhay passay … koo der taylayfon*
I've taken … from the minibar.	**J'ai pris … au mini-bar.** *zhay pree … oa meenee bar*
Can I have an itemized bill?	**Est-ce que je peux avoir une note détaillée?** *ess ker zher pur avwarewn not daytieyay*
Could I have a receipt?	**Est-ce que je peux avoir un reçu?** *ess ker zher pur avwarang rersew*

Tipping

A service charge is generally included in hotel and restaurant bills. However, if the service has been particularly good, you may want to leave an extra tip. The following chart is a guide:

	France	Belgium	Switzerland
Bellman [Porter]	5F	30F	1–2F
Hotel maid, per week	50–100F	100–150F	10F
Waiter	optional	optional	optional

EATING OUT

	ESSENTIAL
A table for	**Une table pour...** *ewn tabler poor*
1/2/3/4	**un/deux/trois/quatre** *ang/dur/trwa/katr*
Thank you.	**Merci.** *mehrsee*
The check [bill], please.	**L'addition, s'il vous plaît.** *ladeesyawng seel voo pleh*

RESTAURANTS

Auberge *oabehrzh*

An inn, often in the country; serves full meals and drinks.

Bistrot *beestroa*

Can vary from a café, selling mostly drinks and basic food (sandwiches, salads, snacks) to a more picturesque restaurant, with traditional French cuisine; usually not very expensive.

Brasserie *brasserree*

A large café serving good, simple food and drinks, very often offering a **plat du jour** (dish of the day).

Buffet *bewfeh*

A restaurant found in principal train stations; the food is generally good.

Café/bar *kafay/bar*

Can be found on virtually every street corner; coffee and drinks served, sometimes light meals, too. Come here for a croissant with your morning coffee; and now many cafés also offer snacks, salads and sandwiches. Beer, wine and liquor are served, but don't ask for any fancy cocktails or highballs.

Crêperie *krepehree*

Offers snacks of light pancakes with various fillings.

Restaurant *restoarang*

These are rated by scores of professional and amateur gourmets. You'll encounter restaurants classified by stars, forks and knives and endorsed by everyone including travel agencies, automobile associations and gastronomic guilds. Bear in mind that any form of classification is relative.

Restoroute *restoaroot*
A large restaurant just off a highway [motorway]; table and/or cafeteria service is available.

Rôtisserie *roateessree*
Very often linked with a **charcuterie** and specializes in meat products: roast chickens, quiches, sausages, ham, hors-d'œuvre, etc.

Routier *rootyay*
Roughly equivalent to a roadside diner; the food is simple but can be surprisingly good if you happen to hit upon the right place.

Meal times

le petit déjeuner *ler pertee dayzhurnay*
Breakfast: from 7-10 a.m. Traditionally just bread, butter, jam, a croissant and **un petit noir** (small black coffee), tea or hot chocolate; hotels are now offering more filling fare.

le déjeuner *ler deayzhurnay*
Lunch: from noon until 2 p.m. If you don't have time for a leisurely meal, try a restaurant offering a **plat du jour** (single dish of the day) or light salad. In a hurry, go for fast-food outlets, pizzerias or crêperies, or just grab a baguette sandwich.

le dîner *ler deenay*
Dinner is usually served late, from 8-10 p.m. The French are likely to linger over their meal, so service may seem on the slow side.

FRENCH CUISINE

There are few countries where you can spend more delightful hours just eating. For, apart from the many regional specialties that do ample justice to the local produce, you can sample, among others, **haute cuisine** (sophisticated dishes made according to time-honored recipes) or **nouvelle cuisine** (a more refined preparation enhancing the delicate flavors of the food).

Most restaurants display a menu (**la carte**) outside. Besides ordering **à la carte**, you can order a fixed price menu – **le menu (à prix fixe)**. Cheaper meals often run to three courses, with or without wine, but service is always included. More expensive menus stretch to four or even five courses, but hardly ever include wine.

FINDING A PLACE TO EAT

Can you recommend a good restaurant?	**Pouvez-vous nous recommander un bon restaurant?** *poovay voo noo rerkommahngday ang bawng restoarahng*
Is there a … restaurant near here?	**Y a-t-il un restaurant … près d'ici?** *ee ateel ang restoarahng … preh deessee*
traditional local	**local traditionnel** *lokal tradeessyonell*
Chinese	**chinois** *sheenwa*
Greek	**grec** *grek*
Italian	**italien** *eetalyang*
French	**français** *frangsay*
inexpensive	**bon marché** *bawng marshay*
vegetarian	**végétarien** *vayzhaytaryang*
Where can I find a(n) …?	**Où puis-je trouver …?** *oo pweezh troovay*
burger stand	**un kiosque à hamburger** *ang keeosk a amburger*
café	**un café** *ang kafay*
restaurant/café with a beer garden	**un café/restaurant avec jardin/terrasse** *ang kafay/restoarahng avek zhardang/tehrass*
fast-food restaurant	**un fast-food** *ang fast food*
tea room	**un salon de thé** *ang salawng der tay*
pizzeria	**une pizzeria** *ewn peetzehreea*
steak house	**un restaurant-grill** *ang restoarahng greel*

RESERVATIONS

I'd like to reserve
a table for 2.

Je voudrais réserver une table pour deux personnes. *zher voodray rayzehrvay ewn tabl poor dur pehrsonn*

For this evening/
tomorrow at …

Pour ce soir/demain à … heures. *poor ser swar/dermang a … urr*

We'll come at 8:00.

Nous viendrons à huit heures. *noo vyangdrawng a weeturr*

A table for 2, please.

Une table pour deux, s'il vous plaît. *ewn tabl poor dur seel voo pleh*

We have a reservation.

Nous avons réservé. *noo zavawng rayzehrvay*

YOU MAY HEAR

C'est à quel nom, s'il vous plaît?	What's the name, please?
Je regrette. Il y a beaucoup de monde/nous sommes complets.	I'm sorry. We're very busy/full.
Nous aurons une table libre dans … minutes.	We'll have a free table in … minutes.
Revenez dans … minutes.	Please come back in … minutes.

WHERE TO SIT

Could we sit …?

Pouvons-nous nous asseoir …? *poovawng noo noo zaswar*

outside

dehors *der or*

in a non-smoking area

dans une zone non-fumeur *dahng zewn zon nawng fewmurr*

by the window

près de la fenêtre *preh der la fernetr*

IN A RESTAURANT

Une table pour deux, s'il vous plaît.
ewn tabl poor dur seel voo pleh
(A table for two, please.)
Fumeur ou non-fumeur? *fewmurroo nawng fewmurr*
(Smoking or non-smoking?)
Non-fumeur. Merci. *nawng fewmurr mehrsee*
(Non-smoking. Thank you.)

IN A RESTAURANT

Mademoiselle (Monsieur)! *mahdmwazel/murssyew*
(Waitress/Waiter!)
Oui, monsieur. *wee murssyew (Yes, sir.)*
La carte, s'il vous plaît. *la kart seel voo pleh*
(The menu, please.)
Entendu. *awngtawngdew (Certainly.)*

YOU MAY HEAR

Vous désirez commander?	Are you ready to order?
Qu'est-ce que vous prendrez?	What would you like?
Voulez-vous prendre un apéritif pour commencer?	Would you like to order drinks first?
Je vous recommande/conseille …	I recommend …
Nous n'avons pas de …	We haven't got …
Il faudra attendre … minutes.	That will take … minutes.
Bon appétit.	Enjoy your meal.

ORDERING

Waiter!/Waitress!	**Monsieur!/Mademoiselle!** *murssyew/madmwazel*
May I see the wine list, please?	**Puis-je avoir la carte des vins, s'il vous plaît?** *pweezh avwar la karter day vang seel voo pleh*
Do you have a set menu?	**Avez-vous un menu à prix fixe?** *avay voo zang mernew a pree feex*
Can you recommend some typical local dishes?	**Pouvez-vous recommander des spécialités régionales?** *poovay voo rerkommahngday day spaysyaleetay rayzhyonal*
Could you tell me what … is?	**Pourriez-vous me dire ce qu'est …?** *pooray voo mer deer ser keh*
What's in it?	**Qu'y a-t-il dedans?** *kee ateel derdahng*
I'd like …	**Je voudrais …** *zher voodray*
a bottle/glass/carafe of …	**une bouteille/un verre/une carafe de …** *ewn bootay/ang verr/ewn karaf de*

Side dishes

Could I have … without the …?	**Est-ce que je pourrais avoir … sans …?** *ess ker zher pooray avwar … sahng*
With a side order of …	**Avec … comme accompagnement.** *avek … ko makawngpañmahng*
Could I have salad instead of vegetables, please?	**Est-ce que je pourrais avoir une salade à la place des légumes?** *ess ker zher pooray avwar ewn salad a la plass day laygewm*
Does the meal come with vegetables/potatoes?	**Le plat est-il servi avec des légumes/ pommes de terre?** *ler pla eteel sehrvee avek day laygewm/pom der tehr*
Do you have any sauces?	**Avez-vous des sauces?** *avay voo day soass*
Would you like … with that?	**Est-ce que vous voulez … avec?** *ess ker voo voolay … avek*
vegetables/salad	**des légumes/de la salade** *day laygewm/der la salahd*
potatoes/French fries [chips]	**des pommes de terre/des frites** *day pom der tehr/day freet*
sauce	**de la sauce** *der la soass*
ice	**des glaçons** *day glassawng*
May I have some …?	**Puis-je avoir …?** *pwee zhavwar*
bread	**du pain** *dew pang*
butter	**du beurre** *dew burr*
lemon	**du citron** *dew seetrawng*
mustard	**de la moutarde** *der la mootard*
pepper	**du poivre** *dew pwavr*
salt	**du sel** *dew sel*
seasoning	**de l'assaisonnement/de la vinaigrette** *der lassayzonmahng/der la veenaygret*
sugar	**du sucre** *dew sewkr*
(artificial) sweetener	**de l'édulcorant** *der laydewlkorahngt*
vinaigrette [dressing]	**de la vinaigrette** *der la veenaygret*

General questions

Could I have a(n) (clean) …, please?
Pourriez-vous m'apporter … (propre)?
pooryay voo maportay … (propr)

ashtray
un cendrier *ang sahngdryay*

cup/glass
une tasse/un verre *ewn tass/ang vehr*

fork/knife
une fourchette/un couteau
ewn foorshett/ang kootoa

napkin
une serviette *ewn sehrvyett*

plate/spoon
une assiette/une cuillère
ewn assyett/ewn kweeyehr

I'd like some more …, please.
Je voudrais un peu plus de …
zher voodray ang pur plews der

Nothing more, thanks.
Ça suffit, merci. *sa sewfee mehrsee*

Where are the restrooms?
Où sont les toilettes?
oo sawng lay twalett

Special requirements

I mustn't eat food containing …
Je ne dois pas manger de plats contenant …
zher ner dwa pa mahngzhay der pla kawngtnahng

salt/sugar
du sel/du sucre *dew sel/dew sewkr*

Do you have meals/ drinks for diabetics?
Avez-vous des repas/boissons pour diabétiques? *avay voo day rerpa/ bwassawng poor dyabayteek*

Do you have vegetarian meals?
Avez-vous des repas végétariens?
avay voo day rerpa vayzhaytaryang

For the children

Do you have children's portions?
Faites-vous des portions enfants?
fet voo day porsyawng ahngfahng

Could we have a child's seat, please?
Pourrions-nous avoir une chaise haute (pour bébé)? *pooryawng noo avvwar ewn shezer oat (poor baybay)*

Where can I nurse/ change the baby?
Où est-ce que je peux allaiter/ changer le bébé? *oo ess ker zher pur aletay/shahngzhay ler baybay*

Something to drink

I'd like a cup of …	**Je voudrais une tasse de …** *zher voodray ewn tass der*
tea/coffee	**thé/café** *tay/kafay*
black/with milk	**noir/au lait** *nwar/oa leh*
I'd like a … of red/white wine.	**Je voudrais … de vin rouge/blanc.** *zher voodray … der vang roozh/blahng*
carafe/bottle/glass	**une carafe/une bouteille/un verre** *ewn karaf/ewn bootay/ang vehr*
Do you have … beer?	**Avez-vous de la bière …?** *avay voo der la byehr*
bottled/draft [draught]	**en bouteille/pression** *ahng bootay/pressyawng*

And to eat

A piece of …, please.	**Un morceau de …, s'il vous plaît.** *ang morsoa der … seel voo pleh*
I'd like two of those.	**J'en voudrais deux.** *zhahng voodray dur*
burger/fries	**un hamburger/des frites** *ang amburger/ day freet*
cake/sandwich	**un gâteau/un sandwich** *ang gatoa/ang sahngdveesh*

une glace *ewn glas*
ice cream: some common flavors are **à la vanille** (vanilla), **au chocolat** (chocolate), **à la fraise** (strawberry).

une pizza *ang peetza*
pizza: popular types include **marguerite** (cheese and tomato), **quatre saisons** (four different toppings, usually ham, mushrooms, cheese and anchovy), **reine** (ham and mushroom).

A … slice, please.	**Une … tranche, s'il vous plaît.** *ewn … trahngsh seel voo pleh*
small	**petite portion** *perteet porsyawng*
regular [medium]	**portion moyenne** *porsyawng mwahyenn*
large	**grosse portion** *gross porsyawng*

| It's to go [take away]. | **C'est pour emporter.** *seh poor ahngportay* |
| That's all, thanks. | **C'est tout, merci.** *seh too mehrsee* |

IN A CAFÉ

Deux cafés, s'il vous plaît. *dur kafay seel voo pleh*
(Two coffees, please.)
Et avec ça? *ay avek sa (Anything else?)*
C'est tout. Merci. *seh too mehrsee (That's all, thanks.)*

COMPLAINTS

I have no knife/fork/spoon.	**Je n'ai pas de couteau/fourchette/cuillère.** *zher nay pa der kootoa/foorshett/kweeyehr*
That's not what I ordered.	**Ce n'est pas ce que j'ai commandé.** *ser neh pa ser ker zhay kommahngday*
I asked for …	**J'ai demandé …** *zhay dermahngday*
The meat is …	**La viande est …** *la vyahngd eh*
overdone	**trop cuite** *tro kweet*
underdone	**pas assez cuite** *pa zassay kweet*
too tough	**trop dure** *tro dewr*
This is too …	**C'est trop …** *seh tro*
bitter/sour	**amer/acide** *amehr/asseed*
The food is cold.	**La nourriture est froide.** *la nooreetewr eh frwad*
How much longer will our food be?	**Il y en a encore pour combien de temps?** *eel yahng na ahngkor poor kawnbyang der tahng*
We can't wait any longer. We're leaving.	**Nous ne pouvons plus attendre. Nous partons.** *noo ner poovawng plew atahngdr. noo partawng*
This isn't clean.	**Ce n'est pas propre.** *ser neh pa propr*
I'd like to speak to the headwaiter/to the manager.	**Je voudrais parler au maître d'hôtel/au patron.** *zher voodray parlay oa metrer doatel/oa patrawng*

Tipping: Service is generally included in the bill (15% in France), but if you are happy with the service, a personal tip for the waiter is appropriate and appreciated – round the bill up 5–10 francs.

The check [bill], please.	**L'addition, s'il vous plaît.** *ladeesyawng seel voo pleh*
We'd like to pay separately.	**Nous voudrions payer séparément.** *noo voodryawng payay sayparaymahng*
It's all together, please.	**Tous les repas ensemble, s'il vous plaît.** *too lay repa ahngsahngbl seel voo pleh*
I think there's a mistake in this bill.	**Je crois qu'il y a une erreur sur l'addition.** *zher krwa keel ee a ewn ehrurr sewr ladeesyawng*
What is this amount for?	**Que représente ce montant?** *ker reprayzahngt ser mawngtahng*
I didn't have that. I had …	**Je n'ai pas pris ça. J'ai pris …** *zher nay pa pree sa. zhay pree*
Is service included?	**Le service est-il compris?** *ler sehrveess eteel kawngpree*
Can I pay with this credit card?	**Puis-je payer avec cette carte de crédit?** *pweezh payay avek set kart der kraydee*
I've forgotten my wallet.	**J'ai oublié mon porte-monnaie.** *zhay oobleeay mawng port monnay*
I don't have enough money.	**Je n'ai pas assez d'argent.** *zher nay pa zassay darzhahng*
Could I have a receipt?	**Puis-je avoir un reçu?** *pweezh avwar ang rersew*
That was a very good meal.	**C'était un très bon repas.** *sayteh ang treh bawng repa*

IN A RESTAURANT

L'addition, s'il vous plaît. *ladeesyawng seel voo pleh* (*The bill please.*)
Bien sûr. Voilà. *byang sewr vwala* (*Of course. Here you are.*)
Merci. *mehrsee* (*Thanks.*)

COURSE BY COURSE

Breakfast

The typical breakfast consists of coffee, rolls, croissants and jam. Most of the larger hotels are used to providing an English or American breakfast.

I'd like some …	**Je voudrais …** *zher voodray*
bread	**du pain** *dew pang*
butter	**du beurre** *dew burr*
eggs	**des œufs** *day zur*
fried eggs	**au plat** *oa plah*
scrambled eggs	**brouillés** *brooay*
grapefruit juice	**un jus de pamplemousse** *ang zhew der pangplermoos*
honey	**du miel** *dew myel*
jelly/jam	**de la confiture** *der lah kawngfeetewr*
marmalade	**de la marmelade** *der lah marmerlad*
milk	**du lait** *dew lay*
orange juice	**un jus d'orange** *ang zhew dorahngzh*
rolls	**des petits pains** *day pertee pang*
toast	**du pain grillé** *dew pang greeyay*

Appetizers/Starters

andouille(tte) *angdooy(ett)*
seasoned, aromatic sausage made from tripe, served grilled or fried.

bouchée à la reine *booshay ah lah ren*
pastry shell usually filled with creamed sweetbreads and mushrooms.

pâté *patay*
liver purée that may be blended with other meat, such as **pâté de campagne**; **pâté de foie gras** indicates a fine paste of duck or goose liver, often with truffles (**truffé**); **pâté en croûte** is enveloped in a pastry crust.

quenelles *kernel*
light dumplings made of fish, fowl or meat, served with a velvety sauce; the best known are **quenelles de brochet**, made of pike.

quiche *keesh*
a flan or open-faced tart with a rich, creamy filling of cheese, vegetables, meat or seafood; **quiche lorraine**, the best known, is garnished with bacon.

43

Soups

Soups appear on menus in various forms: **bouillon**, **consommé**, **crème**, **potage**, **soupe** and **velouté**. Look for these specialties:

aïgo bouïdo	*aeegoa bweedoa*	garlic soup (Provence)
bisque	*beesk*	seafood stew/chowder
bouillabaisse	*booyabess*	fish and seafood soup (Marseilles)
consommé	*kawngssommay*	clear, stock-based soup
à l'œuf	*a lurf*	with a raw egg
au porto	*oa portoa*	with port wine
Célestine	*saylesteen*	with chicken and noodles
Colbert	*kolbehr*	with poached eggs, spring vegetables
garbure	*garbewr*	cabbage soup, often with pork or goose
pot-au-feu	*po toa fur*	meat and vegetable stew
potage	*potazh*	soup
à l'ail	*ah lay*	garlic
au cresson	*oa kressawn*	watercress
bilibi	*beeleebee*	fish and oyster
bonne femme	*bon fam*	potato, leek and sometimes bacon
Condé	*kawngday*	mashed red beans
Crécy	*krehsee*	carrots and rice
du Barry	*dew baree*	cream of cauliflower
julienne	*zhewlyen*	shredded vegetables
Parmentier	*parmahngtyay*	potato
soupe	*soop*	soup
à la bière	*a la byehr*	beer with chicken stock and onions
à l'oignon	*ah lonyawng*	French onion
au pistou	*oa peestoo*	vegetable (Provence)/basil
aux choux	*oa shoo*	cabbage
de Pélous	*der payloo*	crab with tomatoes
de poisson	*der pwassawn*	small fish, simmered and puréed
de volaille	*der volay*	chicken
velouté	*verlootay*	cream

Fish and seafood

In coastal areas, take advantage of the wonderful variety of fresh fish and seafood. You'll recognize: **carpe**, **crabe**, **harengs**, **maquereau**, **perche**, **sardines**, **saumon**, **scampi**, **sole**, **turbot**.

escargots	*eskargoa*	snails
huîtres	*weetr*	oysters
morue	*morew*	cod
moules	*mool*	mussels
thon	*tawng*	tuna
truite	*trweet*	trout

bar aux herbes en chemise *bar oazerb ahng shermeez*
bass stuffed with spinach and herbs, wrapped in lettuce and poached in white wine.

cotriade *kotreeyad*
assorted fish soup/stew with shellfish, onion, carrots, potatoes, garlic, Calvados and white wine (Brittany).

homard à l'américaine *oma rah lamayreeken*
sautéed diced lobster, flamed in cognac and then simmered in wine, aromatic vegetables, herbs and tomatoes.

Meat

I'd like some …	**Je voudrais …** *zher voodreh*
bacon	**du lard** *dew lar*
beef	**du bœuf** *dew burf*
chicken	**du poulet** *dew pooleh*
duck	**du canard** *dew kanar*
goose	**de l'oie** *der lwah*
ham	**du jambon** *dew zhahngbawng*
lamb	**de l'agneau** *der lañoa*
pork	**du porc** *dew por*
rabbit	**du lapin** *dew lapang*
sausages	**des saucisses** *day soasseess*
steak	**du steak** *dew stek*
veal	**du veau** *dew voa*

Meat Cuts

contre-filet	*kawngtre feeleh*	loin strip steak
côte de bœuf	*koat der burf*	T-bone steak
côtelettes	*koaterlet*	chops
entrecôte	*ahngtrerkoat*	rib or rib-eye steak
escalope	*eskalop*	cutlet
filet	*feeleh*	fillet steak
gigot	*zheegoa*	leg
médaillon	*maydahyawng*	tenderloin steak
rognons	*roñawng*	kidneys
selle	*sel*	saddle
tournedos	*toornerdoa*	tenderloin of T-bone steak

Meat dishes

blanquette de veau *blawnket der voa*

veal stew in a white sauce (with eggs and cream), with onions and mushrooms.

bœuf bourguignon *burf boorgeeñawng*

a rich beef stew with vegetables, braised in red Burgundy wine.

canard à l'orange *kahnahrah lorahngzh*

duck braised with oranges and orange liqueur.

cassoulet toulousain *kassoolay tooloozang*

a casserole of white beans, mutton or salt pork, sausages and preserved goose.

civet *seevay*

game stew, with wine, onions and blood sauce; e.g., **civet de lièvre** (jugged hare).

coq au vin *ko koa vang*

chicken stewed with onion, mushroom, bacon in a red wine sauce. Sometimes the menu will tell what kind of wine was used, for instance, **coq au Chambertin**.

couscous *kooskoos*

Arab hot dish based on cracked wheat and topped with vegetables and meat.

lapin à la flamande *lahpang a la flamawnd*

marinated rabbit, braised potatoes, carrots, cabbage, turnip, bacon and sausage, simmered in beer (Belgium).

ragoût *ragoo*

meat stew, generally served in a delicate gravy with vegetables; for example **ragoût de bœuf** (beef stew).

Vegetables

You'll recognize: **artichaut**, **carottes**, **concombre**, **lentilles**, **oignons**, **radis**, **tomates**.

haricots verts	*areekoa vehr*	French (green) beans
laitue	*lehtew*	lettuce
petits pois	*pertee pwah*	peas

champignons *shahngpeeñawng*
button mushrooms. Common wild varieties used in French cuisine include **bolets** (boletus), **cèpes** (flat), **chanterelle** (aromatic) and **morille** (sweet).

pommes (de terre) *pom (der tehr)*
potatoes; which may appear as: **allumettes** (matchsticks), **dauphine** (mashed and deep-fried), **duchesse** (mashed), **en robe des champs** (in their jackets), **frites** (fries), **gaufrettes** (waffles), **mignonettes** (fries), **paille** (straws), **pont-neuf** (straight cut).

truffes *trewf*
truffles: highly prized fungus with a heavy, musky flavor. The black truffle of Périgord is regarded as the supreme delicacy.

chou rouge à la flamande *shoo roo zhah lah flamangd*
red cabbage, cooked with apples, onions, red wine and vinegar (Belg.).

chou fassum *shoo fassang*
cabbage stuffed with rice, eggs, cheese and minced meat (Provence).

Salads

The French will save a side salad until the end of their main course.

salade composée	*salad kawngpoazay*	mixed salad
salade de foies	*salad der fwa*	lettuce with
de volaille	*der volay*	chicken livers
salade russe	*salad rewss*	diced vegetables
salade de thon	*salad der tawng*	tuna salad
salade verte	*salad vehrt*	green salad

salade antiboise *salad awngteebwaz*
cooked diced fish, anchovy fillets, green peppers, beets, rice and capers in vinaigrette dressing.

salade niçoise *salad neeswaz*
a Riviera combination salad with tuna, anchovies, olives and vegetables.

Cheese

With almost 400 cheeses in France alone, there are plenty to suit any palate. Try goat's cheese (**fromage de chèvre**) for a distinctive sharp flavor.

mild	**beaumont, belle étoile, boursin, brie, cantal, coulommiers, mimolette, Port-Salut, reblochon, saint-paulin, tomme**
sharp, tangy	**bleu de Bresse, brousse, camembert, livarot, maroilles, munster, pont-l'évêque, roquefort, vacherin**
goat's milk	**bûcheron, cabécou, crottin de Chavignol, rocamadour, st-marcellin, valençay**
Swiss cheeses	**beaufort, comté, emmental, gruyère**

croque-monsieur *krok mersyur*
toasted ham and cheese sandwich.

croûte au fromage *kroot oa fromazh*
hot, melted cheese served over a slice of toast, sometimes with ham and topped with a fried egg.

fromage blanc *fromazh blahng*
fresh white cheese to be eaten with sugar or with pepper and salt.

raclette *raklet*
a half round of a firm cheese grilled until the surface begins to melt; the melting cheese is then scraped off on to a warmed plate and eaten with cold meats, boiled potatoes, gherkins and pickled pearl onions.

Dessert

crêpe *krep*
Thin pancake; **à la confiture** (with jelly); **au sucre** (with sugar); **normande** (with Calvados and cream); **suzette** (simmered in orange juice and cream).

diplomate *deeplomat*
molded custard dessert with crystallized fruit and lined with sponge cake fingers steeped in liqueur.

sabayon *sabayawng*
creamy dessert of egg yolks, wine, sugar and flavoring.

tarte Tatin *tart tartang*
hot caramelized apples with crust on top and served with vanilla ice cream, **chantilly** or **crème anglaise** (custard).

DRINKS

Beer

Beer is to the Belgians what wine is to the French, and it is often served in its own type of glass. Look for the following types:

bière blanche (white beer): cloudy and honeyish e.g., *Hoegaarden, Kwak*

bière blonde (lager): light, Pilsener-style e.g., *Jupiler, Lamot, Stella Artois*

bière brune (red beer): refreshing and sour e.g., *Rodenbach*

bières trappistes (abbey beers): dark and full bodied e.g., *Chimay, Orval*

Gueuze (blended Lambic beers): e.g., *Kriek* (cherry), *Frambozen* (raspberries), *Faro* (sugar)

Lambic (wheat beer): fermented like wine with a sour, apple-like taste. Elsewhere, popular brews include *Kronenbourg, Pelforth* and *Kanterbraü* (French) and *Cardinal* and *Hürlimann* (Swiss).

Wine

French cuisine and wine are inseparable components that complement each other. The wine waiter (**le sommelier**) will be happy to offer advice – and a tip is appreciated for this service. The main grape varieties are:

red:	**Cabernet-Sauvignon, Carignan, Cinsaut, Gamay, Grenache, Merlot, Mourvedre, Pinot Noir, Syrah**;
white:	**Chardonnay, Chenin Blanc, Gewurztraminer, Muscadet, Muscat, Riesling, Sauvignon Blanc, Sémillon**.

Reading the label

AC (appellation contrôlée)/AOC highest quality wine	**mis en bouteilles par** bottled by
blanc white	**mousseux** sparkling/frothy
brut dry	**rosé** rosé
cépage grape variety	**rouge** red
château wine-making estate	**sec** dry
côte/coteaux slope/hills	**VDQS** good quality regional wine
crémant sparkling	**vignoble** vineyard
cru superior growth	**vin de garde** wine to lay down to mature
demi-sec medium dry/sweet	
doux sweet	**vin de pays** local wine – less strict quality control than AC
millésime vintage	
mis en bouteilles dans nos caves bottled in our cellars	**vin de table** table wine
	vin ordinaire table wine

Wine regions

Alsace (almost only dry white wines) esp. Gewurztraminer, Riesling, Sylvaner

Bordeaux (major wine growing area) sp. Entre-Deux-Mers, Graves, Médoc (red: Listrac, Margaux, Moulis, Pauillac, St-Estèphe, St-Julien), Pessac-Léognan, Pomerol (red: Château-Pétrus, Lalande-de-Pomerol, Néac), Sauternes (white: Château-d'Yquem, Barsac), Sainte-Croix-du-Mont (sweet), St-Émilion (Lussac, Montagne, Parsac, Puisseguin, St-Georges).

Bourgogne (Burgundy: major wine-growing area of 5 regions) Beaujolais (red: Chiroubles, Fleurie, Juliénas, Moulin-à-Vent, Morgon, Régnié, St-Amour); Chablis (white); Côte Chalonnaise (Mercurey); Côte de Beaune (Aloxe-Corton, Beaune, Blagy, Chassagne-Montrachet, Chorley-lès-Beaune, Meursault, Pernand-Vergelesses, Pommard, Puligny-Montrachet, St-Romain, Santenay, Savigny-lès-Beaune, Volnay); Côte de Nuits (Chambolle-Musigny, Fixin, Gevrey-Chambertin, Marsannay, Morey-St-Denis, Nuits-St-Georges, Vosne-Romanée); Mâconnais (red: St-Véran).

Champagne (home of the world-famous sparkling wine) e.g., Bollinger, Jacquart, Krug, Laurent Perrier, Moët & Chandon, Mumm.

Côtes-du-Rhône (wide variety of white, red and rosé) Northern Rhone (Cornas, Côte-Rôtie, Crozes-Hermitage, St-Joseph); Southern Rhone (Châteauneuf-du-Pape, Gigondas, Lirac, Muscat de Beaumes-de-Venise, Rasteau, Tavel-rosé, Vacqueyras); Côtes du Ventoux; Côtes du Lubéron.

Jura (small wine-growing area between Burgundy and Switzerland) esp. Arbois, Château-Chalon, Côtes du Jura, l'Etoile.

Languedoc Blanquette de Limoux, Clairette de Bellegarde, Clairette du Languedoc, Corbières, Costières de Nîmes, Faugères, Fitou, Muscat (sweet: Lunel, Minervois, Mireval, St-Jean-de-Minervois), St-Chinian.

Loire Anjou (Coteaux-de-l'Aubance, Coteaux-du-Layon, Quarts-de-Chaume, Savennières); Berry and Nivernais (Menetou-Salon, Pouilly-Fumé, Quincy, Reuilly, Sancerre); Nantais (Muscadet); Saumur; Touraine (Bourgueil, Chinon, Montlouis, Vouvray).

Lorraine (minor wine-growing area) e.g., Vins de la Moselle, Côtes-de-Toul.

Provence (wide range of red, white and rosé) esp: Bandol, Bellet, Cassis, Coteaux-d'Aix-en-Provence, Côtes-de-Provence, Palette, Coteaux Varois.

Roussillon (produces 3/4 of France's sweet wine) e.g., red: Côtes-du-Roussillon; sweet: Banyuls, Côtes-du-Haut-Roussillon, Grand-Roussillon, Muscat de Rivesaltes, Rivesaltes.

Savoie (bordering Switzerland – primarily dry white wines) e.g., Crépy, Seyssel.

Switzerland (produces primarily light, white wines) esp. Neuchâtel (Auvernier, Cormondrèche, Cortaillod, Hauterive), Valais (Arvine, Dôle, Ermitage, Fendant, Johannisberg, Malvoisie), Vaud (Aigle, Dézaley, Mont-sur-Rolle, Lavaux, Yvorne).

Other drinks

Apéritifs are much more common than cocktails or highballs. Many are wine- and brandy-based with herbs and bitters (e.g., *Amer Picon*®, *Byrrh*®, *Dubonnet*®); typically French is the aniseed-based pastis (e.g., *Pernod*®, *Ricard*®). But you may prefer a liqueur drink such as **blanc-cassis** or **kir** (chilled white wine with black currant syrup). You'll recognize **un gin-tonic**, **un rhum**, **un vermouth**, **une vodka**, **un whisky**.

After a meal, you may like to try a fruit-distilled brandy: **calvados** (apple), **kirsch** (cherry), **marc** (grape), **poire William** (pear) or **quetsche** (plum). Other popular liqueurs include the famous orange-flavored *Grand Marnier*® and *Cointreau*®; and *Bénédictine*® – brandy-based with herbs.

Non-alcoholic drinks

France offers a wide choice of mineral waters, such as *Badoit*®, *Evian*®, *Perrier*®, *Vichy*®, *Vittel*®, *Volvic*®. You'll also have no trouble finding your favorite soft drinks or sodas, such as *Coca-Cola*®, *Fanta*®, *Pepsi*®.

I'd like …	**Je voudrais …** *zher voodray*
(hot) chocolate	**un chocolat (chaud)** *ang shokolah (shoa)*
coke/lemonade	**un coca/une limonade** *ang koka/ewn leemonad*
milkshake	**un frappé** *ang frapay*
mineral water	**de l'eau minérale** *der loa meenayral*
carbonated	**gazeuse** *gazurz*
non-carbonated/still	**non gazeuse** *nawng gazurz*
tonic water	**un Schweppes** *ang shweps*

un café *ang kafay*
Coffee can be served: **au lait** (with milk); **complet** (with bread, rolls, butter and jam); **crème** (with cream); **décaféiné** (decaffeinated); **frappé** (shaken, iced coffee); **noir** (black); **sans caféine** (decaffeinated); **soluble** (instant).

un jus de fruits *ang zhoo der frwee*
Common fruit juices are **jus d'orange** (orange), **jus de pamplemousse** (grapefruit), **jus de poire** (pear), **jus de pomme** (apple), and **jus de tomate** (tomato).

un thé *ang tay*
Tea can be drunk the British way, **au lait** (with milk), but it is more usual to have it **au citron** (with lemon), **à la menthe** (mint tea), **glacé** (iced) or **nature** (black). A **tisane** (herb tea) is also a popular alternative.

MENU READER

à la vapeur	*a la vapurr*	steamed
au four	*oa foor*	baked
bouilli	*booyee*	boiled
braisé	*brezay*	braised
coupé en dés	*koopay ahng day*	diced
en ragoût	*ahng ragoo*	stewed
épicé	*aypeessay*	spicy
farci	*farsee*	stuffed
frit (dans la friture)	*free (dahng la freetewr)*	(deep) fried
fumé	*fewmay*	smoked
grillé	*greeyay*	grilled
mariné	*mareenay*	marinated
pané	*panay*	breaded
poché	*poshay*	poached
rôti	*roatee*	roasted/ oven-browned
sauté	*soatay*	sautéed
velouté de ...	*velootay der*	creamed
bleu	*blur*	very rare
saignant	*señahng*	rare
à point	*a pwang*	medium
bien cuit	*byang kwee*	well-done

A

à la, à l', au, aux in the manner of, as in, with

à l'étouffée stewed

à la croque au sel served raw with salt and French dressing

abricot apricot

agneau lamb

aiglefin (églefin) haddock

aïgo bouïdo garlic soup (*Prov.*)

aiguillettes de canard au vinaigre fillet of duck in raspberry vinegar (*Dord.*)

ail garlic

aïoli garlic mayonnaise

alose shad (fine textured fish with delicate flesh)

alouette lark

alouettes sans têtes stuffed small rolled veal cutlets

amandes almonds

américaine white wine, brandy, garlic, shallots, tomatoes, shrimp or lobster flavoring

amuse-gueule savory biscuits, crackers; appetizers

ananas pineapple
anchois anchovies
anchoïade purée of unsalted anchovies in olive oil (*Prov.*)
andouille(tte) tripe sausage
aneth dill
anglaise boiled or steamed vegetables; breaded and fried
anguille eel
anguille au vert eel flavored with sorrel, sage and parsley (*Belg.*)
anis aniseed
A.O.C. officially recognized wine
apéritifs aperitifs
artichaut artichoke
asperges asparagus
aspic (meat or fish in) aspic
assaisonnement seasoning
assiette anglaise assorted cold cuts
assiette de charcuterie selection of cold meats
attente: 15 min waiting time: 15 minutes
au bleu (especially for trout) poached when it's fresh
au choix choice of …
au citron with lemon
au four baked
au gril grilled
au lait with milk
aubergine eggplant/aubergine
avec de l'eau gazeuse with (seltzer) water
avec des glaçons on the rocks

B

baguette long, thin loaf of French bread
ballon a glass
bananes Baronnet sliced bananas with lemon, cream and kirch ↑
bar sea bass
bar aux herbes en chemise stuffed sea bass
barbue brill (fish like a turbot)
barquette small boat-shaped pastry shell garnished with fruit

basilic basil
bâtard small French bread stick
baudroie angler
bavarois Bavarian cream cakes
béarnaise creamy sauce of vinegar, egg, white wine, shallots, tarragon
bécasse woodcock
bécassine snipe
béchamel white sauce
beignet fritter, generally filled with fruit, vegetables or meat
betterave beet
beurre butter
beurre blanc butter, shallots, vinegar, white wine
beurre noir browned butter, vinegar and/or lemon juice
bien cuit well-done
bière beer
bière blonde/brune light/dark beer
bière en bouteilles bottled beer
bière sans alcool a non-alcoholic beer
bifteck beef steak
bigarade with oranges
bigorneaux winkles
biscuit de Savoie sponge cake
biscuits cookies/biscuits
biscuits apéritifs appetizers, snacks
biscuits salés crackers
bisque seafood chowder/stew
bisque d'écrevisses crayfish chowder/stew
bisque de homard lobster chowder/stew
blanc white (wine); breast (chicken)
blanchaille herring/whitebait
blanquette de veau veal in cream sauce
bleu very rare; blue (cheese); boiled fresh (fish)
bœuf beef
bœuf bourguignon wine beef stew
bœuf mode beef chunks with carrots and onions in red wine
bœuf salé corned beef
boissons drinks

boisson non alcoolisée soft drink/soda
bolets boletus mushrooms
bombe molded ice cream mousse
bordelaise sauce of mushrooms, red wine, shallots, beef marrow (*Bord.*)
bouchée à la reine sweetbreads in pastry
boudin blood sausage/black pudding
bouillabaisse fish and seafood soup (*Mar.*)
bouilleture d'anguilles eel cooked in cream (*Anjou*)
bouilli boiled; boiled beef
bouillon bouillon
bouillon de poulet chicken bouillon
boulettes (de viande) meatballs
bourguignonne red wine, herbs, button mushrooms, shallots
bourride fish chowder/stew (*Prov.*)
braisé braised
brandade de morue creamed salt cod
brème bream (fish)
brioche bun
brioche au sucre bun sprinkled with sugar
(à la) broche (on a) skewer
brochet pike
brochette skewered kebab
brugnon nectarine
brut very dry (wine)
bûche de Noël Christmas log
bulots large whelks (seafood)

C

cabillaud (fresh) cod
cabri kid goat
cacahuètes peanuts
cade chickpea cake (*Riv.*)
café coffee
café au lait coffee with milk
café complet coffee with bread, rolls, butter and jam
café crème coffee with cream
café décaféiné decaffeinated coffee

café frappé shaked cold coffee
café noir black coffee
café sans caféine decaffeinated coffee
café soluble instant coffee
caille quail
calissons ground almonds and marzipan (*Aix*)
cal(a)mars squid
calvados apple brandy (*Norm.*)
canard (sauvage) (wild) duck
canard à l'orange duck in orange
canard laqué Peking duck
caneton duckling
caneton à la rouennaise duckling in red wine sauce (*Norm.*)
cannelle cinnamon
câpres capers
carafe carafe
carbonnade charcoal-grilled meat
carbon(n)ade flamande beef slices and onions in beer (*Belg.*)
caricoles sea snails (*Belg.*)
carottes carrots
carpe carp
carré d'agneau rack of lamb
carré braisé à la niçoise braised loin with vermouth and lemon peel
carrelet plaice (flat fish)
casse-croûte sandwich, snack
cassis black currants; black currant liqueur
cassoulet toulousain beef and pork casserole
céleri(-rave) celeriac
cèpes flap mushrooms
céréales cereal
cerf venison (red deer)
cerfeuil chervil
cerises (noires) (black) cherries
cervelas type of sausage
cervelle brains
chabichou cheese of cow's and goat's milk
champignons (de Paris) mushrooms
chantilly whipped cream
chapon capon

charcuterie cold cuts; assorted pork products

charlotte fruit dessert in mold

Chartreuse herb liqueur

chasseur wine, mushrooms, onions, shallots, herbs

chateaubriand double fillet steak (tenderloin of porterhouse steak)

chaud hot

chaud-froid dressing containing gelatin

chaudrée fish and seafood stew

chausson aux pommes apple turnover

chevreuil venison/roe deer

chichifregi roll doughnuts, sold by the centimeter (Riv.)

chicorée endive/chicory

chips potato chips/crisps

chocolat (chaud) (hot) chocolate

chocolat froid cold chocolate

chocolatine chocolate puff pastry

chou (rouge) (red) cabbage

chou rouge à la flamande red cabbage in red wine (Belg.)

chou fassum
stuffed cabbage (Prov.)

chou-fleur cauliflower

chou-fleur au gratin cauliflower with white cheese sauce

choucroute sauerkraut

choucroute garnie sauerkraut, sausages and cured pork

choux de Bruxelles brussels sprouts

ciboulette chives

citron lemon

citron pressé lemon juice

citron vert lime

civet game stew

clafoutis fruit in pancake batter

clous de girofle clove

cochon de lait suckling pig

(en) cocotte pot-roasted

cœurs d'artichaut artichoke hearts

cognac brandy

colonel lemon (water ice) doused with vodka

communard red wine and black currant liqueur

compris(e) included

concombre cucumber

confit preserve

confiture jam

congolais coconut cake

consommé consommé

consommé à l'œuf consommé with a raw egg

consommé au porto consommé with port wine

consommé Célestine consommé with chicken and noodles

consommé Colbert consommé with poached eggs, spring vegetables

contre-filet loin strip steak

coq au vin chicken in red wine

coq de bruyère woodgrouse

coquelet à l'estragon spring chicken with tarragon sauce

coquilles St-Jacques scallops

coriandre coriander

cornichons pickles/gherkins

corsé full-bodied (wine)

côte rib

côte de bœuf T-bone steak

côtelettes chops

cotriade fish soup (Britt.)

cou d'oie farci stuffed goose neck (Dord.)

coulis soup; creamy sauce

coupe (glacée) ice cream dessert, sundae

courgette zucchini

couronne ring-shaped loaf

couscous Arab dish of cracked wheat with meat

couvert silverware

crabe crab

crème ... cream of ...

crème anglaise custard equivalent

crème brûlée custard with crispy caramel topping

crème caramel caramel pudding

crème Chantilly whipped cream

crème d'asperges cream of asparagus

crème de bolets cream of boletus mushrooms

crème de volaille cream of chicken

crème pâtissière cream with butter

crêpe pancake

crêpe à la confiture pancake with jam

crêpe au sucre pancake with sugar

crêpe dentelle thin biscuity pancake (*Britt.*)

crêpe normande pancake with Calvados and cream

crêpe suzette large, thin pancakes simmered in orange juice and flambéed with orange liqueur

crépinette flat seasoned sausage

cresson watercress

crevettes shrimp

croissants flaky crescent rolls

croquembouche caramel-coated pastry puff

croque-madame a croque-monsieur with an egg on top

croque-monsieur toasted ham and cheese sandwich

crottin de Chavignol goat's cheese

croustade filled pie/pastry shell

croûte au fromage melted cheese on toast, with ham and topped by a fried egg

cru raw; system of grading wine

crudités mixed raw vegetable salad

crustacés shellfish

cuisses de grenouilles frog's legs

cuit à la vapeur steamed

cuit au bleu poached when fresh (esp. trout)

cul de veau à l'angevine veal rump in rich sauce with vegetables (*Loire*)

cumin caraway

dartois jam pastry

dattes dates

daube de bœuf beef stew with tomatoes and olives (*Prov.*)

daurade sea bream (fish)

décaféiné decaffeinated

délice dessert specialty of the chef

délimité de qualité supérieure superior quality (wine)

demi-bouteille a half bottle

demi-poulet grillé half a roasted chicken

dessert desserts

diable hot-pepper sauce

diabolo menthe mint cordial

dinde turkey

dinde aux marrons turkey with chestnuts

dindonneau young turkey (cock)

diplomate molded dessert

doux sweet (wine)

dur hard (egg)

duxelles with mushrooms

eau (chaude) (hot) water

eau minérale mineral water

eau minérale gazeuse carbonated/ mineral water

eau minérale non gazeuse non carbonated mineral water

échalote shallot

éclair au chocolat/café long cake filled with chocolate/coffee cream

écrevisses crayfish

émincé de bœuf aux morilles beef stew with morels

emporter, à to take out

en chemise baked in waxed paper

en saison in season

endives endive

entrecôte rib/rib-eye steak

entrées first course/appetizer

entremets small dish served before cheese; dessert

épaule shoulder

épaule braisée aux marrons braised shoulder stuffed with chestnuts

éperlans smelts/spaling (small fish)

épices spices

épinards spinach

escalope cutlet

escalope à la crème veal scallops cooked with cream
escalope viennoise breaded veal cutlet
escargots snails
espadon swordfish
estouffade de bœuf beef stew
estragon tarragon
expresso espresso coffee

F

faisan pheasant
far sweet batter pudding, often with dried fruit (*Britt.*)
farces stuffing, esp. liver and truffles
farci stuffed
faux-filet sirloin steak
fenouil fennel
féra lake salmon
fèves broad beans
ficelle thin bread stick
figues figs
filet fillet steak
filet mignon au poivre vert meat with green pepper sauce
financière Madeira wine, truffles, olives, mushrooms
fines herbes mixture of herbs; with herbs
flageolets small kidney beans
flamiche savory cheese pie with leeks or onions
flan custard tart
florentin thin crust of almonds and dark chocolate
(à la) florentine with spinach
foie liver
foie de veau grillé à la moutarde grilled calf's liver with mustard and breadcrumbs
foie gras goose or duck liver
fond d'artichaut artichoke heart
fondue melted cheese dip (*Switz.*)
fondue bourguignonne meat fondue with different sauces
fondue chinoise thinly sliced meat plunged into simmering stock

forestière with mushrooms, shallots and white wine
fougasse flat loaf with anchovies, olives, cheese (*Prov.*)
(au) four baked
fraises strawberries
framboises raspberries
frappé chilled, iced; milkshake
fricassée braised meat in a thick sauce
frigousse casserole of chicken, bacon and chestnuts (*Britt.*)
frisée curly lettuce
frit fried
frites French fries
friture de mer small fish, generally deep fried, eaten like chips (fries)
froid cold
fromage cheese
fromage blanc fresh white cheese to be eaten with sugar or with pepper and salt.
fromage blanc à la crème fresh white cheese served with cream
fromage de chèvre goat's cheese
fruits fruit
fruits confits candied fruit
fruits de mer seafood
fruits frais fresh fruits
fruits secs dried fruit
fumé smoked

G

galette flat, plain cake/crêpe
galette complète crêpes filled with egg, ham and cheese
ganses small fried cakes topped with sugar (*Prov.*)
garbure cabbage soup, with pork or goose
garniture au choix choice of vegetable accompaniment
gâteau cake
gâteau au chocolat chocolate cake
gâteau Bigarreau sponge cake with praline filling
gâteau breton rich pound cake
gâteau de riz rice pudding

gâteau de semoule semolina pudding

gâteau lyonnais chocolate and chestnut cake

gaufres waffles

(à la) gelée in aspic

génoise light cake

gibelotte de lapin rabbit stew in wine sauce

gibier game

gigot leg of lamb

gigot à la bretonne roast leg of lamb with dried beans

gin-tonic gin and tonic

gingembre ginger

glace ice cream

glace à la fraise/à la vanille strawberry/vanilla ice cream

glacé iced, glazed

goujon gudgeon (tiny freshwater fish)

grand veneur sauce for game

(au) gratin browned with breadcrumbs or cheese

gratin dauphinois sliced potatoes gratinéed with milk, cream and garlic

gratin de queues d'écrevisses baked crayfish tails

gratinée au four baked with cheese and ham

grattons grilled pork fat (*Lyon*)

grenadine red fruit syrup with water

grillades grilled meat

grillé grilled

grive thrush

grondin gurnard (firm fleshed fish)

groseilles red currants

groseilles à maquereau gooseberries

H
---

hachis Parmentier shepherd's pie

hareng herring

haricots blancs haricot beans, white kidney beans

haricots verts French (green) beans

(aux) herbes with herbs

hollandaise egg yolks, butter, vinegar

homard lobster

homard à l'américaine sautéed lobster

homard thermidor lobster gratinéed with cheese

hors-d'œuvre appetizers

hors-d'œuvre variés assorted appetizers

huîtres oysters

I

île flottante meringue in custard

(à l')indienne (in) curry sauce

J
---

jambon ham

jambon de Bayonne raw, salty ham

jambon-beurre sandwich with ham and butter

jambonneau cured pig's knuckle

jardinière cooked assorted vegetables

jarret knuckle

Joconde almond sponge

julienne vegetables cut into fine strips

jus (fruit) juice

jus d'orange orange juice

jus de fruits fruit juice

jus de pamplemousse grapefruit juice

jus de poire pear juice

jus de pomme apple juice

jus de tomate tomato juice

K

Kig-Ha-Farz mixture of pork, beef, vegetables and buckwheat (*Britt.*)

kir white wine with black currant liqueur

kir royal champagne and black currant liqueur

kirsch cherry liqueur

kouing-aman crisp butter cake (*Britt.*)

L
---

lait milk

laitue lettuce
lamproie lamprey
langouste spiny (rock) lobster
langoustines Dublin bay prawns, scampi
langue tongue
lapin rabbit
lapin à la flamande marinated rabbit (*Belg.*)
lard bacon
laurier bay leaf
léger light (wine)
légumes vegetables
lentilles lentils
lièvre wild hare
limonade soft drink/soda
liqueur liqueur
(à la) lorraine braised in red wine with red cabbage
lotte burbot (firm white flesh fish)
lotte de mer anglerfish, monkfish (chewy, mild, sweet flesh)
loup sea bass
(à la) lyonnaise sautéed with onions

M

madère with Madeira wine
magret de canard fillet breast of fattened duck (*Dord.*)
maïs corn
maison homemade
maître d'hôtel headwaiter (or maitre d')
mandarine tangerine
manons chocolate filled with fresh cream (*Belg.*)
maquereau mackerel
marc grape spirit
marcassin young wild boar
marchand de vin wine merchant
mariné marinated
marinière white wine, mussel broth thickened with egg yolks
marjolaine marjoram; layered nut cake
marrons chestnuts

matelote (d'anguilles) fish (esp. eel) stew with wine (*Tours, Anjou*)
médaillon tenderloin steak
melon melon
menthe mint
menthe à l'eau mint syrup with water
menu à prix fixe set menu
menu gastronomique gourmet menu
menu touristique choice of dishes for each course, for a fixed price
meringue meringue
merlan whiting
méthode champenoise in the champagne style
meunière brown butter, parsley, lemon juice
miel honey
(à la) milanaise with Parmesan and noisette butter
milhassou sweet, cornmeal pudding
milkshake milkshake
mille-feuille flaky pastry with cream filling (napoleon)
(à la) mode in the style of, esp. local recipe
moelle bone marrow
molle, pâte soft (cheese)
mollet soft (egg)
mont-blanc chestnut dessert with whipped cream
morilles morels (mushrooms)
Mornay cheese sauce
mortadelle Bologna sausage
morue cod
moules mussels
moules marinière mussels simmering in white wine with shallots, thyme and parsley
mousse au chocolat chocolate mousse
mousse de foie light liver pâté
mousseline mayonnaise with cream; puréed raw fish with cream
mousseux sparkling (wine)
moutarde mustard; mustard sauce

mûres mulberries, blackberries
muscade nutmeg
myrtilles blueberries

nature plain; black (tea)
navets turnips
nectar d'abricot apricot juice
(à la) niçoise with garlic, anchovies, olives, onions and tomatoes
Noilly Prat® a French vermouth
noir black (coffee/tea)
noisette hazelnut; boneless round piece of meat
noisette de porc aux pruneaux pork tenderloin/fillet with prunes and cream (*Loire*)
noix walnuts
noix de coco coconut
noix de muscade nutmeg
(à la) normande mushrooms, eggs and cream sauce
nouilles noodles

œufs eggs
œuf à la coque boiled egg
œuf dur hard-boiled egg
œufs Argenteuil eggs on tartlet with asparagus and cream sauce
œufs à la Bruxelles eggs with braised chicory and cream sauce
œufs à la diable deviled eggs
œufs à la neige meringue on custard
œufs au bacon bacon and eggs
œufs au jambon ham and eggs
œufs au plat fried eggs
œufs brouillés scrambled eggs
œufs mimosa hard-boiled eggs served with mayonnaise
oie goose
oignons onions
olives olives
omble (chevalier) char (delicate, flavorful fish)
omelette (nature) (plain) omelet

omelette au fromage cheese omelet
omelette au jambon ham omelet
omelette aux champignons mushroom omelet
omelette aux fines herbes herb omelet
onglet prime cut of meat
opéra layered chocolate and nut cake
orange orange
orangeade orangeade
origan oregano
ormeaux abalones (chewy shellfish)
ortolan ortolan bunting

pain bread
pain au chocolat flaky pastry filled with chocolate
pain au levain leaven bread
pain aux raisins snail-shaped bun with raisins
pain blanc/bis white/brown bread
pain complet/intégral whole-wheat/wholemeal bread
pain d'épices gingerbread (*Dijon*)
pain de seigle rye bread
pain de son bran bread
pain grillé toast
paillasson fried, sliced potatoes (*Lyon*)
palourdes clams
pamplemousse grapefruit
panaché selection; shandy
panbagna/pan bagnat tuna and salad sandwich (*Riv.*)
pannequet parcel shaped crêpe
(en) papillote baked in grease-proof paper
parfait glacé frozen dessert
Paris-Brest large pastry ring with cream
(à la) parisienne with mushrooms in white wine sauce
Parmentier with potatoes
pastèque watermelon
pastis aniseed-based drink (*Prov./Midi*); flaky apple pie (*Dord.*)
pâté molded pastry case; liver and pork purée

pâtes pasta
pâtes fraîches fresh pasta, noodles
pâtisseries pastries
paupiettes de veau Valentino
veal "birds" stuffed with asparagus,
with tomato sauce
(à la) paysanne containing vegetables
pêche peach
perche perch
perdreau young partridge
perdrix partridge
Périgueux with a goose – or duck –
liver purée and truffles
Pernod® aniseed flavored aperitif
persil parsley
petit déjeuner breakfast
petit four small cake
petit noir espresso coffee
petit pain roll
petit pain au cumin roll with
caraway seeds
petit pain aux pavots
roll with poppy seeds
petit salé aux lentilles
pork breast with lentils
petit-suisse thick fromage frais (fresh
curd cheese) eaten with sugar or jam
petits pois peas
petits trianons chocolate fudge bars
pieds feet/trotters
pieds (et) paquets stuffed sheep's
trotters (*Mar.*)
pigeon pigeon
pigeonneau squab
pignons buttery croissants with pine-
nuts (*Prov.*)
pilaf rice boiled in a bouillon with
onions
piment pimiento
pintade guinea fowl
pintadeau young guinea cock
pissaladière type of pizza made with
onions and anchovies (*Prov.*)
pistou vegetable and pasta soup; garlic
and fresh basil paste (*Riv.*)
plaque de chocolat chocolate bar (large)

plat (du jour) dish (of the day)
plateau plate
plat principal main course
plie plaice (flat fish)
poché poached
poire pear
poire à la Condé hot pear on bed of
vanilla-flavored rice
poire Belle-Hélène pear with vanilla ice
cream and chocolate sauce
poireaux leeks
pois mange-tout string-peas
poissons fish
poivrade pepper sauce
poivre pepper
poivrons sweet peppers
polenta polenta
pomme apple
pommes de terre potatoes
pommes allumettes potato matchsticks
pommes dauphine potato mashed in
butter and egg yolks, mixed in seasoned
flour and deep-fried
pommes duchesse potato mashed
with butter and egg yolks
pommes en robe des champs
potatoes in their jackets
pommes frites French fries
pommes mousseline mashed potatoes
pommes nature boiled, steamed
potato
pommes nouvelles new potatoes
pommes vapeur steamed, boiled
potato
pompes à l'huile cake flavored with
orange flower water or aniseed (*Riv.*)
porc pork
porto port; with port wine
pot-au-feu beef stew with vegetables
potage soup
potage à l'ail garlic soup
potage au cresson watercress soup
potage bilibi fish and oyster soup
potage bonne femme potato, leek
and sometimes bacon soup
potage Condé shredded vegetables soup

potage du Barry cream of cauliflower
potage julienne mashed red beans soup
potage Parmentier potato soup
potiron pumpkin
poularde fattened pullet
poule stewing fowl
poule au pot stewed chicken with vegetables
poulet chicken
poulet créole chicken in white sauce with rice
poulet Marengo chicken in white wine
poulet rôti roast chicken
poulette with butter, cream and egg yolks
poulpes octopus
pour deux personnes for two
poussin spring chicken
praires clams
pressé fresh (juice)
pression draft beer
profiterole filled choux pastry
(à la) provençale onions, tomatoes, garlic
pruneaux prunes
prunes plums
pudding à la Reine bread pudding with lemon, cream and apricot
puits d'amour pastry shell with liqueur-flavored custard
purée de pommes de terre mashed potatoes

quatre-quarts pound cake
quenelles dumplings
quiche savory flan or open-faced tart

raclette melted cheese dish
radis radishes
ragoût meat stew
raie ray
raifort horseradish
raisin (blanc/noir) (white/black) grapes

raisins secs raisins
ramequin small cheese tart
râpé grated
rascasse fish used in bouillabaisse
ratatouille vegetable casserole
ravigote vinegar sauce with eggs, capers and herbs
religieuse au chocolat/café puff cake with chocolate/coffee filling
rémoulade sauce flavored with mustard and herbs
réserve du patron house wine
rhubarbe rhubarb
rhum rum
Ricard® aniseed-flavored aperitif
rillettes pâté, usually of duck
rillettes de porc minced pork served chilled in earthenware pots
rillons chunky pieces of pork hors-d'œuvre
ris de veau veal sweetbreads
riz rice
rognons kidneys
romarin rosemary
rosbif roast beef
rosé rosé (wine)
rosette dried sausage (*Lyon*)
rôti roast
rouge red (wine)
rouget red mullet
rouille pink, garlicky mayonnaise
rouilleuse white wine sauce, thickened with blood

sabayon creamy dessert
sablé au beurre type of shortbread
sacristains pastry straws with sugar or cheese topping
safran saffron
saignant rare
saint-cyr baked meringue with frozen chocolate mousse
saint-honoré choux cake with cream
saint-pierre John Dory (nutty, sweet-flavored fish)

salade salad

salade composée mixed salad

salade au cabécou goat-cheese salad (*Dord.*)

salade chiffonnade shredded lettuce and sorrel in melted butter

salade de foies de volaille lettuce with chicken livers

salade de museau de bœuf marinated brawn/headcheese

salade de thon tuna salad

salade niçoise a Riviera combination salad, which includes tuna, anchovies, black olives and tomatoes and rice

salade russe diced vegetable salad in mayonnaise

salade verte green salad

sandre pike perch, zander

sandwich sandwich

sandwich au fromage cheese sandwich

sandwich au jambon ham sandwich

sanglier wild boar

sans glaçon straight

sarcelle teal (a duck)

sardines sardines

sauces sauces

sauce bleue vinaigrette with blue cheese (roquefort type)

sauce diable sauce with cayenne, shallots, pepper

sauce Périgueux rich Madeira sauce with cognac and truffles

saucisse sausage

saucisse de Francfort frankfurter

saucisse de Morteau type of pork sausage to cook

saucisse de Strasbourg Strasbourg (pork) sausage, knackwurst

saucisson cold sausage

saucisson brioché large sausage in a bun (*Lyon*)

sauge sage

saumon salmon

sauté sautéed

savarin sponge cake in rum

scallopini breaded escalopes

scampi prawns (shrimp)

Schweppes® tonic water

sec dry (wine)

sel salt

selle saddle

selon arrivage when available

selon grosseur/grandeur (s.g.) price according to size

sirop syrup

socca chickpea cake, eaten hot (Nice)

sole sole

sorbet sherbet

soubise onion-cream sauce

soufflé light fluffy dish with browned egg whites

soufflé au Grand Marnier soufflé made of orange liqueur

soufflé Rothschild vanilla-flavored soufflé with candied fruit

soupe soup

soupe à la bière beer soup with chicken stock and onions (*Belg.*)

soupe à l'oignon French onion soup

soupe au pistou vegetable soup with pesto sauce (*Prov.*)

soupe aux choux cabbage soup

soupe de Pélous crab soup with tomatoes, saffron and bread

soupe de poisson small fish, simmered with tomatoes and saffron, then puréed and sieved

soupe du jour soup of the day

spécialités locales local specialties

steak beef steak

steak au poivre steak with cracked black pepper

steak tartare raw minced fillet with egg, capers and parsley

steak-frites steak and French fries

sucre sugar

supplément/en sus extra charge

suprême thickened chicken broth

suprême de volaille chicken breast in cream sauce

sur commande made to order

tablier de sapeur pig's feet/fried tripe in breadcrumbs
tajine lamb with almonds and sultanas
tapenade spicy mousse of olives and anchovies (*Prov.*)
tartare mayonnaise flavored with mustard and herbs
tarte à la brousse type of cheese cake (*Corsica*)
tarte à la cannelle blueberry-cinnamon flan
tarte au citron meringuée lemon meringue pie
tarte au fromage cheese tart
tarte aux pommes apple tart
tarte de blettes tart with minced chard leaves, cheese, dried currants
tarte frangipane almond cream tart
tarte Tatin upside down apple tart
tartelette small tart
tartine buttered bread with jam, marmelade or honey
tarte tropézienne rich cake filled with crème pâtissière
tasse de thé cup of tea
tellines small triangular shellfish seasoned with garlic and parsley (*Riv.*)
terrine sliced pâté
tête de nègre meringue cake covered with dark chocolate
thé tea
thé à la menthe mint tea
thé au citron tea with lemon
thé au lait tea with milk
thé glacé iced tea
thé nature black tea
thon tuna
thym thyme
tian de courgettes zucchini [courgette] custard (*Riv.*)
(en) timbale cooked in a pastry case or mold
tisane herb tea
tomates tomatoes

tomate aux crevettes tomato filled with shrimps and mayonnaise (*Belg.*)
tourain/tourin soup (*Dord.*)
tournedos tenderloin of T-bone steak
tournedos Rossini beef in Madeira wine sauce
tourte layer cake
tourteau fromager goat cheesecake
tranche slice
tripes à la mode de Caen baked tripe with Calvados
triple sec orange liqueur
truffes truffles
truite trout
truite saumonée salmon trout
turbot turbot

vacherin glacé ice-cream cake
veau veal
velouté cream of
velouté de tomates cream of tomato
velouté de volaille cream of chicken
veloutée thickened chicken or meat stock
verre a glass
verre de lait a glass of milk
verte mayonnaise with spinach, watercress, herbs
viande meat
viande séchée des Grisons cured dried beef
vin wine
vinaigrette oil and vinegar dressing
vin du pays local wine
vin ordinaire table wine
volaille fowl, poultry
V.S.O.P. cognac aged over 5 years

waterzooi de poulet chicken in white wine (*Belg.*)
xérès sherry
yaourt/yoghourt yogurt

TRAVEL

ESSENTIAL	
1/2/3 for …	**Un/deux/trois pour …** *ang/dur/trwa poor*
To …, please.	**À…, s'il vous plaît.** *seel voo pleh*
one-way [single]	**aller-simple** *alay sangpl*
round-trip [return]	**aller-retour** *alay rertoor*
How much?	**C'est combien?** *seh kawnbyang*

SAFETY

Would you accompany me …?	**Pourriez-vous m'accompagner …?** *pooryay voo makawngpañay*
to the bus stop	**jusqu'à l'arrêt d'autobus** *zhewska lareh doatobews*
to my hotel	**jusqu'à mon hôtel** *zhewska mawng noatel*
I don't want to … on my own.	**Je ne veux pas … tout(e) seul(e).** *zher nevur pa … too(t) surl*
stay here	**rester ici** *restay eessee*
walk home	**rentrer chez moi à pied** *rahngtray shay mwa a pyay*
I don't feel safe here.	**Je ne me sens pas en sécurité ici.** *zher nemer sahng pa zahng saykewreetay eessee*

ARRIVAL

Import restrictions between EU countries have been relaxed on items for personal use or consumption that are bought duty-paid within the EU. Suggested maximum: 90L wine or 60L sparkling wine, 20L fortified wine, 10L spirits and 110L beer.

If buying wine directly from a vineyard, check that the VAT has been paid (**capsule-congé** sticker on the bottle or case). Ask for a VAT receipt (**un reçu TVA**) if in doubt.

Document Requirements

UK	valid passport; visitors passport; or British Excursion document (valid 60 hours)
U.S./CAN	valid passport
AUS	visa required for France (check with embassy)

Duty Free Into:	Cigarettes	Cigars	Tobacco	Spirits	Wine
France/Belg.	200 or	50 or	250g	1L	2L
Switzerland 1)	200 or	50 or	250g	1L and	2L
2)	400 or	100 or	500g	1L and	2L
Canada	200 and	50 and	400g	1L or	1L
UK	200 or	50 or	250g	1L and	2L
U.S.	200 and	100 and	discretionary	1L or	1L

1) EU residents; 2) non-EU residents

Passport control

We have a joint passport.	**Nous avons un passeport joint.** *noo zavawng ang passpor zhwang*
The children are on this passport.	**Les enfants sont sur ce passeport.** *lay zahngfahng sawng sewr ser passpor*
I'm here on vacation [holiday]/ business.	**Je suis ici en vacances/pour affaires.** *zher swee eessee ahng vakahngss/ poor afehr*
I'm just passing through.	**Je suis en transit.** *zher swee zahng trahngzeet*
I'm going to …	**Je vais à …** *zher vay a*
I'm …	**Je suis …** *zher swee*
on my own	**tout(e) seul(e)** *too(t) surl*
with my family	**avec ma famille** *avek ma famee*
with a group	**avec un groupe** *avek ang groop*

Customs

I have only the normal allowances.	**Je n'ai que les quantités autorisées.** *zher nay ker lay kahngteetay oatoreezay*
It's a gift.	**C'est un cadeau**. *seh ang kadoa*
It's for my personal use.	**C'est pour mon usage personnel.** *seh poor mawng newzazh pehrsonell*
I would like to declare …	**Je voudrais déclarer …** *zher voodray dayklaray*
I don't understand.	**Je ne comprends pas.** *zher ner kawngprahng pa*
Does anyone here speak English?	**Y a-t-il quelqu'un ici qui parle anglais?** *ee a teel kelkang eessee kee parl ahnggleh*

Duty-free shopping

What currency is this in?	**C'est en quelle monnaie?** *seh tahng kel monayy*
Can I pay in …?	**Est-ce que je peux payer en …?** *ess ker zher pur payay ahng*
dollars	**dollars** *dolar*
francs	**francs** *frahng*
pounds	**livres** *leevr*

YOU MAY SEE

CONTRÔLE DES PASSEPORTS	passport control
POSTE FRONTIÈRE	border crossing
DOUANE	customs
RIEN À DÉCLARER	nothing to declare
MARCHANDISES À DÉCLARER	goods to declare
MARCHANDISES HORS TAXE	duty-free goods

YOU MAY HEAR

Avez-vous quelque chose à déclarer?	Do you have anything to declare?
Il y a des droits de douane à payer sur cet article.	You must pay duty on this.
Où avez-vous acheté ceci?	Where did you buy this?
Pouvez-vous ouvrir ce sac, SVP?	Please open this bag.

PLANE

Air Inter, France's principal domestic airline, runs services between Paris and Bordeaux, Lyon, Marseilles, Montpellier, Mulhouse, Nantes, Nice, Strasbourg and Toulouse. Inquire about discounts based on day and time of flight.

Tickets and reservations

When is the … flight to …?	**À quelle heure est le … vol pour …?** *a kelur reh ler … vol poor*
first/next/last	**premier/prochain/dernier** *prermyay/proshang/dehrnyay*
I'd like 2 … tickets to …	**Je voudrais deux … pour …** *zher voodray dur … poor*
one-way [single]	**aller-simple** *alay sangpl*
round-trip [return]	**aller-retour** *alay rertoor*
first class	**première classe** *prermyehr klass*
business class	**classe affaires** *kla ssafehr*
economy class	**classe économique** *kla ssaykonomeek*
How much is a flight to …?	**Combien coûte un vol pour …?** *kawnbyang koo tang vol poor*
I'd like to … my reservation for flight number …	**Je voudrais … ma réservation pour le vol numéro …** *zher voodray … ma rayzehrvasyawng poor ler vol newmayroa*
cancel	**annuler** *anewlay*
change	**changer** *shahngzhay*
confirm	**confirmer** *kawngfeermay*

Inquiries about the flight

Are there any supplements/discounts?	**Y a-t-il des suppléments/réductions?** *ee a teel day sewplaymahng/raydewksyawng*
What time does the plane leave?	**À quelle heure part l'avion?** *a kelur par lavyawng*
What time will we arrive?	**À quelle heure arriverons-nous?** *a kelur areevrawng noo*
What time do I have to check in?	**À quelle heure est l'enregistrement?** *a kelur reh lahngrerzheestrermahng*

Checking in

Where is the check-in desk for flight …?	**Où est le bureau d'enregistrement pour le vol …?** *oo eh ler bewroa dahngrerzheestrermahng poor ler vol*
I have …	**J'ai …** *zhay*
3 suitcases to check in	**trois valises à faire enregistrer** *trwa valee za feh rahngrerzheestray*
2 pieces of hand luggage	**deux bagages à main** *dur bagazh a mang*

YOU MAY HEAR

Votre billet/passeport, s'il vous plaît.	Your ticket/passport, please.
Voulez-vous un siège côté hublot ou côté couloir?	Would you like a window or an aisle seat?
Fumeur ou non-fumeur?	Smoking or non-smoking?
Veuillez vous rendre dans la salle de départ.	Please go through to the departure lounge.
Combien de bagages avez-vous?	How many pieces of luggage do you have?
Vos bagages sont trop lourds.	You have excess luggage.
Vous devrez payer un supplément de …	You'll have to pay a supplement of …
Ceci est trop lourd/grand pour les bagages à main.	That's too heavy/large for hand luggage.
Avez-vous fait vos valises vous-même?	Did you pack these bags yourself?
Est-ce qu'ils contiennent des objets pointus ou électriques?	Do they contain any sharp or electrical items?

YOU MAY SEE

ARRIVÉES	arrivals
DÉPARTS	departures
CONTRÔLE DE SÉCURITÉ	security check
NE LAISSEZ PAS VOS BAGAGES SANS SURVEILLANCE	do not leave luggage unattended

69

Information

Is there any delay on flight …?	**Est-ce que le vol … a du retard?** *ess ker ler vol … a dew rertar*
How late will it be?	**Il a combien de retard?** *eel a kawnbyang der rertar*
Has the flight from … landed?	**Est-ce que le vol de … est arrivé?** *ess ker ler vol der … eh tareevay*
Which gate does flight … leave from?	**De quelle porte part le vol …?** *der kel port par ler vol*

Boarding/In-flight

Your boarding pass, please.	**Votre carte d'embarquement, s'il vous plaît.** *votr kart dahngbarkermahng seel voo pleh*
Could I have a drink/ something to eat?	**Est-ce que je pourrais avoir quelque chose à boire/à manger?** *ess ker zher pooray avwar kelker shoaz a bwar/a mahngzhay*
Please wake me for the meal.	**Pouvez-vous me réveiller pour le repas, s'il vous plaît?** *poovay voo mer rayvayay poor ler rerpa seel voo pleh*
What time will we arrive?	**À quelle heure arriverons-nous?** *a kelur rareevrawng noo*

Arrival

Where is/are …?	**Où est/sont …?** *oo eh/sawng*
currency exchange office	**le bureau de change** *ler bewroa der shahngzh*
buses	**les autobus** *lay zoatobews*
car rental (office)	**le bureau de location de voitures** *ler bewroa der lokasyawng der vwatewr*
exit	**la sortie** *la sortee*
taxis	**les taxis** *lay taxee*
Is there a bus into town?	**Est-ce qu'il y a un bus pour aller en ville?** *ess keel ee a ang bewss poor alay ahng veel*
How do I get to the … Hotel?	**Comment est-ce que je peux me rendre à l'hôtel …?** *kommahng ess ker zher pur mer rahngdr a loatel*

Luggage/Baggage

Tipping: If you want to give a bellman [porter] a tip, the following amounts (per bag) are usual: France: 5F, Belgium: 30F, Switzerland: 1–2F.

Bellman [Porter]!	**Porteur! S'il vous plaît!**
Excuse me!	*porturr seel voo pleh*
Could you take my luggage to …?	**Pourriez-vous emporter mes bagages à …?** *pooryay voo ahngportay meh bagazh a*
a taxi/bus	**jusqu'à un taxi/bus** *zhewska ang taxee/bewss*
Where is/are …?	**Où est/sont …?** *oo eh/sawng*
luggage carts [trolleys]	**les chariots à bagages** *lay sharyoa a bagazh*
baggage check	**la consigne** *la kawngseeñ*
Where is the luggage from flight …?	**Où sont les bagages du vol …?** *oo sawng laybagazh dew vol*

Loss, damage and theft

I've lost my baggage.	**J'ai perdu mes bagages.** *zhay pehrdew meh bagazh*
My baggage has been stolen.	**On m'a volé mes bagages.** *awng ma volay meh bagazh*
My suitcase was damaged.	**Ma valise a été abîmée.** *ma valee za aytay abeemay*
Our baggage has not arrived.	**Nos bagages ne sont pas arrivés.** *no bagazh ner sawng pazareevay*

TRAIN

TGV *tay zhay vay*

extra-high speed train (**Train à Grande Vitesse**); compulsory reservation when you buy your ticket; a surcharge may be payable.

Eurostar/Le Shuttle *urroastar/ler shutel*

car and passenger Channel Tunnel link from London Waterloo to Paris and Brussels (car from Folkstone to Calais only); no reservation necessary.

EuroCity	*urrosseettee*	international express train
Rapide	*rapeed*	long-distance express; luxury coaches (*Fr.*)
Intercity	*angtehrsseettee*	intercity express with few stops
Express	*express*	ordinary long-distance train (*Fr.*)
Direct	*deerekt*	ordinary long-distance train (*Bel., Sw.*)
Omnibus	*omneebewss*	local train (*Fr., Bel.*)
Train régional	*trang rayzhyonal*	local train (*Sw.*)
Autorail	*oatorie*	small diesel used on short runs
RER (Réseau Express Régional)	*ehr er ehr*	Paris regional network, linked to the métro
Train-Auto-Couchette	*trang oato kooshett*	autotrain service; advance reservation required
wagon-restaurant	*vagawng restoarahng*	dining car
wagon-lit	*vagawng lee*	sleeping car with individual compartments and washing facilities
couchette	*kooshett*	berth with bedding; **supérieure** (upper) or **inférieure** (lower)

Check out the various discounts and travel passes available:

For children (**Carte Kiwi, Carte Jeune**); families (**Rail Europ F, Zoom**); Senior Citizens (**Carte Vermeil, Rail Europ Senior**); under-26 (**Domino, Eurail Youthpass; BIJ** [Belg.]; **InterRail**); couples (**Carte couple**); advance bookings (**Joker**); Off-peak (**Carrissimo, billet séjour**).

Paris has several main stations – so don't go to the wrong one: gare du Nord (north, incl. Eurostar, U.K.), gare de l'Est (east), gare d'Austerlitz (southwest, Bordeaux, Spain), gare Saint-Lazare (Normandy, Dieppe), Montparnasse (west, Brittany) and gare de Lyon (Riviera, Switzerland and Italy).

To the station

How do I get to the (main) train station?	**Pour aller à la gare (principale)?**	*poo ralay a la gar (prangseepal)*
Do trains to … leave from … Station?	**Est-ce que les trains pour … partent de la gare …?**	*ess ker lay trang poor … part der la gar …*
Is it far?	**(Est-ce que) c'est loin?**	*(ess ker) seh lwang*
Can I leave my car there?	**Est-ce que je peux y laisser ma voiture?**	*ess ker zher pur ee layssay ma vwatewr*

At the station

Where is/are the …?	**Où est/sont …?**	*oo eh/sawng*
currency exchange office	**le bureau de change**	*ler bewroa der shahngzh*
information desk	**le bureau des renseignements**	*ler bewroa day rahngseñermahng*
baggage check	**la consigne**	*la kawngseeñ*
lost-and-found [lost property office]	**le bureau des objets trouvés**	*ler bewroa day zobzheh troovay*
luggage lockers	**la consigne automatique**	*la kawngsee ñoatomateek*
platforms	**les quais**	*lay kay*
snack bar	**le snack-bar/buffet**	*ler snak bar/bewfeh*
ticket office	**le guichet**	*ler geesheh*
waiting room	**la salle d'attente**	*la sal datahngt*

YOU MAY SEE

ENTRÉE	entrance
SORTIE	exit
RÉSERVATIONS	reservations
RENSEIGNEMENTS	information
ACCÈS AUX QUAIS	to the platforms
ARRIVÉES	arrivals
DÉPARTS	departures

Tickets

Remember to validate your train ticket by inserting it in an orange validating machine (**machine à composter** or **composteur**) at the stations; otherwise the conductor (**contrôleur**) is entitled to fine you.

Where can I buy a ticket?	**Où puis-je acheter un billet?** *oo pweezh ashertay ang beeyeh*
I'd like a … ticket to …	**Je voudrais un billet … pour …** *zher voodray ang beeyeh … poor*
one-way [single]	**aller-simple** *alay sangpl*
round-trip [return]	**aller-retour** *alay rertoor*
first/second class	**de première/deuxième classe** *der prermyehr/durzyem klass*
reduced price	**à prix réduit** *a pree raydwee*
I'd like to reserve a seat.	**Je voudrais réserver une place.** *zher voodray rayzehrvay ewn plass*
aisle seat	**siège côté couloir** *syezh kotay coolwar*
window seat	**siège côté fenêtre** *syezh kotay fernehtr*
Is there a sleeping car [sleeper]?	**Est-ce qu'il y a un wagon-lit?** *ess kee lee a ang vagawng lee*
I'd like a … berth.	**Je voudrais une couchette.** *zher voodray ewn kooshett*
upper/lower	**supérieure/inférieure** *sewpayryurr/angfayryurr*

Price

How much is that?	**C'est combien?** *seh kawnbyang*
Is there a discount for …?	**Y a-t-il une réduction pour …?** *ee a teel ewn raydewksyawng poor*
children/families	**les enfants/les familles** *lay zahngfahng/lay famee*
senior citizens	**les personnes âgées** *lay pehrson azhay*
students	**les étudiants** *lay zaytewdyahng*
Do you offer a cheap same-day round-trip [return] ticket?	**Est-ce que vous offrez un aller-retour dans la même journée bon marché?** *ess ker voo zofray ang nalay rertoor dahng la mem zhoornay bawng marshay*

Queries

Do I have to
change trains?

Est-ce que je dois changer de train?
ess ker zher dwa shahngzhay der trang

It's a direct train.

C'est un train direct.
seh tang trang deerekt

You have to change at …

Vous avez une correspondance à …
voo zavay ewn korespawngdahngss a

How long is this
ticket valid for?

**Ce billet est valable pour combien de
temps?** *ser beeyeh eh valabl poor
kawnbyang der tahng*

Can I take my bicycle
on the train?

**Est-ce que je peux emporter mon vélo
dans le train?** *ess ker zher pur ahng
portay mawng vaylo dahng
ler trang*

Which car [coach] is
my seat in?

Dans quel wagon est mon siège?
dahng kel vagawng eh mawng syezh

Is there a dining car on
the train?

**Est-ce qu'il y a un wagon-restaurant
dans le train?** *ess keel ee a ang
vagawng restoarahng dahng
ler trang*

Train timetable

Could I have a timetable?

Est-ce que je pourrais avoir un horaire?
ess ker zher pooray avwar ang norehr

When is the … train to …?

À quelle heure est le … train pour …?
a kel urr eh ler … trang poor

first/next/last

premier/prochain/dernier
prermyay/proshang/dehrnyay

IN A TRAIN STATION

Un billet pour Lyon, s'il vous plaît. *ang beeyeh poor
leeawng seel voo pleh (Two tickets to Lyon, please.)*
Aller-simple ou aller-retour? *alay sangpl oo alay rertoor
(One way or round trip?)*
Aller-retour, s'il vous plaît. *alay rertoor seel voo pleh
(Round trip, please.)*

75

How frequent are the trains to …?	**Combien de fois par jour (est-ce qu')il y a des trains pour …?** *kawnbyang der fwa par zhoor (ess k)eel ee a day trang poor*
once/twice a day	**une/deux fois par jour** *ewn/dur fwa par zhoor*
5 times a day	**cinq fois par jour** *sangk fwa par zhoor*
every hour	**toutes les heures** *toot lay zurr*
What time do they leave?	**À quelle heure partent-ils?** *a kel urr part teel*
every hour/on the hour	**toutes les heures/à l'heure juste** *toot lay zurr/a lurr zhewst*
20 minutes past the hour	**vingt minutes après l'heure** *vang meenewt apreh lurr*
What time does the train stop at …?	**À quelle heure le train s'arrête-t-il à …?** *a kel urr ler trang sarett teel a*
What time does the train arrive in …?	**À quelle heure le train arrive-t-il à …?** *a kel urr ler trang areev teel a*
How long is the trip [journey]?	**Combien de temps dure le voyage?** *kawnbyang der tahng dewr ler vwahyazh*
Is the train on time?	**Est-ce que le train est à l'heure?** *ess ker ler trang eh a lurr*

Departures

Which platform does the train to … leave from?	**De quel quai part le train pour …?** *der kel kay par ler trang poor*
Where is platform 4?	**Où est le quai numéro 4?** *oo eh ler kay newmayroa katr*
over there	**là-bas** *la ba*
on the left/right	**à gauche/à droite** *a goash/a drwat*
Where do I change for …?	**Où est-ce que je dois changer pour …?** *oo ess ker zher dwa shahngzhay poor*
How long will I have to wait for a connection?	**Combien de temps dois-je attendre pour une correspondance?** *kawnbyang der tahng dwazh atahngdr poor ewn korespawngdahngss*

Boarding

Is this the right platform for the train to …?	**Est-ce bien le bon quai pour le train pour …?** *ess byang ler bawng kay poor ler trang poor*
Is this the train to …?	**Est-ce que c'est bien le train pour …?** *ess ker seh byang ler trang poor*
Is this seat taken?	**Est-ce que cette place est occupée/prise?** *ess ker set plass eh okewpay/preez*
I think that's my seat.	**Je crois que c'est ma place.** *zher krwa ker seh ma plass*
Are there any available seats/berths?	**Est-ce qu'il y a des places/couchettes libres?** *ess keel ee a day plass/kooshett leebr*
Do you mind if …?	**Est-ce que ça vous dérange si …?** *ess ker sa voo dayrahngzh see*
I sit here.	**je m'asseois ici** *zher maswa eessee*

During the trip

How long are we stopping here?	**Combien de temps est-ce que nous nous arrêtons ici?** *kawnbyang der tahng ess ker noo noo aretawng eessee*
When do we get to …?	**À quelle heure arrivons-nous à …?** *a kel urr areevawng noo a*
Have we passed …?	**Est-ce que nous sommes passés à …?** *ess ker noo som passay a*
Where is the dining/ sleeping car?	**Où est le wagon-restaurant/wagon-lit?** *oo eh ler vagawng restoarahng/vagawng lee*
Where is my berth?	**Où est ma couchette?** *oo eh ma kooshett*
I've lost my ticket.	**J'ai perdu mon billet.** *zhay pehrdew mawng beeyeh*

YOU MAY SEE

ARRÊT D'URGENCE	emergency brake
SONNETTE D'ALARME	alarm
PORTES AUTOMATIQUES	automatic doors

LONG-DISTANCE BUS

Services are efficient and relatively cheap. Find details at the bus terminal (**gare routière**), generally located near the railway station.

When's the next bus [coach] to …?
À quelle heure est le prochain car pour …?
a kel urr eh ler proshang kar poor

Which stop does it leave from?
De quel arrêt part-il?
der kel areh par teel

Where are the bus [coach] stops?
Où sont les arrêts de car?
oo sawng lay areh der kar

Does the bus [coach] stop at ,..?
Est-ce que le car s'arrête à …?
ess ker ler kar sarett a

How long does the trip [journey] take?
Combien de temps dure le voyage?
kawnbyang der tahng dewr ler vwahyazh

BUS

Tickets can normally be purchased from the driver, but remember that you must always validate your ticket (**compostez votre billet**) in the machine.

Where is the bus station/terminal?
Où est la gare routière?
oo eh la gar rootyehr

Where can I get a bus to …?
Où est-ce que je peux prendre un bus pour …? *oo ess ker zher pur prahngdr ang bewss poor*

What time is the … bus to …?
À quelle heure part le … bus pour …?
a kel urr par ler … bewss poor

YOU MAY HEAR	
Vous devez prendre le bus numéro …	You need bus number …
Vous devez changer de bus à …	You must change buses at …

YOU MAY SEE	
ARRÊT D'AUTOBUS	bus stop
ARRÊT FACULTATIF	request stop
DÉFENSE DE FUMER	no smoking
SORTIE DE SECOURS	(emergency) exit

Buying tickets

Where can I buy tickets?	**Où est-ce que je peux acheter des tickets?** *oo ess ker zher pur ashertay day teekeh*
A … ticket to …, please.	**Un ticket … pour …, s'il vous plaît.** *ang teekeh … poor … seel voo pleh*
one-way [single]	**aller** *alay*
round-trip [return]	**aller-retour** *alay rertoor*
A booklet of tickets, please.	**Un carnet de tickets, s'il vous plaît.** *ang karneh der teekeh seel voo pleh*
How much is the fare to …?	**Combien coûte un ticket pour …?** *kawnbyang koot ang teekeh poor*

Traveling

Is this the right bus/streetcar [tram] to …?	**C'est bien le bon bus/tram pour …?** *seh byang ler bawng bewss/tram poor*
Could you tell me when to get off?	**Pourriez-vous me dire quand il faut descendre?** *pooryay voo mer deer kahng eel foa dessahngdr*
Do I have to change buses?	**Est-ce que je dois changer de bus?** *ess ker zher dwa shahngzhay der bewss*
How many stops are there to …?	**Combien d'arrêts est-ce qu'il y a jusqu'à …?** *kawnbyang dareh ess keel ee a zhewska*
Next stop, please!	**Prochain arrêt, s'il vous plaît!** *proshang nareh seel voo pleh*

AT A BUS STOP

C'est bien le bon bus pour le centre-ville?
seh byang ler bawng bews poor ler sahngtr veel
(Excuse me, is this the bus to downtown?)
Oui, le numéro huit. *wee ler newmayroa weet*
(Yes, bus number 8.)
Merci. *mehrsee (Thanks.)*
De rien. *de reeangh (You're welcome.)*

SUBWAY

There are excellent subway systems in Paris, Brussels, Lille and Lyon. Big maps in each station make the systems easy to use. The fare is standard, irrespective of the distance you travel. Tickets can be bought cheaper in a book of ten (**un carnet**).

The Paris metro closes 12:50am – 5:30am.

General Inquiries

Where's the nearest subway station?
Où est la station de métro la plus proche?
oo eh la stasyawng der maytroa la plew prosh

Where can I buy a ticket?
Où est-ce que je peux acheter un ticket?
oo ess ker zher pur ashertay ang teekeh

Could I have a map of the subway [metro]?
Est-ce que je pourrais avoir un plan du métro? *ess ker zher pooray avwar ang plahng dew maytroa*

Traveling

Which line should I take for …?
Quelle ligne dois-je prendre pour …?
kel leeñ dwazh prahngdr poor

Is this the right train for …?
Est-ce que c'est bien la bonne rame pour …?
ess ker seh byang la bon ram poor

Which stop is it for …?
C'est quelle station pour …?
seh kel stasyawng poor

How many stops is it to …?
Combien de stations est-ce qu'il y a jusqu'à …? *kawnbyang der stasyawng ess keel ee a zhewska*

Is the next stop …?
Est-ce que la prochaine station est bien …?
ess ker la proshayn stasyawng eh byang

Where are we?
Où sommes-nous?
oo som noo

Where do I change for …?
Où est-ce que je dois changer pour …?
oo ess ker zher dwa shahngzhay poor

What time is the last train to …?
À quelle heure est la dernière rame pour …?
a kel urr eh la dehrnyehr ram poor

FERRY

Ferry companies operating services from the UK include: Stena Sealink, Hoverspeed, Brittany Ferries, P&O, Sally Ferries, North Sea Ferries.

When is the … car ferry to …?	**À quelle heure est le … car-ferry pour …?** *a kel urr eh ler … kar fehrree poor*
first/next/last	**premier/prochain/dernier** *prermyay/proshang/dehrnyay*
hovercraft/ship	**l'hovercraft/le bateau** *lovehrkraft/ler batoa*
A round-trip [return] ticket for …	**Un billet aller et retour pour …** *ang beeyeh alay ay rertoor poor*
1 car and 1 trailer [caravan]	**une voiture et une caravane** *ewn vwatewr ay ewn karavahn*
2 adults and 3 children	**deux adultes et trois enfants** *dur zadewlt ay trwa zahngfahng*
I want to reserve a … cabin.	**Je voudrais réserver une cabine …** *zher voodray rayzehrvay ewn kabeen*

YOU MAY SEE

ACCÈS AUX GARAGES INTERDIT	no access to car decks
CANOT DE SAUVETAGE	life boat
GILETS DE SAUVETAGE	life jacket
POINT DE RASSEMBLEMENT	meeting point

Boat trips

For a relaxing way to see Paris, take a cruise in a **bateau-mouche** or **vedette** along the Seine.

Is there a …?	**Est-ce qu'il y a …?** *ess keel ee a*
boat trip	**un voyage en bateau** *ang vwahyazh ahng batoa*
river cruise	**une croisière sur la rivière** *ewn krwazyehr sewr la reevyehr*
What time does it leave/return?	**À quelle heure part/revient le bateau?** *a kel urr par/rervyang ler batoa*
Where can we buy tickets?	**Où pouvons-nous acheter des billets?** *oo poovawng noo zashertay day beeyeh*

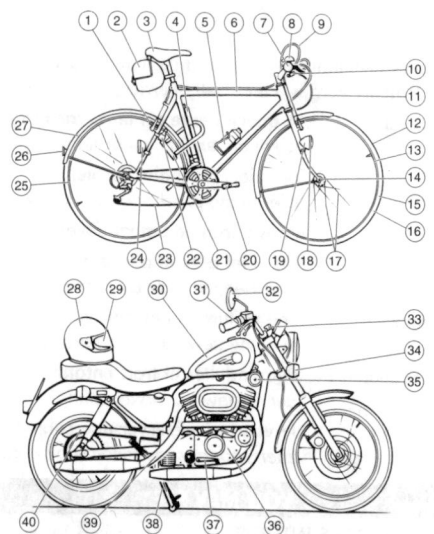

1	brake pad **plaquette de frein** f	19	headlamp **phare** m
2	bicycle bag **sacoche de bicyclette** f	20	pedal **pédale** f
3	saddle **selle** f	21	lock **antivol** m
4	pump **pompe** f	22	generator **dynamo** f
5	water bottle **bidon d'eau** m	23	chain **chaîne** f
6	frame **cadre** m	24	rear light **feu arrière** m
7	handlebars **guidon** m	25	rim **jante** f
8	bell **sonnette** f	26	reflectors **réflecteurs** mpl
9	brake cable **câble de frein** m	27	fender [mudguard] **garde-boue** m
10	gear/shift **levier de changement de vitesse** m	28	helmet **casque** m
11	gear/control cable **câble de changement de vitesse** m	29	visor **visière** f
12	inner tube **chambre à air** f	30	fuel tank **réservoir** m
13	front/back wheel **roue avant/arrière** f	31	clutch **embrayage** m
14	axle **essieu** m	32	mirror **rétroviseur** m
15	tire **pneu** m	33	ignition switch **contact** m
16	wheel **roue** f	34	turn signal (indicator) **clignotant** m
17	spokes **rayons** mpl	35	horn **klaxon** m
18	bulb **ampoule** f	36	engine **moteur** m
		37	stick shift **levier de vitesse** m
		38	kick stand **béquille** f
		39	exhaust pipe **pot d'échappement** m
		40	chain guard **couvre-chaîne** m

BICYCLE/MOTORBIKE

Bicycle rental shops are plentiful; SNCF (French railways) operates a cycle rental service at railway stations (passport, deposit or credit card required). Many towns also have mopeds (**vélomoteurs**, **cyclomoteurs** or **mobylettes**) for rent. In Belgium, it is compulsory to use low headlights on motorcycles at all times.

I'd like to rent a …	**Je voudrais louer …**	*zher voodray looay*
3-/10-gear bicycle	**un vélo à trois/dix vitesses** *ang vaylo a trwa/dees veetess*	
moped	**une mobylette** *ewn mobeelett*	
motorbike	**une moto** *ewn moto*	
How much does it cost per day/week?	**Ça coûte combien par jour/semaine?** *sa koot kawnbyang par zhoor/sermayn*	
Do you require a deposit?	**Est-ce qu'il faut verser une caution?** *ess keel foa vehrsay ewn kosyawng*	
The brakes don't work.	**Les freins ne marchent pas.** *lay frang ner marsh pa*	
There are no lights.	**Il n'y a pas de feux.** *eel nee a pa der fur*	
The front/rear tire [tyre] has a flat [puncture].	**Le pneu avant/arrière est crevé.** *ler pnur avahng/aryehr eh krervay*	

HITCHHIKING

Hitchhiking is permitted everywhere except on highways. Always take care before hitchhiking anywhere.

Where are you heading?	**Où allez-vous?** *oo alay voo*	
I'm heading for …	**Je vais vers …** *zher vay vehr*	
Is that on the way to …?	**Est-ce que c'est sur la route de …?** *ess ker seh sewr la root der*	
Could you drop me off …?	**Est-ce que vous pourriez me déposer …?** *ess ker voo pooryay mer daypoazay*	
here/at …	**ici/à …** *eessee/a*	
at the … exit	**à la sortie …** *a la sortee*	
in the center	**dans le centre** *dahng ler sahngtr*	
Thanks for giving me a lift.	**Merci de m'avoir emmené.** *mehrsee der mavwar ahngmernay*	

TAXI/CAB

Many French taxis will only take 3 passengers; traveling in the front passenger seat is not usual. Taxis ordered by telephone will pick you up with the meter already running.

Tipping suggestions: France: 10–15%; Belgium: optional; Switzerland: 15% (sometimes included).

Where can I get a taxi?	**Où est-ce que je peux trouver un taxi?** *oo ess ker zher pur troovay ang taxee*
Do you have the number for a taxi?	**Avez-vous le numéro de téléphone pour appeler un taxi?** *avay voo ler newmay roa der taylayfon poor aperlay ang taxee*
I'd like a taxi …	**Je voudrais un taxi …** *zher voodray ang taxee*
now	**maintenant** *mangtnahng*
in an hour	**dans une heure** *dahng zewn urr*
tomorrow at 9:00	**demain à neuf heures** *dermang a nurf urr*
The address is …	**L'adresse est …** *ladress eh*
I'm going to …	**Je vais à …** *… zher vay a*
Please take me to the …	**Emmenez-moi à …, s'il vous plaît.** *ahngmernay mwa a … seel voo pleh*
airport	**l'aéroport** *layropor*
train station	**la gare** *la gar*
this address	**cette adresse** *set adress*
How much is that?	**C'est combien?** *seh kawnbyang*
You said … Francs.	**Vous m'aviez dit … francs.** *voo mavyay dee … frahng*
On the meter it's …	**Le compteur indique …** *ler kawngturr angdeek*
Keep the change.	**Gardez la monnaie.** *garday la monay*

AT A BUS STOP

C'est combien pour l'aéroport? *seh kawnbyang poor layropor (How much is it to the airport?)*
Cent francs. *sahng frahng (100 francs.)*
Merci. *mehrsee (Thanks.)*

CAR/AUTOMOBILE

While driving, the following documents must be carried at all times: valid driver's license (**permis de conduire**), vehicle registration (**certificat d'immatriculation**) and insurance documentation (**certificat d'assurance**).

Insurance for minimum Third Party risks is compulsory in Europe. It is recommended that you take out International motor insurance (or a "Green Card") through your insurer.

Essential equipment: warning triangle and nationality plate; headlight beams must be adjusted for right-hand drive vehicles; wearing seat belts is compulsory.

Minimum driving age: 18; minimum rental age: 21 (25 with some firms).

Tolls are payable on many French autoroutes; usually pick up a ticket at point of entry and pay at the exit; Visa and Access (MasterCard) are accepted. Some barriers are operated automatically by depositing exact toll in coins.

For travel on Swiss highways/motorways, a pass/vignette is required – available from tourist offices, customs, post offices and garages. It is valid for 1 year, non-transferable and is to be attached to your windshield.

Traffic police can give on-the-spot fines (ask for a receipt).

Alcohol limit in blood: max. 80mg/100ml. Note that any alcohol may impair ability to drive safely.

Speed conversion chart

km	1	10	20	30	40	50	60	70	80	90	100	110	120	130
miles	0.6	6	12	19	25	31	37	44	50	56	62	68	75	81

Road network

France	A (**autoroute**) - highway (blue sign; generally tolls); N (**route nationale**) - main road (green sign); D - secondary road (white sign); V - local road (white sign)
Belgium	A and E - highway (green signs, toll free); N - main road
Switzerland	A - highway (toll free); N - main road; E - secondary road

Speed limits mph (km/ph)	Built-up area	Outside built-up area	highway/ toll road
France	31 (50)	56 (90)	68 (110)/81 (130)
in bad weather		50 (80)	62 (100)/68 (110)
Belgium	31 (50)	56 (90)	74 (120)
Switzerland	31 (50)	50 (80)	62-74 (100-120)

Car rental

You will need to produce a valid driver's license (held for at least a year) and your passport. The minimum age ranges from 21 to 25, depending on the rental firm.

Many firms now require you to have a major credit card.

Where can I rent a car?	**Où est-ce que je peux louer une voiture?** *oo ess ker zher pur looay ewn vwatewr*
I'd like to rent a(n) …	**Je voudrais louer une …** *zher voodray looay ewn*
2-/4-door car	**voiture deux portes/quatre portes** *vwatewr dur port/katr port*
automatic	**voiture automatique** *vwatewr oatomateek*
car with air conditioning	**voiture avec climatisation** *vwatewr avek kleemateezassyawng*
I'd like it for a day/a week.	**Je la voudrais pour un jour/une semaine.** *zher la voodray poor ang zhoor/ewn sermayn*
How much does it cost per day/week?	**Quel est le tarif par jour/semaine?** *keleh ler tareef par zhoor/sermayn*
Is mileage/insurance included?	**Est-ce-que le kilométrage/l'assurance est compris(e)?** *ess ker ler keelomaytrazh/ lassewrahngss eh kawngpree(z)*
Are there special weekend rates?	**Y a-t-il des tarifs spéciaux pour le week-end?** *ee a teel day tareef spaysyoa poor ler weekend*
Can I return the car at …?	**Est-ce que je peux rapporter la voiture à …?** *ess ker zher pur raportay la vwatewr a*
What kind of fuel does it take?	**Qu'est-ce qu'il faut mettre comme carburant?** *kess keel foa metr kom karbewrahng*
Where is the high/low [full/dipped] beam?	**Où sont les phares/les codes?** *oo sawng lay far/lay kod*
Could I have full insurance?	**Est-ce que je peux prendre une assurance tous risques?** *ess ker zher pur prahngdr ewn assewrahngss too reesk*

Gas [Petrol] station

Where's the next gas [petrol] station?	**Où est la station-service la plus proche?** *oo eh la stasyawng sehrveess la plew prosh*
Is it self-service?	**Est-ce que c'est un self-service?** *ess ker seh ang self sehrveess*
Fill it up, please.	**Le plein, s'il vous plaît.** *ler plang seel voo pleh*
premium [super]/regular	**super/ordinaire** *sewpehr/ordeenehr*
unleaded/diesel	**sans plomb/diesel** *sahng plawng/diaysel*
I'm pump number …	**Je suis à la pompe numéro …** *zher swee za la pawngp newmayroa*
Where is the air pump/water?	**Où est le compresseur pour l'air/l'eau?** *oo eh ler kawngpressurr poor lehr/loa*

Parking

In Blue Zones, parking tokens/discs are required (available from police stations, tourist offices and some shops).

Unilateral parking on alternate days is marked by signs: **côté du stationnement, jours pairs** (even dates) and **jours impairs** (odd dates).

In one-way streets parking is permitted on the left-hand side only.

No parking where curbs are marked yellow or on Paris red routes (**axes rouges**).

Is there a parking lot [car park] nearby?	**Est-ce qu'il y a un parking près d'ici?** *ess keel ee a ang parking preh deessee*
What's the charge per hour/per day?	**Quel est le tarif par heure/jour?** *kel eh ler tareef par urr/zhoor*
Do you have some change for the parking meter?	**Avez-vous de la monnaie pour le parcmètre?** *avay voo der la mon nay poor ler parkmetr*
My car has been booted [clamped]. Who do I call?	**On a mis un sabot à ma voiture. À qui dois-je téléphoner?** *awng a mee ang saboa a ma vwatewr.a kee dwazh taylayfonay*

YOU MAY SEE

PRIX AU LITRE	price per liter

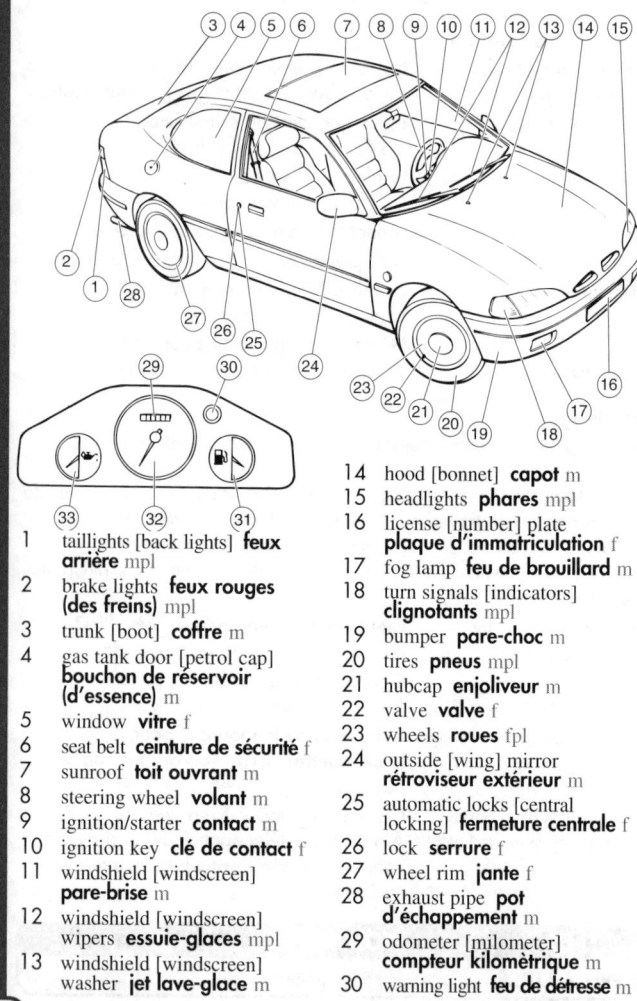

1	taillights [back lights] **feux arrière** mpl
2	brake lights **feux rouges (des freins)** mpl
3	trunk [boot] **coffre** m
4	gas tank door [petrol cap] **bouchon de réservoir (d'essence)** m
5	window **vitre** f
6	seat belt **ceinture de sécurité** f
7	sunroof **toit ouvrant** m
8	steering wheel **volant** m
9	ignition/starter **contact** m
10	ignition key **clé de contact** f
11	windshield [windscreen] **pare-brise** m
12	windshield [windscreen] wipers **essuie-glaces** mpl
13	windshield [windscreen] washer **jet lave-glace** m

14	hood [bonnet] **capot** m
15	headlights **phares** mpl
16	license [number] plate **plaque d'immatriculation** f
17	fog lamp **feu de brouillard** m
18	turn signals [indicators] **clignotants** mpl
19	bumper **pare-choc** m
20	tires **pneus** mpl
21	hubcap **enjoliveur** m
22	valve **valve** f
23	wheels **roues** fpl
24	outside [wing] mirror **rétroviseur extérieur** m
25	automatic locks [central locking] **fermeture centrale** f
26	lock **serrure** f
27	wheel rim **jante** f
28	exhaust pipe **pot d'échappement** m
29	odometer [milometer] **compteur kilomètrique** m
30	warning light **feu de détresse** m

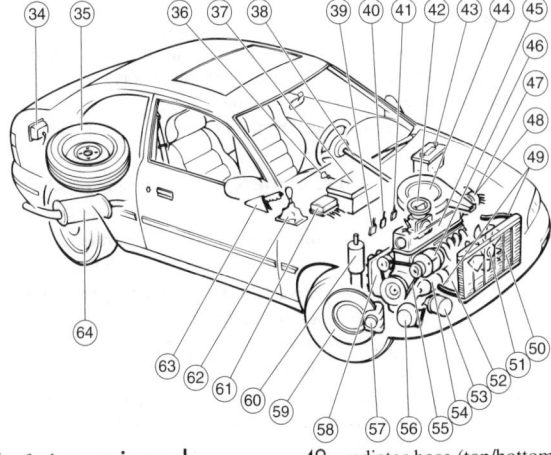

31	fuel gauge **jauge de carburant** f
32	speedometer **compteur de vitesse** m
33	oil gauge **jauge à huile** f
34	backup [reversing] lights **feux de recul** mpl
35	spare tire [wheel] **roue de secours** f
36	choke **starter** m
37	heater **radiateur** m
38	steering column **colonne de direction** f
39	accelerator **accélérateur** m
40	pedal **pédale** f
41	clutch **embrayage** m
42	carburetor **carburateur** m
43	battery **batterie** f
44	alternator **alternateur** m
45	camshaft **arbre à cames** m
46	air filter **filtre à air** m
47	distributor **distributeur** m
48	points **vis platinées** fpl

49	radiator hose (top/bottom) **durite** f
50	radiator **radiateur** m
51	fan **ventilateur** m
52	engine **moteur** m
53	oil filter **filtre à huile** m
54	starter motor **démarreur** m
55	fan belt **courroie de ventilateur** f
56	horn **klaxon** m
57	brake pads **plaquettes de freins** fpl
58	transmission [gearbox] **boîte de vitesses** f
59	brakes **freins** mpl
60	shock absorbers **amortisseurs** mpl
61	fuses **fusibles** mpl
62	gear shift [lever] **levier de vitesses** m
63	emergency [hand] brake **frein à main** m
64	muffler **pot d'échappement** m

Breakdown

For help in the event of a breakdown refer to your breakdown assistance documents; or contact the nearest garage or agent for your type of car; or contact the police, who often have a list of 24-hour garages.

Orange emergency telephones can be found every 2km on highways and main roads.

Where is the nearest garage?	**Où se trouve le garage le plus proche?** *oo ser troov ler garazh ler plew prosh*
I've had a breakdown.	**Ma voiture est tombée en panne.** *ma vwatewr eh tawngbay ahng pan*
Can you send a mechanic/ tow [breakdown] truck?	**Pouvez-vous m'envoyer un mécanicien/ une dépanneuse?** *poovay voo mahngvwahyay ay maykaneesyang/ ewn daypanurz*
I belong to … road assistance service.	**Je suis membre du service d'assistance routière …** *zher swee mahngbr dew sehrveess dasseestahngss rootyehr*
My license plate number is …	**Mon numéro d'immatriculation est …** *mawng newmayroa deematreekewlasyawng eh*
The car is …	**La voiture est …** *la vwatewr eh*
on the highway [motorway]	**sur l'autoroute** *sewr loatoroot*
2 km from …	**à deux kilomètres de …** *a dur keelometr der*
How long will you be?	**Combien de temps allez-vous mettre?** *kawnbyang der tahng alay voo metr*

What is wrong?

My car won't start.	**Ma voiture ne démarre pas.** *ma vwatewr ner daymar pa*
The battery is dead.	**La batterie est à plat.** *la batree eh a pla*
I've run out of gas [petrol].	**Je suis en panne d'essence.** *zher swee zahng pan dessahngss*
I have a flat [puncture].	**J'ai un pneu à plat.** *zhay ang pnur a pla*
There is something wrong with …	**J'ai un problème avec …** *zhay ang problemm avek*
I've locked the keys in the car.	**J'ai enfermé mes clés dans la voiture.** *zhay ahngfehrmay meh klay dahng la vwatewr*

Repairs

Do you do repairs?	**Faites-vous des réparations?** *fet voo day rayparasyawng*
Can you repair it (temporarily)?	**Est-ce que vous pouvez faire une réparation (temporaire)?** *ess ker voo poovay fehr ewn rayparasyawng (tahngporehr)*
Please make only essential repairs.	**Faites seulement les réparations essentielles.** *fett surlmahng lay ray parasyawng essahngsyell*
Can I wait for it?	**Est-ce que je peux attendre?** *ess ker zher pur atahngdr*
Can you repair it today?	**Est-ce que vous pouvez la réparer aujourd'hui?** *ess ker voo poovay la rayparay oazhoordwee*
When will it be ready?	**Quand est-ce qu'elle sera prête?** *kahng ess kel serra pret*
How much will it cost?	**Ça coûtera combien?** *sa kootra kawnbyang*
That's outrageous!	**C'est du vol!** *seh dew vol*
Can I have a receipt for the insurance?	**Est-ce que je peux avoir un reçu pour l'assurance?** *ess ker zher pur avwar ang rersew poor lassewrahngss*

YOU MAY HEAR

... ne marche pas.	The ... isn't working.
Je n'ai pas les pièces nécessaires.	I don't have the necessary parts.
Il faut que je commande les pièces.	I will have to order the parts.
Je ne peux faire qu'une réparation temporaire.	I can only repair it temporarily.
Ça ne vaut pas la peine de la faire réparer.	Your car is totaled/a write-off.
On ne peut pas la réparer.	It can't be repaired.
Elle sera prête ...	It will be ready ...
dans la journée	later today
demain	tomorrow
dans ... jours	in ... days

Accidents

In the event of an accident:

1. report the accident to the police (compulsory if there is personal injury);
2. give your name, address, insurance company to the other party;
3. report it to the appropriate insurance company of the third party and your own company;
4. don't make any written statement without advice of a lawyer or automobile club official;
5. Get a police officer (**agent de police**) to make a report of major accidents in towns; on country roads send for the **gendarme**.

There has been an accident.	**Il y a un accident.** *eel ee a ang nakseedahng*
It's …	**Il est …** *eel eh*
on the highway [motorway]	**sur l'autoroute** *sewr loatoroot*
near …	**près de …** *preh der*
Where's the nearest telephone?	**Où est le téléphone le plus proche?** *oo eh ler taylayfon ler plew prosh*
Call …	**Téléphonez …** *taylayfonay*
an ambulance	**une ambulance** *ewn ambewlahngss*
a doctor	**un docteur** *ang dokturr*
the fire department	**les pompiers** *lay pawngpyay*
the police	**la police** *la poleess*
Can you help me please?	**Pourriez-vous m'aider, s'il vous plaît?** *pooryay voo mayday seel voo pleh*

Injuries

There are people injured.	**Il y a des blessés.** *eel ee a day blessay*
No one is hurt.	**Personne n'est blessé.** *pehrson neh blessay*
He is seriously injured.	**Il est gravement blessé.** *eel eh gravmahng blessay*
She's unconscious.	**Elle a perdu connaissance.** *el a pehrdew konayssahngss*
He can't breathe/move.	**Il ne peut pas respirer/bouger.** *eel ner pur pa respeeray/boozhay*
Don't move him.	**Ne le déplacez pas.** *ner ler dayplassay pa*

Legal matters

What's your insurance company?	**Quelle est votre compagnie d'assurance?** *kel eh votr kawngpañee dassewrahngss*
What's your name and address?	**Quels sont vos nom et adresse?** *kel sawng vo nawng ay adress*
He ran into me.	**Il m'est rentré dedans.** *eel meh rahngtray derdahng*
She was driving too fast/too close.	**Elle conduisait trop vite/trop près.** *el kawngdweezeh tro veet/tro preh*
I had the right of way.	**J'avais la priorité.** *zhaveh la preeoreetay*
I was (only) driving … km/h.	**Je ne faisais que … km à l'heure.** *zher ner ferzeh ker … keelometr a lurr*
I'd like an interpreter.	**Je voudrais un interprète.** *zher voodray ang nangtehrpret*
I didn't see the sign.	**Je n'ai pas vu le panneau.** *zher nay pa vew ler panoa*
He/She saw it happen.	**Il/Elle a vu ce qui s'est passé.** *eel/el a vew ser kee seh passay*
The license plate number was …	**Le numéro d'immatriculation était …** *ler newmayroa deematreekew-lasyawng ayteh*

YOU MAY HEAR

Est-ce que je peux voir votre …	Can I see your …
permis de conduire	driver's license
certificat d'assurance	insurance certificate
carte grise	vehicle registration document
À quelle heure est-ce que ça s'est passé?	What time did it happen?
Où est-ce que ça s'est passé?	Where did it happen?
Est-ce qu'il y avait quelqu'un d'autre (impliqué)?	Was anyone else involved?
Est-ce qu'il y a des témoins?	Are there any witnesses?
Vous alliez trop vite.	You were speeding.
Vos feux ne marchent pas.	Your lights aren't working.
Vous devez payer une amende (sur place).	You'll have to pay a fine (on the spot).
Vous devez venir au commissariat pour faire une déposition.	You have to make a statement at the station.

ASKING DIRECTIONS

Excuse me, please.	**Excusez-moi, s'il vous plaît.** *exkewzay mwa seel voo pleh*
How do I get to …?	**Pour aller à …?** *poor alay a*
Where is …?	**Où est …?** *oo eh*
Can you show me on the map where I am?	**Est-ce que vous pouvez me montrer où je suis sur la carte?** *ess ker voo poovay mer mawngtray oo zher swee sewr la kart*
I've lost my way.	**Je me suis perdu(e).** *zher mer swee pehrdew*
Can you repeat that?	**Est-ce que vous pouvez répéter?** *eh ser ker voo poovay raypaytay*
Thanks for your help.	**Merci pour votre aide.** *mehrsee poor votr ayd*

Traveling by car

Is this the right road for …?	**Est-ce que c'est bien la bonne route pour …?** *ess ker seh byang la bon root poor*
How far is it to … from here?	**… est à combien de kilomètres d'ici?** *eh a kawnbyang der keelometr deessee*
How do I get onto the highway [motorway]?	**Comment est-ce que je peux accéder à l'autoroute?** *kommahng ess ker zher pur aksayday a loatoroot*
What's the next town called?	**Comment s'appelle la prochaine ville?** *kommahng sapell la proshayn veel*
How long does it take by car?	**Il faut combien de temps en voiture?** *eel foa kawnbyang der tahng ahng vwatewr*

ON THE STREET

La gare, c'est loin d'ici? *la gar seh lwang deessee*
(Is the train station far from here?)
Non, non. C'est à cinq minutes à pied.
nawng nawng seh a sangk meenewt a peeay
(No, no. It's 5 minutes on foot.)
Merci. beaucoup. *mehrsee boakoo* *(Thank you very much.)*
De rien. *de reeangh* *(You're welcome.)*

YOU MAY HEAR

C'est ...	It's ...
tout droit	straight ahead
à gauche	on the left
à droite	on the right
de l'autre côté de la rue	on the other side of the street
au coin	on the corner
après le coin	round the corner
en direction de ...	in the direction of ...
en face de .../derrière ...	opposite .../behind ...
à côté de .../après ...	next to .../after ...
Descendez la	Go down the ...
rue transversale/rue principale	side street/main street
Traversez ...	Cross the ...
la place/le pont	square/bridge
Prenez la troisième route à droite.	Take the third turn on the right.
Tournez à gauche ...	Turn left ...
après les premiers feux	after the first traffic light
au deuxième carrefour	at the second intersection [crossroad]

Road signs

YOU MAY SEE

ALLUMEZ VOS PHARES	use headlights
BIS	alternative route
CÉDEZ LE PASSAGE	yield/give way
DÉVIATION	detour [diversion]
ÉCOLE	school
HAUTEUR LIMITÉE	low bridge
PRENEZ LA BONNE FILE	stay in lane/get in lane
ROUTE BARRÉE	road closed
SAUF RIVERAINS	local access only
SENS UNIQUE	one-way street

Is it far?

C'est ...	It's ...
près d'ici/loin	close/a long way
à cinq minutes à pied	5 minutes on foot
à dix minutes en voiture	10 minutes by car
à environ dix kilomètres	about 10 km away

Town plans

aéroport	a ayropor	airport
arrêt d'autobus	areh doatobews	bus stop
bâtiment public	bateemahng pewbleek	public building
(bureau de) poste	(bewroa der) post	post office
cinéma	seenayma	movie theater [cinema]
commissariat	komeessarya	police station
église	aygleez	church
gare	gar	station
itinéraire des bus	eeteenayrehr day bewss	bus route
office du tourisme	ofeess dew tooreezm	information office
parc	park	park
parking	parking	parking lot [car park]
passage piétons	passazh pyaytawng	pedestrian crossing
passage souterrain	passazh sootehrang	underpass
rue principale	rew prangseepal	main [high] street
stade	stad	stadium
station de métro	stasyawng der maytroa	subway [metro] station
station de taxi	stasyawng der taxee	taxi stand [rank]
terrain de sports	tehrrang der spor	playing field [sports ground]
théâtre	tayatr	theater
vieille ville	vyay veel	old town
vous êtes ici	voo zet eessee	you are here
zone piétonnière	zoan pyaytonyehr	pedestrian zone

SIGHTSEEING

TOURIST INFORMATION

Tourist information offices are often situated in the town center; look for **office du tourisme**, **syndicat d'initiative** or simply **informations**.

    Son et Lumière shows (telling the history of the town using special lighting and sound effects), wine tastings and markets, along with many other events, are advertised at the tourist information office.

Where's the tourist information office?	**Où est l'office du tourisme?** *oo eh loffeess dew tooreezm*
What are the main points of interest?	**Qu'est-ce qu'il y a d'intéressant à voir?** *kess keel ee a dangtayressahng a vwar*
We're here for …	**Nous restons …** *noo restawng*
only a few hours	**seulement quelques heures** *surlmahng kelker zurr*
a day	**une journée** *ewn zhoornay*
a week	**une semaine** *ewn sermayn*
Can you recommend …?	**Pouvez-vous recommander …?** *poovay voo rerkommahngday*
a sightseeing tour	**une visite touristique** *ewn veezeet tooreesteek*
an excursion	**une excursion** *ewn exkewrsyawng*
a boat trip	**une promenade en bateau** *ewn promnad ahng batoa*
Do you have any information on …?	**Avez-vous des renseignements sur …?** *avay voo day rahngsayñmahng sewr*
Are there any trips to …?	**Y a-t-il des voyages à …?** *ee ateel day vwahyazh a*

Reserving a tour

How much does the tour cost?	**Combien coûte cette excursion?** *kawnbyang koot set exkewrsyawng*
Is lunch included?	**Le déjeuner est-il compris?** *ler dayzhurnay eteel kawngpree*

Where do we leave from?	**D'où partons-nous?** *doo partawng noo*
What time does the tour start?	**À quelle heure commence l'excursion?** *a kel urr kommahngss lexkewrsyawng*
What time do we get back?	**À quelle heure revenons-nous?** *a kel urr rervnawng noo*
Do we have free time in …?	**Est-ce que nous aurons du temps libre à …?** *ess ker noo zoarawng dew tahng leebr a*
Is there an English-speaking guide?	**Y a-t-il un guide qui parle anglais?** *ee ateel ang geed kee parl ahnggleh*

On tour

Are we going to see …?	**Est-ce que nous allons voir …?** *ess ker noo zalawng vwar*
We'd like to have a look at the …	**Nous aimerions voir …** *noo zaymryawng vwar*
Can we stop here …?	**Est-ce que nous pouvons nous arrêter ici …?** *ess ker noo poovawng noo zarettay eessee*
to take photographs	**pour prendre des photos** *poor prahngdr day foto*
to buy souvenirs	**pour acheter des souvenirs** *poor ashtay day soovneer*
to use the restrooms [toilets]	**pour aller aux toilettes** *poor alay oa twalett*
Would you take a photo of us, please?	**Pourriez-vous nous prendre en photo, s'il vous plaît?** *pooryay voo noo prahngdr ahng foto seel voo pleh*
How long do we have here/in …?	**Combien de temps avons-nous ici/à …?** *kawnbyang der tahng avawng noo zeessee/a*
Wait! … isn't back yet.	**Attendez! … n'est pas encore là!** *atahngday … neh pa zahngkor la*

Sights

Town maps are displayed in major squares and streets and in the tourist information office.

Where is the …?	**Où est …?**	*oo eh*
abbey	**l'abbaye**	*labayee*
art gallery	**la galerie d' art**	*la galree dar*
battleground	**le champ de bataille**	*ler shahng der batie*
botanical garden	**le jardin botanique**	*ler zhardang botahneek*
castle	**le château**	*ler shatoa*
cathedral	**la cathédrale**	*la kataydral*
cemetery	**le cimetière**	*ler seemtyehr*
church	**l'église**	*laygleez*
downtown area	**le centre-ville**	*ler sahngtr veel*
fountain	**la fontaine**	*la fawngtayn*
market	**le marché**	*ler marshay*
(war) memorial	**le monument (aux morts)**	*ler monewmahng (oa mor)*
monastery	**le monastère**	*ler monastehr*
museum	**le musée**	*ler mewzay*
old town	**la vieille ville**	*la vyay veel*
opera house	**l'opéra**	*lopayra*
palace	**le palais**	*ler paleh*
park	**le parc**	*ler park*
parliament building	**le parlement**	*ler parlmahng*
ruins	**les ruines**	*lay rween*
shopping area	**les rues commerçantes**	*lay rew komehrsahngt*
statue	**la statue**	*la statew*
theater	**le théâtre**	*ler tayatr*
tower	**la tour**	*la toor*
town hall	**l'hôtel de ville**	*loatel der veel*
viewpoint	**le belvédère**	*ler belvaydehr*
Can you show me on the map?	**Pouvez-vous me montrer sur la carte?**	*poovay voo mer mawngtray sewr la kart*

ADMISSION

In France, national museums are usually closed on Tuesdays and on important holidays (Christmas, New Year's Day, etc.).

Is the … open to the public?	**Est-ce que … est ouvert(e) au public?** *ess ker … eh oovehr(t) oa pewbleek*
Can we look around?	**Est-ce que nous pouvons regarder?** *ess ker noo poovawng regarday*
What are the hours?	**Quelles sont les heures d'ouverture?** *kel sawng lay zurr doovehrtewr*
Is … open on Sundays?	**Est-ce que … est ouvert(e) le dimanche?** *ess ker … eh oovehr(t) ler deemahngsh*
When's the next guided tour?	**À quelle heure est la prochaine visite guidée?** *a kel urr eh la proshayn veezeet geeday*
Do you have a guide book (in English)?	**Avez-vous un guide (en anglais)?** *avay voo ang geed (ahng nahngleh)*
Can I take photos?	**Est-ce que je peux prendre des photos?** *ess ker zher pur prahngdr day foto*
Is there access for the handicapped?	**Est-ce accessible aux handicapés?** *ess aksesseebl oa ahngdeekapay*

Paying/Tickets

How much is the entrance fee?	**Combien coûte l'entrée?** *kawnbyang koot lahngtray*
Are there any discounts for …?	**Y a-t-il des réductions pour …?** *ee ateel day raydewksyawng poor*
children	**les enfants** *lay zahngfahng*
the handicapped	**les handicapés** *lay ahngdeekapay*
groups	**les groupes** *lay groop*
senior citizens	**les retraités** *lay rertretay*
students	**les étudiants** *lay zaytewdyahng*
1 adult and 2 children, please.	**Un adulte et deux enfants, s'il vous plaît.** *ang nadewlt ay dur zahngfahng seel voo pleh*
I've lost my ticket.	**J'ai perdu mon billet.** *zhay pehrdew mawng beeyeh*

AT THE TICKET COUNTER

Deux adultes, s'il vous plaît. *dur zadewlt seel voo pleh*
(Two adults, please.)

Ça fait quatre-vingt francs. *sa feh katr vang frahng*
(That's 80 francs.)

Voilà. *vwala* (Here you are.)

YOU MAY SEE

OUVERT	open
FERMÉ	closed
MAGASIN DE SOUVENIRS	gift shop
DÉFENSE D'ENTRER	no entry
HEURES DES VISITES	visiting hours
ENTRÉE GRATUITE/LIBRE	admission free
PROCHAINE VISITE À … H	next tour at …
DERNIER BILLET À 17H	last entry at 5 p.m.
PHOTOS AU FLASH INTERDITES	no flash photography

IMPRESSIONS

It's …	**C'est …**	*seh*
amazing	**incroyable**	*angkrwayyabl*
beautiful	**beau**	*boa*
boring	**ennuyeux**	*ahngnweeyur*
breathtaking	**époustouflant**	*aypoostooflahng*
brilliant	**fantastique**	*fahngtasteek*
interesting	**intéressant**	*angtayressahng*
magnificent	**magnifique**	*mañeefeek*
romantic	**romantique**	*romahngteek*
stunning	**stupéfiant**	*stewpayfyahng*
superb	**superbe**	*sewpehrb*
ugly	**laid**	*lay*

It's a good value. **On en a pour son argent.**
awng nahng na poor sawng narzhahng

It's a rip-off. **C'est du vol.** *seh dew vol*

I (don't) like it. **Ça (ne) me plaît (pas).** *sa (ner) mer pleh (pa)*

à chevrons herringbone
à colombages half-timbered
à l'échelle 1/100 scale 1:100
à poutres apparentes half-timbered
abside apse
aile (d'un bâtiment) wing (of building)
appartements royaux apartments (royal)
aquarelle watercolor
arc-boutant hanging buttress
argent silver
argenterie silverware
argile clay
arme weapon
arsenal armory
artisanat crafts
autel altar(piece)
bains baths
bâtiment building
beaux-arts fine arts
bibliothèque library
bijoux jewelry
bois wood
brique brick
cage d'escalier staircase
chaire pulpit
chef-d'œuvre masterpiece
chœur choir (stall)
cimetière churchyard
clef de voûte headstone
commandé par commissioned by
commencé en started in
complété en completed in
conception design
conçu par designed by
conférence lecture

construit en built in
contrefort buttress
cour courtyard
couronne crown
créneau battlement
dans le style de in the style of
découvert en discovered in
dessin drawing/design
dessiné par designed by
détail detail
détruit par destroyed by
doré à l'or fin gilded
douves moat
école de ... school of ...
émail enamel
en or gold(en)
en saillie overhanging
en surplomb overhanging
entrée doorway
érigé en erected in
escalier stairs
esquisse sketch
exposition display, exhibition
exposition temporaire temporary exhibit
fenêtre window
ferronnerie ironwork
flèche spire
fondé en founded in
fonts baptismaux font
fossé moat
fresque fresco
frise frieze
fronton pediment
fusain charcoal
gargouille gargoyle
grande salle de réception stateroom
gravure à l'eau-forte etching
gravure engraving

habitait lived (place)
hall d'entrée foyer
hauteur height
horloge clock
image picture
impératrice empress
jardin à la française formal garden
joyaux jewelry
lambris paneling
légué par donated by
maître master
maquette model
marbre marble
meubles furniture
moulures molding
mourut en died in
mur wall
nature morte still life
né en/à born in
nef nave
niveau 1 level 1
objet exposé exhibit
ombre shadow
orgue organ
œuvres works
panneau panel
par by (person)
paysage landscape/painting
paysage marin seascape
peint par painted by
peintre painter
peinture murale mural
peintures à l'huile oils
pendule clock
personnage en cire waxwork
pièce coin
pierre stone
pierre angulaire cornerstone
pierre précieuse gemstone
pierre tombale headstone

pignon gable
pilier pillar
plafond ceiling
pont-levis drawbridge
portail door, gate
porte doorway
poutre beam
prêté à on loan to
rebâti en rebuilt in
reconstruit en rebuilt in
reigne reign
reine queen
remparts battlement
renfoncement alcove
restauré en restored in
rinceau foliage
roi king
scène stage
sculpture carving, sculpture
siècle century
tableau painting
tableau vivant tableau
tapisserie tapestry
tenture hanging
terre cuite terracotta
thermes baths
toile canvas
toit roof
tombe grave/tomb
tombeau tomb
tour tower
tourelle turret
verrière (stained) glass window
vestibule foyer
vitrail (pl vitraux) stained glass window
vitrine display cabinet
vivait lived (time)
voûte vault

Who/What/When?

What's that building?	**Quel est ce bâtiment?** *kel eh ser bateemahng*
When was it built?	**Quand a-t-il été construit?** *kahng a teel aytay kawngstrwee*
Who was the …?	**Qui était …?** *kee ayteh*
architect/artist	**l'architecte/l'artiste** *larsheetekt/larteest*
What style is that?	**C'est quel style?** *seh kel steel*

Roman ca. 11th–12th century
The romanesque style was characterized by simple lines and round arches; esp. religious architecture in Burgundy (e.g., Tournus and Cluny).

Gothique ca. 12th–end 15th century
Very complex architectural forms, using pointed arches, rib vaults and flying buttresses; esp. cathedrals of Reims, Chartres, Strasbourg, Notre-Dame and Sainte-Chapelle in Paris.

Renaissance ca. 15th–16th century
Cultural and artistic movement, derived from the Italian Renaissance that aimed to imitate the ancient Roman stability and poise, esp. châteaux of the Loire and at Fontainebleau.

Baroque ca. 17th–18th century
Artistic movement; its music was finely polished, esp. Lully, Rameau and Couperin; its architectural style was large-scale and elaborately decorated, esp. many churches in the Savoie region.

Classicisme ca. mid 18th–mid 19th century
The Classical movement brought about a return to classical values such as simplicity and methodical order, esp. the Louvre and its famous colonnade (by Perrault); artist: David.

Art nouveau 1880s–1910s
Simplified forms, ranging from the emulation of nature to abstract forms; esp. the use of undulating lines seen in glassware, jewelry and art.

Impressionnisme 1874–1886
Movement rejecting the true-to-life style of Réaliste art; moved toward a greater use of color and light to create an "impression"; esp. artists: Manet, Degas, Cézanne, Monet; composers: Debussy, Ravel.

Rulers

What period is that? **C'est quelle période?** *seh kel payryod*

gallo-romain 59 BC–476 AD

Julius Caesar brought the whole of Gaul (now France, Belgium and Switzerland), under Roman rule. The western Roman Empire flourished, esp. in Lyon and Provence; on its collapse, Gaul was invaded by numerous barbarian tribes, including the Franks.

médiéval 476–1500

Dynasties and major figures of the Middle Ages include mérovingiens (486–751) – Clovis I; carolingiens (751–987) – Charlemagne; capétiens (987–1328) – Saint Louis; les Valois (1328–1589) – François I.

les Bourbons 1589–1793, 1815–1848

Dynasty founded by Henri IV; reached the pinnacle of power under Louis XIV (le Roi-Soleil – Sun King) with the magnificence of Versailles and Paris during le grand siècle (ca. 17th); ended with the execution of Louis XVI; briefly restored 1815–1848.

la Révolution 1789–1799

The French Revolution began with the storming of La Bastille prison (14 July 1789). Peasant uprisings (**la Grande Peur**) and Revolutionary wars follow. The Republic is declared, Louis XVI is executed and Robespierre leads a Reign of Terror (**la Terreur**).

l'Empire 1799–1814, 1852–1870

The Empire of Napoléon Bonaparte with its initial prosperity and military expansion across Europe crumbled with a disastrous campaign in Russia (1812) and final defeat at Waterloo. The Second Empire under Napoléon III saw Paris transformed by wide boulevards; but it also ended in defeat, followed by the Third Republic (1870–1940).

Religion

France and Belgium are predominantly Roman Catholic, although places of worship for most faiths can be found, especially in large cities. Switzerland is equally divided between Roman Catholic and Protestant.

Catholic/Protestant church	**une église catholique/protestante** *ewn aygleez katoleek/protestahngt*
mosque	**une mosquée** *ewn moskay*
synagogue	**une synagogue** *ewn seenagog*

IN THE COUNTRYSIDE

I'd like a map of …	**Je voudrais une carte …** *zher voodray ewn kart*
this region	**de cette région** *der seht rayzhyawng*
walking routes	**des sentiers de randonnée** *day sahngtyay der rahngdonnay*
cycle routes	**des circuits cyclistes** *day seerkwee seekleest*
How far is it to …?	**Il y a combien de kilomètres jusqu'à …?** *eel ee a kawnbyang der keelometr zhewska*
Is there a right of way?	**Y a-t-il un droit de passage?** *ee ateel ang drwa der passazh*
Is there a trail/scenic route to …?	**Y a-t-il une route touristique pour aller à …?** *ee ateel ewn root tooreesteek poor alay a*
Can you show me on the map?	**Pouvez-vous me le montrer sur la carte?** *poovay voo mer ler mawngtray sewr la kart*
I'm lost.	**Je me suis perdu(e).** *zher mer swee pehrdew*

Guided tours

When does the walk/hike start?	**À quelle heure commence la promenade?** *a kel urr kommahngss la promnahd*
When will we return?	**À quelle heure reviendrons-nous?** *a kel urr rervyangdrawng noo*
I'm exhausted.	**Je suis épuisé(e).** *zher swee zaypweezay*
What is the walk like?	**C'est quel genre de promenade?** *seh kel zhahngr der promnad*
gentle/medium/tough	**facile/moyenne/difficile** *fasseel/mwahyenn/deefeesseel*
What kind of … is that?	**C'est quel genre …?** *seh kel zhahngr*
animal/bird	**d'animal/d'oiseau** *dahneemal/dwazoa*
flower/tree	**de fleur/d'arbre** *der flurr/darbr*

Geographic features

bridge	**le pont**	*ler pawng*
cave	**la grotte**	*la grot*
cliff	**la falaise**	*la falez*
farm	**la ferme**	*la fehrm*
field	**le champ**	*ler shahng*
(foot)path	**le sentier/le chemin**	*ler sahngtyay/ler shermang*
forest	**la forêt**	*la foreh*
hill	**la colline**	*la koleen*
lake	**le lac**	*ler lak*
mountain	**la montagne**	*la mawngtañ*
mountain pass	**le col (de montagne)**	*ler kol (der mawngtañ)*
mountain range	**la chaîne de montagnes**	*la shen der mawngtañ*
nature reserve	**le parc naturel**	*ler park natewrel*
panorama	**le panorama**	*ler pahnorama*
park	**le parc**	*ler park*
peak	**le pic/le sommet**	*ler peek/ler someh*
picnic area	**l'aire de pique-nique**	*lehr der peek neek*
pond	**l'étang**	*laytahng*
rapids	**les rapides**	*lay rapeed*
river	**la rivière**	*la reevyehr*
sea	**la mer**	*la mehr*
stream	**le ruisseau**	*ler rweessoa*
valley	**la vallée**	*la valay*
viewpoint	**le point de vue/le belvédère**	*ler pwang der vew/le belvaydehr*
village	**le village**	*ler veelazh*
winery [vineyard]	**la vigne**	*la veeñ*
waterfall	**la cascade**	*la kaskad*
wood	**le bois**	*ler bwa*

LEISURE

WHAT'S ON?

Local papers and, in large cities, weekly entertainment guides will tell you what's on. In Paris look for L'Officiel des Spectacles and Pariscope; in Brussels, Le Bulletin. You'll be spoiled for choice by the range of dance, music and theater offered.

Do you have a program of events?	**Avez-vous un programme des spectacles?** *avay voo ang program day spektakl*
Can you recommend a good …?	**Pouvez-vous me conseiller …?** *poovay voo mer kawngsayay*
Is there a … somewhere?	**Y a-t-il … quelque part?** *ee ateel … kelker par*
ballet/concert	**un ballet/un concert** *ang baleh/ang kawngsehr*
movie [film]	**un film** *ang feelm*
opera	**un opéra** *ang nopayra*
museum	**le musée** *ler mewseh*

AVAILABILITY

When does it start?	**À quelle heure est-ce que ça commence?** *a kelur ess ker sa kommahngss*
When does it end?	**À quelle heure est-ce que ça finit?** *a kelur ess ker sa feenee*
Are there any seats for tonight?	**Est-ce qu'il reste des places pour ce soir?** *ess keel rest day plass poor ser swar*
Where can I get tickets?	**Où est-ce que je peux me procurer des billets?** *oo ess ker zher pur mer prokewray day beeyeh*
There are … of us.	**Nous sommes …** *noo som*
2/4/6	**deux/quatre/six/** *dur/katr/seess*

TICKETS

How much are the seats?	**Combien coûtent les places?** *kawnbyang koot lay plass*
I'd like to make reservations.	**J'aimerais réserver des places.** *zhaymeray rayzehrvay day plass*
Do you have anything cheaper?	**Avez-vous quelque chose de moins cher?** *avay voo kelker shoaz der mwang shehr*
I'd like to reserve ...	**Je voudrais réserver ...** *zher voodray rayzehrvay*
3 for Sunday evening	**trois places pour dimanche soir** *trwa plass poor deemahngsh swar*
1 for Friday matinee	**une place pour vendredi en matinée** *ewn plass poor vahngdrerdee ahng mateenay*
May I have a program?	**Est-ce que je peux avoir un programme?** *ess ker zher pur avwar ang program*
Where's the coat room?	**Où est le vestiaire?** *oo eh ler vestyehr*

YOU MAY HEAR

Quel(le) est ... de votre carte de crédit?	What's your credit card ...?
le numéro/le nom/ la date d'expiration	number/type/ expiration [expiry] date
Venez chercher les billets ... avant ... heures (du soir)	Please pick up the tickets ... by ... p.m.

AT THE BOX OFFICE

Avez-vous un programme des spectacles? *avay voo ang program day spektakl (Do you have a program of events?)*

Bien sûr. Voilà. *byang sewr vwala (Of course. Here you are.)*

Merci. *mehrsee (Thanks.)*

109

MOVIES [CINEMA]

For movies in their original English (with French subtitles), look for those marked VO (**version originale**). However, you'll find most American and British films are dubbed.

Is there a movie theater [cinema] near here?	**Y a-t-il un cinéma près d'ici?** *ee ateel ang seenayma mewlteeplex preh deessee*
What's playing at the movie theater [cinema]?	**Qu'y a-t-il au cinéma ce soir?** *kee ateel oa seenayma ser swar*
Is the film dubbed/subtitled?	**Est-ce que le film est doublé/sous-titré?** *ess ker ler feelm eh dooblay/soo teetray*
Is the film in the original English?	**Est-ce que le film est en version originale (en anglais)?** *ess ker ler feelm eh ahng vehrsyawng oreezheenal (ahng ahngleh)*
A ..., please.	**..., s'il vous plaît.** *seel voo pleh*
box [carton] of popcorn	**une boîte de pop-corn** *ewn bwat der popkorn*
chocolate ice cream	**une glace au chocolat** *ewn glass oa shokola*
hot dog	**un hot dog** *ang ot dog*
soft drink/soda	**une boisson gazeuse** *ewn bwassawng gazurz*
small/regular/large	**petit/moyen/grand** *pertee/mwahyang/grahng*

THEATER

What's playing at the ... Theater?	**Qu'est-ce qu'on joue au théâtre ...?** *kess kawng zhoo oa tayatr*
Who's the playwright?	**Qui est l'auteur?** *kee eh loaturr*
Do you think I'd enjoy it?	**Pensez-vous que ça me plairait?** *pahngsay voo ker sa mer plehreh?*
I don't know much French.	**Je ne connais pas beaucoup de français.** *zher ner konneh pa boakoo der frahngseh*

OPERA/BALLET/DANCE

Where's the opera house?	**Où est l'opéra?** *oo eh lopayra*
Who's the composer/soloist?	**Qui est le compositeur/soliste?** *kee eh ler kawngpozeeturr/soleest*
Is formal dress required?	**Faut-il être en tenue de soirée?** *foa teel etr ahng tenew der swaray*
Who's dancing?	**Qui est-ce qui danse?** *kee ess kee dahngss*
I'm interested in contemporary dance.	**Je m'intéresse à la danse contemporaine.** *zher mangtayress a la dahngss kawngtahngporayn*

MUSIC/CONCERTS

Where's the concert hall?	**Où est la salle de concerts?** *oo eh la sal der kawngsehr*
Which orchestra/ band is playing?	**Quel orchestre/groupe joue?** *kel orkestr/groop zhoo*
What are they playing?	**Qu'est-ce qu'ils jouent?** *kess keel zhoo*
Who is the conductor/soloist?	**Qui est le chef d'orchestre/le soliste?** *kee eh ler shef dorkestr/ler soleest*
Who is the support band?	**Qui est le groupe en première partie?** *kee eh ler groop ahng prermyehr partee*
I really like …	**J'aime beaucoup …** *zhem boakoo*
country music	**la musique country** *la mewzeek country*
folk music	**la musique folk** *la mewzeek folk*
jazz	**le jazz** *ler dzhazz*
music of the '60s	**la musique des années soixante** *la mewzeek day zahnay swassahngt*
pop	**la musique pop** *la mewzeek pop*
rock music	**la musique rock** *la mewzeek rok*
soul music	**la musique soul** *la mewzeek soul*
Have you ever heard of her/him?	**Est-ce que vous en avez déjà entendu parler?** *ess ker voo zahng navay dayzha ahngtahngdew parlay*
Are they popular?	**Est-ce qu'ils sont connus?** *ess keel sawng konnew*

NIGHTLIFE

What is there to do in the evenings?	**Qu'est-ce qu'il y a à faire le soir?** *kess keel ee a a fehr ler swar*
Can you recommend a …?	**Pouvez-vous me recommander un(e) …?** *poovay voo mer rekommahngda y ang (ewn)*
Is there a … in town?	**Est-ce qu'il y a … en ville?** *ess keel ee a … ahng veel*
bar	**un bar** *ang bar*
casino	**un casino** *ang kazeeno*
discotheque	**une discothèque/une boîte (de nuit)** *ewn deeskotek/ewn bwat (der nwee)*
gay club	**un club gay** *ang klurb gay*
nightclub	**un night-club** *ang naytklurb*
restaurant	**un restaurant** *ang restoarahng*
What type of music do they play?	**Quel genre de musique jouent-ils?** *kel zhahngr der mewzeek zhoo teel*
How do I get there?	**Comment est-ce que je peux m'y rendre?** *kommahng ess ker zher pur mee rahngdr*

ADMISSION

What time does the show start?	**À quelle heure commence le spectacle?** *a kel urr kommahngss ler spektakl*
Is evening dress required?	**Faut-il être en tenue de soirée?** *foa teel etr ahng ternew der swaray*
Is there a cover charge?	**Faut-il payer pour rentrer?** *foa teel payay poor rahngtray*
Is a reservation necessary?	**Faut-il réserver?** *foa teel rayzehrvay*
Do we need to be members?	**Faut-il être membre?** *foa teel etr mahngbr*
How long will we have to stand in line [queue]?	**Combien de temps devrons-nous faire la queue?** *kawnbyang der tahng dervrawng noo fehr la kur*
I'd like a good table.	**Je voudrais une bonne table.** *zher voodray ewn bon tabl*

CHILDREN

Can you recommend something for the children?	**Pouvez-vous recommander quelque chose pour les enfants?** *poovay voo rerkommahngday kelker shoaz poor lay zahngfahng*
Are there changing facilities here for infants?	**Y a-t-il une salle de change pour bébé ici?** *ee ateel ewn sal der shahngzh poor baybay eessee*
Where are the restrooms [toilets]?	**Où sont les toilettes?** *oo sawng lay twalett*
game/amusement arcade	**la salle de jeux** *la sal der zhur*
fairground	**la fête foraine** *la fet forayn*
kiddie [paddling] pool	**le petit bassin** *ler pertee bassang*
playground	**la cour de récréation** *la koor der raykrayasyawng*
playgroup/nursery school	**la garderie/l'école maternelle** *la garderree/laykol matehrnel*
zoo	**le zoo** *ler zoa*

Baby-sitting

Can you recommend a reliable baby-sitter?	**Pouvez-vous recommander une gardienne d'enfants sérieuse?** *poovay voo rerkommahngday ewn gardyenn dahngfahng sayryurz*
Is there constant supervision?	**Sont-ils surveillés tout le temps?** *sawng teel sewrvayay too ler tahng*
Are the helpers properly trained?	**Le personnel est-il qualifié?** *ler pehrsonel eteel kaleefyay*
When can I drop them off?	**À quelle heure est-ce que je peux les amener?** *a kel urr ess ker zher pur lay zamnay*
I'll pick them up at …	**Je viendrai les chercher à …** *zher vyangdray lay shehrshay a*
We'll be back by …	**Nous reviendrons à …** *noo rervyangdrawng a*
She's 3 and he's 18 months.	**Elle a trois ans et il a dix-huit mois.** *el a trwa zahng ay eel a deezwee mwa*

SPORTS

Soccer, tennis and racing (bicycles, cars and horses) are popular spectator sports in France. You'll also find plenty of opportunity yourself for sailing, fishing, horseback riding, golf, tennis, hiking, cycling, swimming and skiing.

Spectator Sports

Is there a soccer game this Saturday?	**Y a-t-il un match de football samedi?** *ee ateel ang match der footbal samdee*
Which teams are playing?	**Quelles sont les équipes?** *kel sawng lay zaykeep*
Can you get me a ticket?	**Pouvez-vous me procurer un ticket?** *poovay voo mer prokewray ang teekeh*
What's the admission charge?	**Combien coûtent les places?** *kawnbyang koot lay plass*
Where's the racetrack [race course]?	**Où est l'hippodrome?** *oo eh leepodrom*
athletics	**athlétisme** *atlayteezm*
basketball	**basket(ball)** *basket(bal)*
cycling	**cyclisme** *seekleezm*
soccer [football]	**football** *footbal*
golf	**golf** *golf*
horseracing	**courses de chevaux** *koorss der shervoa*
swimming	**natation** *natasyawng*
tennis	**tennis** *teneess*
volleyball	**volley(ball)** *voleh(bal)*

la pétanque

Provençal name for **boules**, in which metal balls/boules are thrown at the wooden jack (**cochonnet**); the game is played throughout France, wherever there is an available gravel area.

le Tour de France

The world's most prestigious cycle tour (June-July annually) winds a demanding route around France, with the **maillot vert** (green jersey) for the King of the Mountains (Pyrenees and Alps), and the award of the prized **maillot jaune** (yellow jersey) to the winner back in Paris.

Participating sports

Where's the nearest …?	**Où est … le plus proche?** *oo eh … ler plew prosh*
golf course	**le terrain de golf** *ler tehrang der golf*
sports club	**le club sportif** *ler klurb sporteef*
Where are the tennis courts?	**Où sont les courts de tennis?** *oo sawng lay koor der tenneess*
What's the charge per …?	**Combien ça coûte par …?** *kawnbyang sa koot par*
day/round/hour	**jour/partie/heure** *zhoor/partee/urr*
Do I need to be a member?	**Faut-il être membre du club?** *foa teel etr mahngbr dew klurb*
Where can I rent …?	**Où est-ce que je peux louer …?** *oo ess ker zher pur looay*
boots	**des chaussures** *day shoassewr*
clubs	**des clubs (de golf)** *day klurb (der golf)*
equipment	**du matériel** *dew matayryell*
racket	**une raquette** *ewn rakett*
Can I take lessons?	**Est-ce que je peux prendre des leçons?** *ess ker zher pur prahngdr day lerssawng*
Do you have a fitness center?	**Avez-vous une salle de musculation?** *avay voo ewn sal der mewskewlasyawng*
Can I join in?	**Est-ce que je peux vous tenir compagnie?** *ess ker zher pur voo terneer kawngpañee*

At the beach

Most beaches are supervised (**plage/baignade surveillée**) by lifeguards unless specified **non surveillée**.

Always follow the flags regarding swimming safety: green – no danger; orange – danger, be cautious; black – no bathing.

Topless bathing is accepted on most French beaches, although in some places it may be frowned upon: be wise and do what other people do.

Is the beach …?	**Est-ce que c'est une plage …?** *ess ker seh tewn plazh*

pebbly/sandy	**de galets/de sable** *der galeh/der sabl*
Is there a … here?	**Y a-t-il … ici?** *ee ateel … eessee*
children's pool	**une piscine pour enfants** *ewn peesseen poor ahngfahng*
swimming pool	**une piscine …** *ewn peesseen*
indoor/outdoor	**couverte/en plein air** *koovehrt/ahng plang ehr*
Is it safe to swim/dive here?	**Est-ce qu'on peut se baigner/plonger ici sans danger?** *ess kawng pur ser bayñay/ plawngzhay eessee sahng dahngzhay*
Is it safe for children?	**Est-ce que c'est sans danger pour les enfants?** *ess ker seh sahng dahngzhay poor lay zahngfahng*
Is there a lifeguard?	**Y a-t-il un maître-nageur?** *ee ateel ang metr nazhurr*
I want to rent a/some …	**Je voudrais louer …** *zher voodray looay*
deck chair	**une chaise longue** *ewn shez lawngg*
jet ski	**un scooter de mer** *ang skooturr der mehr*
motorboat	**un canot automobile** *ang kahnoa oatomobeel*
umbrella [sunshade]	**un parasol** *ang parassol*
surfboard	**une planche de surf** *ewn plahngsh der surrf*
waterskis	**des skis nautiques** *day skee noateek*
For … hours.	**Pendant … heures.** *pahngdahng … urr*

YOU MAY HEAR

Je regrette, nous sommes complets.	I'm sorry, we're booked.
Il faut verser … francs de caution/d'arrhes.	There is a deposit of …
Quelle pointure faites-vous?	What size are you?
Il vous faut une photo d'identité.	You need a passport-size photo.

Skiing

Generally speaking, the Alps are the best for downhill skiing (**descente**) and the Pyrenees for cross-country (**ski de fond**). French resorts tend to be modern and efficient; in Switzerland the emphasis is more on tradition and character. However, excellent skiing is to be found in both countries.

Is there much snow?	**Est-ce qu'il y a beaucoup de neige?** *ess keel ee a boakoo der nayzh*
What's the snow like?	**Comment est la neige?** *kommahng eh la nayzh*
heavy/icy	**lourde/gelée (verglacée)** *loord/zherlay (vehrglassay)*
powdery/wet	**poudreuse/mouillée** *poodrurz/mooyay*
I'd like to rent some …	**Je voudrais louer …** *zher voodray looay*
poles	**des bâtons** *day batawng*
skates	**des patins** *day patang*
ski boots	**des chaussures de ski** *day shoassewr der skee*
skis	**des skis** *day skee*
These are too …	**Ils sont trop …** *eel sawng tro*
big/small	**grands/petits** *grahng/pertee*
They're uncomfortable.	**Ils ne sont pas confortables.** *eel ner sawng pa kawngfortabl*
A lift pass for a day/5 days, please.	**Un forfait pour une journée/cinq jours, s'il vous plaît.** *ang forfeh poor ewn zhoornay/sangk zhoor seel voo pleh*
I'd like to join the ski school.	**Je voudrais prendre des leçons à l'école de ski.** *zher voodray prahngdr day lerssawng a laykol der skee*
I'm a beginner.	**Je suis débutant.** *zher swee daybewtahng*
I'm experienced.	**J'ai déjà de l'expérience.** *zhay dayzha der lexpayryahngss*

YOU MAY SEE

REMONTE-PENTE/TIRE-FESSES	ski lift
TÉLÉPHÉRIQUE/ŒUFS	cable car/gondolas
TÉLÉSIÈGE	chair lift

MAKING FRIENDS
INTRODUCTIONS

Greetings vary according to how well you know someone.

It's polite to shake hands, both when you meet and say good-bye to a French person, especially when it is for the first time.

The titles **monsieur**, **madame**, **mademoiselle** (sir, madam, miss) are used in French much more than in English and do not sound as formal. In fact, it is polite to add them after **bonjour**, especially when addressing someone you do not know.

In French, there are two forms for "you" (taking different verb forms):

tu (informal/familiar) is used when talking to relatives, close friends and children (and between young people);

vous (formal) is used in all other cases, and is also the plural form of **tu**.

Hello, I don't think we've met.	**Bonjour, nous ne nous connaissons pas, je crois?** *bawngzhoor noo ner noo konessawng pa zher krwa*
My name is …	**Je m'appelle …** *zher mappell*
May I introduce …?	**Puis-je vous présenter …?** *pweezh voo prayzahngtay*
Pleased to meet you.	**Enchanté.** *ahngshahngtay*
What's your name?	**Comment vous appelez-vous?** *kommahng voo zaplay voo*
How are you?	**Comment allez-vous?** *kommahng talay voo*
Fine, thanks. And you?	**Très bien, merci. Et vous [toi]?** *treh byang mehrsee et voo [twa]*

AT A RECEPTION

Je m'appelle Sheryl. *zher mappell sheryl* (*My name is Sheryl.*)

Enchanté. Je m'appelle Yves. *ahngshahngtay zher mappell eve* (*Pleased to meet you. My name is Yves.*)

Enchanté. *ahngshahngtay* (*Pleased to meet you.*)

WHERE ARE YOU FROM?

Where do you come from?	**D'où venez-vous ?**	*doo vernay voo*
Where were you born?	**Où êtes-vous né(e)?**	*oo ayt voo nay*
I'm from …	**Je viens …**	*zher vyang*
Australia	**d'Australie**	*doastralee*
Britain	**de Grande-Bretagne**	*der grahngd brertañ*
Canada	**du Canada**	*dew kahnada*
England	**d'Angleterre**	*dahnglertehr*
Ireland	**d'Irlande**	*deerlahngd*
Scotland	**d'Écosse**	*daykoss*
U.S.	**des États-Unis**	*day zayta zewnee*
Wales	**du Pays de Galles**	*dew payee der gal*
Where do you live?	**Où habitez-vous?**	*oo abeetay voo*
What part of … are you from?	**Vous êtes de quelle région de …?** *voo zayt der kel rayzhyawng der*	
Belgium	**Belgique**	*belzheek*
France	**France**	*frahngss*
Switzerland	**Suisse**	*sweess*
We come here every year.	**Nous venons ici tous les ans.** *noo vernawng eessee too lay zahng*	
It's my/our first visit.	**C'est la première fois que je viens/ nous venons.** *seh la prermyehr fwa ker zher vyang/noo vernawng*	
Have you ever been to …?	**Est-ce que vous êtes déjà allés … ?** *ess ker voo zayt dayzha alay*	
Britain/the U.S.	**en Grande-Bretagne/aux États-Unis** *ahng grahngd brertañ/oa zayta zewnee*	
Do you like it here?	**Ça vous plaît ici?**	*sa voo pleh eessee*
What do you think of the …?	**Que pensez-vous de …?** *ker pahngsay voo der*	
I love the … here.	**J'adore … ici.**	*zhador … eessee*
I don't really like the … here.	**Je n'aime pas beaucoup … ici.** *zher naym pa boakoo … eessee*	
food/people	**la cuisine/les gens**	*la kweezeen/lay zhang*

WHO ARE YOU WITH?

Who are you with?	**Avec qui êtes-vous?** *avek kee ayt voo*
I'm on my own.	**Je suis tout(e) seul(e).** *zher swee too(t) surl*
I'm with a friend.	**Je suis avec un(e) ami(e).** *zher swee zavek ang (ewn) amee*
I'm with my …	**Je suis avec …** *zher swee zavek*
wife	**ma femme** *ma fam*
husband	**mon mari** *mawng maree*
family	**ma famille** *ma famee*
children	**mes enfants** *may zahngfahng*
parents	**mes parents** *may parahng*
boyfriend/girlfriend	**mon copain/ma copine** *mawng kopang/ma kopeen*
father/son	**mon père/fils** *mawng pehr/feess*
mother/daughter	**ma mère/fille** *ma mehr/fee*
brother/uncle	**mon frère/oncle** *mawng frehr/awngkl*
sister/aunt	**ma sœur/tante** *ma surr/tahng*
What's your son's/wife's name?	**Comment s'appelle votre fils/femme?** *kommahng sappell votrer feess/fam*
Are you married?	**Êtes-vous marié(e)?** *ayt voo maryay*
I'm …	**Je suis …** *zher swee*
married/single	**marié(e)/célibataire** *maryay/sayleebatehr*
divorced/separated	**divorcé(e)/séparé(e)** *deevorsay/separay*
engaged	**fiancé(e)** *feeahngsay*
We live together.	**Nous vivons ensemble.** *noo veevawng zahngsahngbl*
Do you have any children?	**Avez-vous des enfants?** *avay voo day zahngfahng*
2 boys and a girl.	**Deux garçons et une fille.** *dur garsawng ay ewn fee*
How old are they?	**Quel âge ont-ils?** *kel azh awng teel*
They're ten and twelve.	**Ils ont dix et douze ans.** *eel zawng dees ay dooz ahng*

WHAT DO YOU DO?

What do you do?	**Qu'est-ce que vous faites dans la vie/comme travail?** *kess ker voo fet dahng la vee/kom travie*
What line are you in?	**Dans quelle branche êtes-vous?** *dahng kel brahngsh ayt voo*
What are you studying?	**Qu'est-ce que vous étudiez?** *kess ker voo zaytewdyay*
I'm studying …	**J'étudie …** *zhaytewdee*
I'm in …	**Je suis dans …** *zher swee dahng*
business	**le commerce** *ler komehrss*
engineering	**l'ingénierie** *langzhaynyeree*
retail	**la vente au détail** *la vahngt oa daytay*
sales	**la vente** *la vahngt*
Who do you work for …?	**Pour qui travaillez-vous …?** *poor kee travieyay voo*
I work for …	**Je travaille pour …** *zher traviey poor*
I'm a(n) …	**Je suis …** *zher swee*
accountant	**comptable** *kawngptabl*
housewife	**femme au foyer** *fam oa fwayay*
student	**étudiant(e)** *aytewdyahng(t)*
retired	**retraité(e)** *rertretay*
self-employed	**à mon compte** *a mawng kawngt*
unemployed	**au chômage** *oa shoamazh*
What are your interests/hobbies?	**Quels sont vos intérêts/hobbies?** *kel sawng vo zangtayreh/obbee*
I like …	**J'aime …** *zhaym*
music	**la musique** *la mewzeek*
reading	**la lecture** *la lektewr*
I play …	**Je joue …** *zher zhoo*
cards	**aux cartes** *oa kart*
chess	**aux échecs** *oa zayshek*

WHAT WEATHER!

What a lovely day!	**Quelle belle journée!**	*kel bell zhoornay*
What awful weather!	**Quel temps horrible!**	*kel tahng zoreebl*
Isn't it cold/hot today!	**Qu'est-ce qu'il fait froid/chaud aujourd'hui!**	*kess keel feh frwa/shoa oazhoordwee*
Is it usually as warm as this?	**Est-ce qu'il fait aussi chaud d'habitude?**	*ess keel feh oassee shoa dabeetewd*
Do you think it's going to … tomorrow?	**Croyez-vous qu'il va … demain?**	*krwahyay voo keel va … dermang*
be a nice day	**faire beau**	*fehr boa*
rain	**pleuvoir**	*plurvwar*
snow	**neiger**	*nayzhay*
What is the weather forecast?	**Quelles sont les prévisions météo?**	*kel sawng lay prayveezyawng maytayo*
It's …	**Il y a …**	*eel ee a*
cloudy	**des nuages**	*day newazh*
foggy	**du brouillard**	*dew brooyar*
frosty	**du givre**	*dew zheevr*
icy	**du verglas**	*dew vehrgla*
thundering	**du tonnerre**	*dew tonehr*
windy	**du vent**	*dew vahng*
It's raining.	**Il pleut.**	*eel plur*
It's snowing.	**Il neige.**	*eel nayzh*
It's sunny.	**Il fait du soleil.**	*eel feh dew solayy*
Has the weather been like this for long?	**Il fait ce temps-là depuis longtemps?**	*eel feh ser tahng la derpwee lawnggtahng*
What's the pollen count?	**Quel est le taux de pollen?**	*kel eh ler toa der pollenn*
high/medium/low	**élevé/moyen/bas**	*aylervay/mwahyang/ba*
What's the forecast for skiing?	**Quelle est la météo pour le ski?**	*kel eh la maytayo poor ler skee*

ENJOYING YOUR TRIP?

I'm here on …	**Je suis ici en …** *zher swee zeessee ahng*
a business trip	**voyage d'affaires** *vwahyazh dafehr*
vacation [holiday]	**vacances** *vakahngss*
We came …	**Nous sommes venus …** *noo som vernew*
by train/by bus/by plane	**en train/en bus/par avion** *ahng trang/ahng bews/par avyawng*
by car/by ferry	**en voiture/par le ferry** *ahng vwatewr/par ler fehree*
I have a rented car.	**J'ai une voiture de location.** *zhay ewn vwatewr der lokasyawng*
We're staying …	**Nous logeons …** *noo lozhawng*
in an apartment	**dans un appartement** *dahng zang napartmahng*
at a hotel/campsite	**à l'hôtel/dans un camping** *a loatel/dahng zang kahngpeeng*
with friends	**chez des amis** *shay day zamee*
Can you suggest …?	**Pouvez-vous nous conseiller …?** *poovay voo noo kawngsayay*
things to do	**quelque chose à faire** *kelker shoaz a fehr*
places to eat	**des endroits pour manger** *day zahngdrwa poor mahngzhay*
places to visit	**des endroits à visiter** *day zahngdrwa a veezeetay*

YOU MAY HEAR

Est-ce que vous êtes en vacances?	Are you on vacation?
Comment êtes-vous venu(s) ici?	How did you travel here?
Où logez-vous?	Where are you staying?
Depuis combien de temps êtes-vous ici?	How long have you been here?
Combien de temps restez-vous?	How long are you staying?
Où allez vous ensuite?	Where are you going next?
Est-ce que vous profitez bien de vos vacances?	Are you enjoying your vacation?

INVITATIONS

Would you like to have dinner with us on …?	**Voulez-vous venir dîner avec nous …?** *voolay voo verneer deenay avek noo*
May I invite you to lunch?	**Est-ce que je peux vous inviter à déjeuner?** *ess ker zher pur voo zangveetay a dayzhurnay*
Can you come for a drink this evening?	**Est-ce que vous pouvez venir prendre un verre ce soir?** *ess ker voo poovay verneer prahngdr ang vehr ser swar*
We are having a party. Can you come?	**Nous donnons une soirée. Pouvez-vous venir?** *noo donawng ewn swaray. poovay voo verneer*
May we join you?	**Est-ce que nous pouvons nous joindre à vous?** *ess ker noo poovawng noo zhwangdr a voo*
Would you like to join us?	**Voulez-vous vous joindre à nous?** *voolay voo voo zhwangdr a noo*

Going out

What are your plans for …?	**Qu'avez-vous de prévu pour …?** *kavay voo der prayvew poor*
today/tonight	**aujourd'hui/ce soir** *oazhoordwee/ser swar*
tomorrow	**demain** *dermang*
Are you free this evening?	**Est-ce que vous êtes libre ce soir?** *ess ker voo zayt leebr ser swar*
Would you like to …?	**Est-ce que vous aimeriez …?** *ess ker voo aymeryay*
go dancing	**aller danser** *alay dahngsay*
go for a drink	**aller prendre un verre** *alay prahngdr ang vehr*
go out for a meal	**aller manger** *alay mahngzhay*
go for a walk	**faire une promenade** *fehr ewn promnahd*
go shopping	**aller faire des courses** *alay fehr day koorss*
I'd like to go to …	**J'aimerais aller à …** *zhaymray alay a*
I'd like to see …	**J'aimerais voir …** *zhaymray vwar*
Do you enjoy …?	**Aimez-vous …?** *aymay voo*

Accepting or declining

Great. I'd love to.	**Avec plaisir.**	*avek playzeer*

Thank you, but I'm busy.
Merci mais j'ai à faire.
mehrsee meh zhay a fehr

May I bring a friend?
Est-ce que je peux amener un(e) ami(e)? *ess ker zher pur amnay ang namee (ewn amee)*

Where shall we meet?
Où nous retrouvons-nous?
oo noo rertroovawng noo

I'll meet you …
Je vous [te] retrouverai …
zher voo [ter] rertroovray

in front of your hotel
devant votre [ton] hôtel
devahngt votr [tawngn] oatel

I'll pick you up at 8.
Je passerai vous [te] chercher à huit heures.
zher passray voo [ter] shehrshay a weet urr

Could we make it a
bit later/earlier?
Un peu plus tard/tôt si c'est possible?
ang pur plew tar/toa see seh posseebl

How about another day?
Peut-être un autre jour?
pur tetr ang noatr zhoor

That will be fine.
D'accord. *dakor*

Dining out/in

The French don't tend to "go dutch" in restaurants. The person who has invited usually pays – with the others offering to return the favor next time.

If you are invited home for a meal, always take a gift – a box of chocolates, a nice bouquet of flowers or possibly a good wine (but not a **vin de table**).

Let me buy you a drink.
Permettez-moi de vous offrir quelque chose à boire.
pehrmettay mwa der voo zofreer kelker shoaz a bwar

Do you like …?
Aimez-vous [aimes-tu] …?
aymay voo [aym tew]

What are you going
to have?
Qu'est-ce que vous prenez [tu prends]?
kess ker voo prenay [tew prahng]

That was a lovely meal.
C'était un très bon repas.
sayteh ang treh bawng repa

ENCOUNTERS

Do you mind if …?	**Ça vous dérange si …?** *sa voo dayrahngzh see*
I sit here	**Je m'asseois ici** *zher masswa eessee*
I smoke	**Je fume** *zher fewm*
Can I get you a drink?	**Puis-je vous offrir quelque chose à boire?** *pweezh voo zofreer kelker shoaz a bwar*
I'd love to have some company.	**J'aimerais bien que vous veniez me tenir compagnie.** *zhaymray byang ker voo vernyay mer teneer kawngpañee*
Why are you laughing?	**Pourquoi riez-vous [ris-tu]?** *poorkwa reeay voo [ree tew]*
Is my French that bad?	**Est-ce que mon français est si mauvais que ça?** *ess ker mawng frahngseh eh see moaveh ker sa*
Shall we go somewhere quieter?	**Si on allait dans un endroit un peu plus calme?** *see awng aleh dahng zang nahngdrwa ang pur plew kalm*
Leave me alone, please!	**Laissez-moi tranquille, s'il vous plaît!** *layssay mwa trahngkee seel voo pleh*
You look great!	**Tu es très beau (belle)!** *tew eh treh boa (bell)*
Thanks for the evening.	**Merci pour cette bonne soirée.** *mehrsee poor set bon swaray*
I'm afraid we've got to leave now.	**Il faut que nous partions maintenant.** *eel foa ker noo partyawng mangtnahng*
Can I see you again tomorrow?	**Est-ce que je peux vous [te] revoir demain?** *ess ker zher pur voo [ter] revwar dermang*
See you soon.	**À bientôt.** *a byangtoa*
Can I have your address?	**Est-ce que je peux avoir votre [ton] adresse?** *ess ker zher pur zavwar votr [tawngn] adress*

TELEPHONING

It's now almost impossible in France to phone using coins, except in rural areas or some cafés. Public telephone booths take phonecards, available at the post office or wherever you see the **Télécarte** sign. Simply lift the receiver, wait for the dial tone, insert the card and dial.

To phone home from French-speaking countries, dial 00 followed by: Australia 61; Canada 1; Ireland 353; New Zealand 64; UK 44; USA 1.

Can I have your telephone number?	**Pouvez-vous me donner votre numéro de téléphone?** *poovay voo mer donnay votr newmayroa der taylayfon*
Here's my number.	**Voilà mon numéro.** *vwala mawng newmayroa*
Please call me.	**Appelez-moi.** *applay mwa*
I'll give you a call.	**Je vous appellerai.** *zher vooz appellray*
Where's the nearest telephone booth?	**Où est la cabine téléphonique la plus proche?** *oo eh la kabeen taylayfoneek la plew prosh*
May I use your phone?	**Est-ce que je peux me servir de votre téléphone?** *ess ker zher pur mer sehrveer der votrer taylayfon*
It's an emergency.	**C'est urgent.** *set ewrzhahng*
I'd like to call someone in England.	**Je voudrais téléphoner en Angleterre.** *zher voodray taylayfonay ahng nahnglertehr*
What's the area [dialling] code for …?	**Quel est le code pour …?** *kel eh ler kod poor*
I'd like a phone card, please.	**Je voudrais une Télécarte, s'il vous plaît.** *zher voodray ewn taylaykart seel voo pleh*
What's the number for Information [Directory Enquiries]?	**Quel est le numéro des Renseignements?** *kel eh ler newmayroa day rahngssayñmahng*
I'd like the number for …	**Je voudrais le numéro de …** *zher voodray ler newmayroa der*
I'd like to call collect [reverse the charges].	**Je voudrais faire un appel en P.C.V.** *zher voodray fehr ang nappell ahng pay say vay*

ON THE PHONE

Hello. This is …	**Allô. C'est …** *aloa. seh*
I'd like to speak to …	**Je voudrais parler à …** *zher voodray parlay a*
Extension …	**Poste …** *posst*
Speak louder/more slowly, please.	**Pouvez-vous parler plus fort/plus lentement, s'il vous plaît.** *poovay voo parlay plew for/plew lahngtmahng seel voo pleh*
Could you repeat that, please?	**Pouvez-vous répéter, s'il vous plaît?** *poovay voo raypaytay seel voo pleh*
I'm afraid he/she's not in.	**Je regrette, il/elle n'est pas là.** *zher rergrett eel/el neh pa la*
You have the wrong number.	**Vous avez fait un faux numéro.** *voo zavay feh ang foa newmayroa*
Just a moment, please.	**Un instant, s'il vous plaît.** *ang nangstahng seel voo pleh*
Hold on, please.	**Ne raccrochez pas, s'il vous plaît.** *ner rakroshay pa seel voo pleh*
When will he/she be back?	**Quand reviendra-t-il/elle?** *kahng rervyangdra teel/tel*
Will you tell him/her that I called?	**Pouvez-vous lui dire que j'ai appelé?** *poovay voo lwee deer ker zhay applay*
My name is …	**Je m'appelle …** *zher mapl*
Would you ask him/her to phone me?	**Pouvez-vous lui demander de me rappeler?** *poovay voo lwee dermahngday der mer rapplay*
I must go now.	**Il faut que je vous quitte, maintenant.** *eel foa ker zher voo keet mangtnahng*
Nice to speak to you.	**J'ai été content(e) de vous parler.** *zhay aytay kawngtahng(t) der voo parlay*
I'll be in touch.	**Je vous [te] téléphonerai.** *zher voo [ter] taylayfonray*
Bye.	**Au revoir.** *oa rervwar*

STORES & SERVICES

France still places the emphasis on small, traditional specialty stores, offering a more personal experience, although modern shopping malls are to be found in most town centers.

There are department stores. Common chains include **Galeries Lafayette, Printemps** and **Nouvelles Galeries.**

Local markets can be found everywhere, from big cities to the smallest regional towns. Flea markets (**marchés aux puces**) are also common, as are **brocantes** (secondhand/junk shops).

I'd like …	**Je voudrais …**	*zher voodray*
Do you have …?	**Avez-vous …?**	*avay voo*
How much is that?	**C'est combien?**	*seh kawnbyang*
Thank you.	**Merci.**	*mehrsee*

Where is …?

Where's the nearest …?	**Où est … le/la plus proche?** *oo eh … ler/la plew prosh*
Where's there a good …?	**Où y a-t-il un(e) bon(ne) …?** *oo ee ateel ang (ewn) bawng (bon)*
Where's the main mall [shopping centre]?	**Où est le centre commercial principal?** *oo eh ler sahngtr komehrsyal prangseepal*
Is it far from here?	**Est-ce loin d'ici?** *ess lwang deessee*
How do I get there?	**Comment puis-je y aller?** *kommahng pweezh ee alay*

Stores

antiques shop	**l'antiquaire** *lahngteekehr*
bakery	**la boulangerie** *la boolahngzhree*
bank	**la banque** *la bahngk*
bookstore [shop]	**la librairie** *la leebrehree*
butcher shop	**la boucherie** *la boosheree*
camera shop	**le magasin de photos** *ler magazang der foto*
cigarette kiosk [tobacconist]	**le (bureau de) tabac** *ler (bewroa der) taba*

clothing store [clothes shop]	**le magasin de vêtements** *ler magazang der vetmahng*
delicatessen	**le charcutier/le traiteur** *ler sharkewtyay/ler treturr*
department store	**le grand magasin** *ler grahng magazang*
drugstore	**la droguerie** *la drogree*
fish store [fishmonger]	**la poissonnerie** *la pwassonree*
florist	**le fleuriste** *ler flurreest*
gift shop	**le magasin de cadeaux** *ler magazang der kadoa*
greengrocer	**le marchand de fruits et légumes** *ler marshahng der frwee ay laygewm*
grocery store/grocer	**l'épicerie** *laypeesree*
health food store	**le magasin de diététique** *ler magazang der dyaytayteek*
jewelry store [jeweller]	**la bijouterie** *la beezhootree*
market	**le marché** *ler marshay*
newsstand [newsagent]	**le kiosque à journaux** *ler keeosk a zhoornoa*
pastry shop	**la pâtisserie** *la pateesree*
pharmacy [chemist]	**la pharmacie** *la farmassee*
record/music store	**le magasin de disques** *ler magazang der deesk*
shoe store	**le magasin de chaussures** *ler magazang der shoassewr*
shopping mall [centre]	**le centre commercial** *ler sahngtr komehrsyal*
souvenir store	**le magasin de souvenirs** *ler magazang der soovneer*
sporting goods store	**le magasin d'articles de sport** *ler magazang darteekl der spor*
supermarket	**le supermarché** *ler sewpehrmarshay*
toy and game store	**le magasin de jouets** *ler magazang der zhooeh*
liquor store [off-licence]	**le marchand de vins** *ler marshahng der vang*

Services

dentist	**le dentiste**	*ler dahngteest*
doctor	**le médecin**	*ler maydsang*
dry cleaner	**le pressing/nettoyage à sec** *ler presseeng/netwahyazh a sek*	
hairdresser (ladies/men)	**le coiffeur (femmes/hommes)** *ler kwafurr (fam/om)*	
hospital	**l'hôpital**	*loapeetal*
laundromat	**la laverie automatique**	*la lavree oatomateek*
library	**la bibliothèque**	*la beebleeotek*
optician	**l'opticien**	*lopteesyang*
police station	**le commissariat (de police)** *ler komeessarya (der poleess)*	
post office	**la poste**	*la posst*
travel agency	**l'agence de voyages**	*lazhahngss der vwahyazh*

Hours

When does the … open/close?	**À quelle heure … ouvre-t-il/ferme-t-il?** *a kel urr … oovr teel/fehrm teel*
Are you open in the evening?	**Êtes-vous ouverts le soir?** *ayt voo oovehr ler swahr*
Do you close for lunch?	**Fermez-vous pour le déjeuner?** *fehrmay voo poor ler dayzhurnay*
Where is the …?	**Où est …?** *oo eh*
escalator	**l'escalier roulant** *leskalyay roolahng*
store guide	**le plan du magasin** *ler plahng dew magazang*
first [ground] floor	**rez-de-chaussée** *ray der shoassay*
second [first] floor	**premier étage** *prermyay aytazh*
Where's the … department?	**Où est le rayon des …?** *oo eh ler rayawng deh*

YOU MAY SEE

OUVERT	open
FERMÉ	closed

131

	Opening	Closing	Lunch break	Closed
stores	9/8	5.30-7 (6) [6.30]	12-2	Sun, Mon
department stores	9/9.30	7/7.30	none	Sun
supermarkets	9	9/10	none	Sun, Mon
post office	8 (7.30) [9]	6.30/7 (6.30) [6]	12-2 12-2 [1.45]	Sat p.m., Sun weekend
banks	8.30/9 (9) [8.30]	4.30/5 (3.30/4) [4.30–5.30]	12-1.30 12.30–1.30	weekend weekend

Service

Can you help me?	**Pouvez-vous m'aider?** *poovay voo mayday*
I'm looking for …	**Je cherche …** *zher shehrsh*
I'm just browsing.	**Je regarde seulement.** *zher rergard surlmahng*
It's my turn.	**C'est à moi.** *se ta mwa*
Do you have any …?	**Avez vous …?** *avay voo*
I'd like to buy …	**Je voudrais acheter …** *zher voodray ashtay*
Could you show me …?	**Pouvez-vous me montrer …?** *poovay voo mer mawngtray*
How much is this/that?	**Combien coûte ceci/cela?** *kawnbyang koot sersee/serla*
That's all, thanks.	**C'est tout, merci.** *seh too mehrsee*

YOU MAY SEE

HEURES D'OUVERTURE	business hours
FERMÉ POUR LE DÉJEUNER	closed for lunch
OUVERT TOUTE LA JOURNÉE	open all day
SORTIE	exit
SORTIE DE SECOURS	emergency/fire exit
ENTRÉE	entrance
ESCALIERS	stairs
ASCENSEUR	elevator
SOLDES	sale

Choices

It must be …	**Ça doit être …**	sa dwa tetr
large/small	**grand/petit**	grahng/pertee
cheap/expensive	**bon marché/cher**	bawng marshay/shehr
dark/light	**foncé/clair**	fawngsay/klehr
light/heavy	**léger/lourd**	layzhay/loor
oval/round/square	**ovale/rond/carré**	ovahl/rawng/karay
genuine/imitation	**un original/d'imitation**	ang oreezheenal/deemeetasyawng
I don't want anything too expensive.	**Je ne veux pas quelque chose de trop cher.**	zher ner vur pa kelker shoaz der tro shehr
Do you have anything …?	**Avez-vous quelque chose de …?**	avay voo kelker shoaz der
larger	**plus grand**	plew grahng
better quality	**meilleure qualité**	mayurr kaleetay
cheaper	**moins cher**	mwang shehr
smaller	**plus petit**	plew pertee

ESSENTIAL

Quel(le) … voulez vous?	What … would you like?
couleur/forme	color/shape
qualité/quantité	quality/quantity
Quel genre voulez-vous?	What kind would you like?
Dans quel ordre de prix cherchez-vous?	What price range are you thinking of?

YOU MAY HEAR

Bonjour, madame/monsieur.	Good morning/afternoon.
Je peux vous aider?	Can I help you?
Vous désirez?/Qu'est-ce que vous voulez?	What would you like?
Je vais vérifier.	I'll just check that for you.
Ce sera tout?	Is that everything?
Et avec ça?/Il vous faut autre chose?	Anything else?

Can you show me …?	**Pouvez-vous me montrer …?**
	poovay voo mer mawngtray
that/this one	**celui-là (celle-là)/celui-ci (celle-ci)**
	serlwee la (sel la)/serlwee see (sel see)
these/those	**ceux-ci (celles-ci)/ceux-là (celles-là)**
	sur see (sel see)/sur la (sel la)

Conditions of purchase

Is there a guarantee?	**Y a-t-il une garantie?**
	ee ateel ewn garahngtee
Are there any instructions with it?	**Est-ce qu'il y a des instructions?**
	ess keel ee a day zangstrewksyawng

Out of stock

Can you order it for me?	**Pouvez-vous me le commander?**
	poovay voo mer ler kommahngday
How long will it take?	**Il faudra combien de temps?**
	eel foadra kawnbyang der tahng

YOU MAY HEAR

Je regrette, nous n'en avons plus.	I'm sorry, we don't have any left.
L'article/Le stock est épuisé.	We're out of stock.
Est-ce que je peux vous montrer quelque chose d'autre?	Can I show you something else?
Voulez-vous que nous le commandions?	Shall we order it for you?

Decision

That's not quite what I want.	**Ce n'est pas vraiment ce que je veux.**
	ser neh pa vraymahng ser ker zher vur
That's too expensive.	**C'est trop cher.** *seh tro shehr*
I'll take it.	**Je le prends.**
	zher ler prahng

IN A STORE

Je peux vous aider? *zher pur voo zayday* (Can I help you?)
Merci. Je regarde seulement. *mehrsee zher rergard surlmahng* (Thanks. I'm just browsing.)

PAYING

Sales tax (**TVA**) is imposed on almost all goods and services; this is included in the TTC (**toutes taxes comprises**) price. Tax can be reclaimed on larger purchases when returning home (outside the EU).

Where do I pay? **Où dois-je payer?** *oo dwazh payay*

How much is that? **C'est combien?** *seh kawnbyang*

Could you write it down, please? **Pourriez-vous l'écrire, s'il vous plaît?** *pooryay voo laykreer seel voo pleh*

Do you accept traveler's checks [cheques]? **Acceptez-vous les chèques de voyage?** *akseptay voo lay shek der vwahyazh*

I'll pay … **Je paie …** *zher payy*

by cash **en liquide** *ahng leekeed*

by credit card **avec une carte de crédit** *avek ewn kart der kraydee*

Sorry, I don't have enough money. **Je regrette, je n'ai pas assez d'argent.** *zher rergret, zher nay pa zassay darzhahng*

Could I have a receipt please? **Est-ce que je peux avoir un ticket de caisse?** *ess ker zher pur avwar ang teekeh der kess*

I think you've given me the wrong change. **Je crois que vous vous êtes trompé en me rendant la monnaie.** *zher krwa ker voo voo zayt trawngpay ahng mer rahngdahng la monayy*

135

Complaints

This doesn't work.	**Ça ne marche pas.**
	sa ner marsh pa
Can you exchange this, please?	**Pouvez-vous échanger ceci, s'il vous plaît?**
	poovay voo ayshahngzhay sersee seel voo pleh
I'd like a refund.	**Je voudrais être remboursé(e).**
	zher voodray zetrer rahngboorsay
Here's the receipt.	**Voici le ticket de caisse.**
	vwasee ler teekeh der kess
I don't have the receipt.	**Je n'ai pas le ticket de caisse.**
	zher nay pa ler teekeh der kess
I'd like to see the manager.	**Je voudrais voir le directeur du magasin**
	zher voodray vwar ler deerekturr dew magazang

Repairs/Cleaning

A **teinturerie** or a **pressing** is a dry cleaner, sometimes combined with a laundry (**blanchisserie**). If you want a self-service laundromat, look for **laverie automatique.**

This is broken. Can you repair it?	**C'est cassé. Pouvez-vous le réparer?**
	seh kassay. poovay voo ler rayparay
Do you have … for this?	**Avez-vous … pour ceci?**
	avay voo … poor sersee
a battery	**une pile** *ewn peel*
replacement parts	**des pièces de rechange**
	day pyes der rershahngzh
Can you … this?	**Pouvez-vous le …?** *poovay voo ler*
clean	**nettoyer** *netwahyay*
press	**repasser** *rerpassay*
patch	**raccommoder** *rakomoday*
When will it be ready?	**Quand sera-t-il prêt?**
	kahng sera teel preh
This isn't mine.	**Ce n'est pas à moi.** *ser neh pa za mwa*
There's … missing.	**Il manque …** *eel mahngk*

BANK/CURRENCY EXCHANGE OFFICE

Cash can be obtained from ATMs [cash machines] with Visa, Eurocard, American Express and many other international cards.

Remember your passport when you want to change money.

Not all banks provide currency exchange services – hotels will sometimes provide an exchange facility, but only to their guests.

Currency	100 centimes (ct.) = 1 franc (F, FF, FB, Fr.)
France	*Coins:* 5, 10, 20, 50 ct.; 1, 2, 5, 10, 20 FF
	Notes: 20, 50, 100, 200, 500 FF
Belgium	*Coins:* 50ct; 1, 5, 20, 50 FB
	Notes: 100, 500, 1000, 2000, 5000 FB
Switzerland	*Coins:* 5, 10, 20, 50 ct.; 1, 2, 5 Fr.
	Notes: 10, 20, 50, 100, 500, 1000 Fr.

Where's the nearest …?	**Où est … le/la plus proche?** *oo eh … ler/la plew prosh*
bank	**la banque** *la bahngk*
currency exchange office	**le bureau de change** *ler bewroa der shahngz*

Changing money

Can I exchange foreign currency here?	**Est-ce que je peux changer des devises étrangères ici?** *ess ker zher pur shahngzhay day derveez aytrahngzhehr eessee*
I'd like to change some dollars/pounds into francs.	**Je voudrais changer des dollars/livres en francs.** *zher voodray shahngzhay day dolar/leevr ahng frahng*
I want to cash some traveler's checks.	**Je voudrais encaisser des chèques de voyage.** *zher voodray ahngkessay day shek der vwahyazh*
What's the exchange rate?	**Quel est le taux (de change)?** *kel eh ler toa (der shahngzh)*
How much commission do you charge?	**Quelle commission prenez-vous?** *kel komeesyawng prernay voo*
Could I have some small change?	**Est-ce que je pourrais avoir de la petite monnaie?** *essker zher pooray avwar der la perteet monayy*

OUVERT/FERMÉ	open/closed
POUSSEZ/TIREZ/APPUYEZ	push/pull/press
CAISSES	cashiers
TOUTES TRANSACTIONS	all transactions

Security

Est-ce que je peux voir…?	Could I see …?
votre passeport	your passport
une pièce d'identité	some identification
votre carte bancaire	your bank card
Quelle est votre adresse?	What's your address?
Où logez-vous?	Where are you staying?
Pouvez-vous remplir cette fiche?	Can you fill in this form?
Signez ici, s'il vous plaît.	Please sign here.

ATMs [Cash machines]

Can I withdraw money on my credit card here?	**Est-ce que je peux retirer de l'argent avec ma carte de crédit ici?** *ess ker zher pur rerteeray der larzhahng avek ma kart der kraydee eessee*
Where are the ATMs [cash machines]?	**Où sont les distributeurs automatiques?** *oo sawng lay deestreebewturr oatomateek*
Can I use my card in the ATM [cash machine]?	**Est-ce que je peux me servir de ma carte dans ce distributeur?** *ess ker zher pur mer sehrveer der ma kart … dahng ser deestreebewturr*
The machine has eaten my card.	**Le distributeur a avalé ma carte.** *ler deestreebewturr a avalay ma kart*

DISTRIBUTEUR AUTOMATIQUE	automated teller/cash machine

PHARMACY

Pharmacies are easily recognized by their sign: a green cross, usually lit up.

If you are looking for a pharmacy at night or during weekends, you'll find a list of **pharmacies de garde** (emergency pharmacies) in the window of any pharmacy or in the local newspaper.

In addition to pharmaceutical products, pharmacies in France also sell toiletries and cosmetics. A **parfumerie** or **grand magasin** (department store) will usually have a more extensive range of perfumes and cosmetics, while a **droguerie** generally sells toiletries and household products only.

Where's the nearest (all-night) pharmacy?	**Où est la pharmacie (de garde) la plus proche?** *oo eh la farmassee (der gard) la plew prosh*
Can you make up this prescription for me?	**Pouvez-vous me préparer cette ordonnance?** *poovay voo mer prayparay set ordonahngss*
Shall I wait?	**Est-ce que je dois attendre?** *ess ker zher dwa atahngdr*
I'll come back for it.	**Je reviendrai la chercher.** *zher rvyangdray la shehrshay*

Dosage instructions

How much should I take?	**Combien dois-je en prendre?** *kawnbyang dwazh ahng prahngdr*
How often should I take it?	**Combien de fois dois-je le prendre?** *kawnbyang der fwa dwazh ler prahngdr*
Is it suitable for children?	**Est-ce que ça convient aux enfants?** *ess ker sa kawngvyang oa zahngfahng*

YOU MAY HEAR

Prenez ... comprimés/ cuillerées à café ...	Take ... tablets/... teaspoons ...
avant/après les repas	before/after meals
avec un verre d'eau	with water
entier (sans croquer)	whole (without chewing)
le matin/le soir	in the morning/at night
pendant ... jours	for ... days

USAGE EXTERNE	for external use only
NE PAS AVALER	not to be taken internally

Asking advice

What would you recommend for …?	**Qu'est-ce que vous me recommandez pour …?** *kess ker voo mer rerkommahngday poor*
a cold	**le rhume** *ler rewm*
a cough	**la toux** *la too*
diarrhea	**la diarrhée** *la deearay*
a hangover	**la gueule de bois** *la gurl der bwa*
hay fever	**le rhume des foins** *ler rewm day fwang*
insect bites	**les piqûres d'insectes** *lay peekewr dangsekt*
a sore throat	**le mal de gorge** *ler mal der gorzh*
sunburn	**les coups de soleil** *lay koo der solayy*
motion [travel] sickness	**le mal des transports** *ler mal day trahngspor*
an upset stomach	**le mal de ventre** *ler mal der vahngtr*
Can I get it without a prescription?	**Puis-je l'obtenir sans ordonnance?** *pweezh lobterneer sahng zordonahngss*

Over-the-counter treatment

Can I have …?	**Pouvez-vous me donner …?** *poovay voo mer donay*
antiseptic cream	**une crème antiseptique** *ewn la krem ahngteessepteek*
(soluble) aspirin	**de l'aspirine (soluble)** *der laspeereen (solewbl)*
gauze [bandage]	**un bandage** *ang bahngdazh*
condoms	**des préservatifs** *day prayzehrvateef*
cotton [cotton wool]	**du coton (hydrophile)** *dew kotawng (ydrofeel)*
insect repellent	**une crème/lotion contre les insectes** *ewn krem/losyawng kawngtr lay zangsekt*
pain killers	**des analgésiques** *day zanalzhayzeek*
vitamin pills	**des vitamines** *day veetameen*

Toiletries

I'd like …	**Je voudrais …** *zher voodray*
aftershave	**de la lotion après-rasage** *der la losyawng apreh razazh*
deodorant	**un déodorant** *ang dayodorahng*
moisturizing cream	**de la crème hydratante** *der la krem ydratahngt*
razor blades	**des lames de rasoir** *day lam der razwar*
sanitary napkins [towels]	**des serviettes hygiéniques** *day sehrvyet yzhyayneek*
soap	**du savon** *dew savawng*
sun block	**de l'écran total** *der laykrahng total*
suntan lotion	**de la crème solaire** *der la krem solehr*
tampons	**des tampons** *day tahngpawng*
tissues	**des mouchoirs en papier** *day mooshwar ahng papyay*
toilet paper	**du papier toilette** *dew papyay twalet*
toothpaste	**du dentifrice** *dew dahngteefreess*

Hair care

comb	**un peigne** *ang payn*
conditioner	**de l'après-shampooing** *der lapreh shahngpwang*
hair mousse	**de la mousse pour cheveux** *der la mooss poor shervur*
hair spray	**de la laque** *der la lak*
shampoo	**du shampooing** *dew shahngpwang*

For the baby

baby food	**des aliments pour bébé** *day zaleemahng poor baybay*
baby wipes	**des lingettes** *day langzhet*
diapers [nappies]	**des couches** *day koosh*
sterilizing solution	**de la solution de stérilisation** *der la solewsyawng der stayreeleezasyawng*

CLOTHING

Paris is renowned for its haute couture houses and their prêt-à-porter boutiques, for example: **Dior**, **Givenchy**, **Lanvin**, **Saint-Laurent**, **Ungaro**, **Féraud**, **Gaultier**, **Yamamoto**, **Hermès**.

You'll find that airport boutiques offering tax-free shopping may have cheaper prices but less selection.

General

I'd like …	**Je voudrais …** *zher voodray*
Do you have any …?	**Avez-vous des …?** *avay voo deh*

Color

I'm looking for something in …	**Je cherche quelque chose en …** *zher shehrsh kelker shoaz ahng*
beige	**beige** *bayzh*
black	**noir** *nwar*
blue	**bleu** *blur*
brown	**marron** *marawng*
green	**vert** *vehr*
gray	**gris** *gree*
orange	**orange** *orahngzh*
pink	**rose** *roz*
purple	**violet** *veeoleh*
red	**rouge** *roozh*
white	**blanc** *blahng*
yellow	**jaune** *zhoan*
I want a darker/. lighter shade	**Je veux une teinte plus foncée/claire.** *zher vur ewn tangt plew fawngsay/klehr*
Do you have the same in …?	**Avez-vous le même en …?** *avay voo ler mem ahng*

Clothes and accessories

belt	**une ceinture**	*ewn sangtewr*
bikini	**un bikini**	*ang beekeenee*
blouse	**un chemisier**	*ang shermeezyay*
bra	**un soutien-gorge**	*ang sootyang gorzh*
shorts/briefs	**une culotte**	*ewn kewlot*
cap	**une casquette**	*ewn kasket*
coat	**un manteau**	*ang mahngtoa*
dress	**une robe**	*ewn rob*
handbag	**un sac à main**	*ang sak a mang*
hat	**un chapeau**	*ang shapoa*
jacket	**une veste**	*ewn vest*
jeans	**un jean**	*ang dzheen*
leggings	**un legging**	*ang legging*
pants	**un pantalon**	*ang pahngtalawng*
pantyhose [tights]	**un collant**	*ang kolahng*
pullover	**un pull-over/pull**	*ang pewlovehr/pewl*
raincoat	**un imperméable**	*ang nangpehrmayabl*
scarf	**une écharpe**	*ewn aysharp*
shirt	**une chemise**	*ewn shermeez*
shorts	**un short**	*ang short*
skirt	**une jupe**	*ewn zhewp*
socks	**des chaussettes**	*day shoasset*
stockings	**des bas**	*day ba*
suit	**un costume**	*ang kostewm*
sweatshirt	**un sweat-shirt**	*ang sweatshirt*
swimming trunks	**un slip de bain**	*ang sleep der bang*
swimsuit	**un maillot de bain**	*ang mahyo der bang*
tie	**une cravate**	*ewn kravat*
underpants	**un slip**	*ang sleep*
with long/short sleeves	**à manches longues/courtes**	*a mahngsh lawngg/koort*
with V-/round neck	**à encolure en V/ronde**	*a ahngkolewr ahng v/rawng*

Shoes

A pair of ...	**Une paire de ...** *ewn pehr der*
boots	**bottes** *bott*
flip-flops	**tongs** *tawng*
sandals	**sandales** *sahngdal*
shoes	**chaussures** *shoassewr*
slippers	**pantoufles** *pahngtoofl*
trainers	**chaussures de sport** *shoassewr der spor*

Hiking/walking gear

windbreaker	**un coupe-vent** *ang koop vahng*
knapsack	**un sac à dos** *ang sak a doa*
walking boots	**des chaussures de marche** *day shoassewr der marsh*
waterproof jacket	**un blouson imperméable** *ang bloozawng angpehrmayabl*

Fabric

I want something in ...	**Je veux quelque chose en ...** *zher vur kelker shoaz ahng*
cotton/lace	**coton/dentelle** *kotawng/dahngtel*
denim/leather	**jean/cuir** *dzheen/kweer*
linen	**lin** *lang*
wool	**laine** *layn*
Is this ...?	**Est-ce ...?** *ess*
pure cotton	**pur coton** *pewr kotawng*
synthetic	**en synthétique** *ahng sangtayteek*
Is it hand washable/ machine washable?	**Est-ce lavable à la main/lavable en machine?** *ess lavabl a la mang/ lavabl ahng masheen*

GRAND TEINT/NE DÉTEINT PAS	colorfast
LAVAGE MAIN SEULEMENT	handwash only
NE PAS REPASSER	do not iron
NETTOYAGE À SEC SEULEMENT	dry clean only

Does it fit?

Can I try this on?	**Est-ce que je peux essayer ça?**
	ess ker zher pur essayay sa
Where's the fitting room?	**Où sont les cabines d'essayage?**
	oo sawng lay kabeen dessayazh
It doesn't fit.	**Ça ne va pas.** *sa ner va pa*
It's too …	**C'est trop …** *seh tro*
short/long	**court/long** *koort/lawng*
tight/loose	**étroit/ample** *aytrwa/ahngpl*
Do you have this in size …?	**Est-ce que vous avez ceci en taille …?**
	ess ker voo zavay sersee ahng tie
What size is this?	**C'est quelle taille?** *seh kel tie*
Could you measure me, please?	**Pouvez-vous prendre mes mesures?**
	poovay voo prahngdr may mezuwr
I don't know French sizes.	**Je ne connais pas les tailles françaises.**
	zher ner koneh pa lay tie frahngsayz

Size

Note: In French, clothes size is **la taille**, shoe (and glove) size is **la pointure**.

	Dresses/Suits						Women's shoes			
American	8	10	12	14	16	18	6	7	8	9
British	10	12	14	16	18	20	4½	5½	6½	7½
Continental	38	40	42	44	46	48	37	38	39	40

	Shirts				Men's shoes							
American **British**	15	16	17	18	6	7	8	8½	9	9½	10	11
Continental	38	41	43	45	38	39	41	42	43	43	44	44

YOU MAY SEE

EXTRA GRAND	extra large (XL)
GRAND	large (L)
MOYEN	medium (M)
PETIT	small (S)

145

I'd like a …	**Je voudrais …** *zher voodray*
facial	**des soins du visage** *day swang dew veezazh*
manicure	**une manucure** *ewn manewkewr*
massage	**un massage** *ang massazh*
waxing	**une épilation à la cire** *ewn aypeelasyawng a la seer*

HAIRDRESSER'S/HAIRSTYLIST

Tipping: France: 10% (generally included in price); Belgium: 15% (generally included); Switzerland: included.

I'd like to make an appointment for …	**Je voudrais prendre un rendez-vous pour …** *zher voodray prahngdr ang rahngday voo poor*
Can you make it a bit earlier/later?	**Est-ce que je peux venir un peu plus tôt/tard?** *ess ker zher pur verneer ang pur plew toa/tar*
I'd like a …	**Je voudrais …** *zher voodray*
cut and blow-dry	**une coupe et un brushing** *ewn koop ay ang brursheeng*
shampoo and set	**un shampooing et une mise en plis** *ang shahngpwang ayt ewn meez ahng plee*
I'd like a trim.	**Je voudrais me faire égaliser les pointes.** *zher voodray mer fehr aygaleezay lay pwangt*
I'd like my hair …	**Je voudrais …** *zher voodray*
highlighted	**des mèches** *day mesh*
permed	**une permanente** *ewn pehrmanahngt*
A little more off the …	**Pouvez-vous en couper un peu plus …** *poovay voo zahng koopay ang pur plews*
back/front	**derrière/devant** *dehrryehr/devahng*
neck/sides	**dans le cou/sur les côtés** *dahng ler koo/sewr lay koatay*
top	**sur le dessus** *sewr ler derssew*
That's fine, thanks.	**Très bien, merci.** *treh byang mehrsee*

HOUSEHOLD ARTICLES

I'd like …	**Je voudrais …** *zher voodray*
adapter	**un adaptateur** *ang nadaptaturr*
aluminum foil	**du papier aluminium** *dew papyay alewmeenyom*
bottle opener	**un ouvre-bouteilles** *ang noovr bootayy*
clothespins [pegs]	**des pinces à linge** *day pangss a langzh*
corkscrew	**un tire-bouchon** *ang teer booshawng*
light bulb	**une ampoule** *ewn ahngpool*
matches	**des allumettes** *day zalewmett*
paper napkins	**des serviettes en papier** *day sehrvyett ahng papyay*
plastic wrap [cling film]	**du film alimentaire** *dew feelm aleementair*
scissors	**des ciseaux** *day seezoa*
can [tin] opener	**un ouvre-boîte** *ang noovr bwat*

Cleaning products

bleach	**de l'eau de Javel** *der loa der zhavel*
dish cloth [tea towel]	**une lavette** *ewn lavet*
dishwashing [washing-up] detergent	**de la poudre pour lave-vaisselle** *der la poodr poor lav vessel*
garbage [refuse] bags	**des sacs poubelles** *day sak poobel*
sponge	**une éponge** *ewn aypawngzh*
detergent [washing powder]	**de la lessive** *der la lesseev*
dishwashing liquid	**du liquide vaisselle** *dew leekeed vessell*

Dishes/Utensils [Crockery/Cutlery]

cups	**des tasses** *day tass*
forks	**des fourchettes** *day foorshet*
glasses	**des verres** *day vehr*
knives	**des couteaux** *day kootoa*
mugs	**des chopes** *day shop*
plates	**des assiettes** *day zassyet*
spoons	**des cuillères** *day kweeyehr*
teaspoons	**des cuillères à café** *day kweeyehr a kafay*

Could I see …?	**Est-ce que je pourrais voir …?** *ess ker zher pooray vwar*	
this/that	**ceci/cela** *sersee/serla*	
It's in the window/ display case.	**C'est en vitrine.** *se tahng veetreen*	
I'd like …	**Je voudrais …** *zher voodray*	
alarm clock	**un réveil** *ang rayvayy*	
battery	**une pile** *ewn peel*	
bracelet	**un bracelet** *ang brasleh*	
brooch	**une broche** *ewn brosh*	
chain	**une chaîne(tte)** *ewn shen(ett)*	
clock	**une pendule** *ewn pahngdewl*	
earrings	**des boucles d'oreilles** *day bookler dorayy*	
necklace	**un collier** *ang kolyay*	
ring	**une bague** *ewn bag*	
watch	**une montre** *ewn mawngtr*	

Materials

Is this real silver/gold?	**Est-ce de l'argent/de l'or véritable?** *ess der larzhahng/der lor vayreetabl*
Is there a certificate for it?	**Y a-t-il un certificat?** *ee ateel ang sehrteefeeka*
Do you have anything in …?	**Avez-vous quelque chose en …?** *avay voo kelker shoaz ahng*
copper/pewter	**cuivre/étain** *kweever/ aytang*
cut glass	**verre taillé** *vehr tieyay*
diamond/ crystal	**diamant/ cristal** *deeamahng/ kreestal*
enamel	**émail** *aymie*
gold/goldplate	**or/plaqué or** *or/plakay or*
pearl	**perle de culture** *pehrl der kewltewr*
platinum/silver	**platine/argent** *plateen/ arzhahng*
silverplate	**plaqué argent** *plakay arzhahng*
stainless steel	**acier inoxydable** *asyay eenoxeedabl*

Newsstands (**maison de la presse** or **bureau de presse**), identifiable by their yellow sign with a red feather, sell magazines, newspapers, some paperbacks and stationery and sometimes cigarettes. Foreign newspapers can usually be found at railroad stations or airports or on newsstands in Paris and other major cities.

Do you sell English-language books/newspapers?	**Vendez-vous des livres/journaux en anglais?** *vahngday voo day leevr/zhoornoa ahng ahnggleh*
I'd like a/an …	**Je voudrais …** *zher voodray*
book	**un livre** *ang leevr*
candy [sweets]	**des bonbons** *day bawngbawng*
chewing gum	**un chewing-gum** *ang shooweeng gom*
chocolate bar	**une tablette de chocolat** *ewn tablet der shokola*
pack of cigarettes	**un paquet de cigarettes** *ang pakeh der seegarett*
cigars	**des cigares** *day seegar*
dictionary	**un dictionnaire** *ang deeksyonehr*
French-English	**français-anglais** *frahngseh ahnggleh*
envelopes	**des enveloppes** *day zahngvlop*
guidebook of …	**un guide de/sur …** *ang geed der/sewr*
lighter	**un briquet** *ang breekeh*
map of the town	**un plan de la ville** *ang plahng der la veel*
road map of …	**une carte routière de …** *ewn kart rootyehr der*
matches	**des allumettes** *day zalewmet*
newspaper	**un journal** *ang zhoornal*
American/English	**américain/anglais** *amayreekamg/ahnggleh*
paper	**du papier** *dew papyay*
pen	**un stylo** *ang steelo*
postcard	**une carte postale** *ewn kart postal*
stamps	**des timbres** *day tangbr*
candy	**des bonbons** *day bawngbawng*
tobacco	**du tabac** *dew taba*

PHOTOGRAPHY

I'm looking for a/an … camera.	**Je cherche un appareil photo …** *zher shehrsh ang naparayy foto*
automatic	**automatique** *oatomateek*
compact	**compact** *kawngpakt*
disposable	**jetable** *zhertabl*
SLR (single lens reflex)	**reflex** *rerflex*
I'd like a/an…	**Je voudrais** *zher voodray*
battery	**une pile** *ewn peel*
camera case	**un sac photo** *ang sak foto*
(electronic) flash	**un flash (électronique)** *ang flash (aylektroneek)*
filter	**un filtre** *ang feeltr*
lens	**un objectif** *ang nobzhekteef*
lens cap	**un couvercle** *ang koovehrkl*

Film/Processing

I'd like a … film for this camera.	**Je voudrais une pellicule … pour cet appareil photo.** *zher voodray ewn peleekewl … poor set aparayy foto*
black and white	**noir et blanc** *nwar ay blahng*
color	**couleur** *koolurr*
24/36 exposures	**24/36 poses** *vangtkatr/trahngtsee poz*
I'd like this film developed.	**Je voudrais faire développer cette pellicule.** *zher voodray fehr dayvlopay set peleekewl*
Would you enlarge this, please?	**Pourriez-vous agrandir ceci?** *pooryay voo agrahngdeer sersee*
When will the photos be ready?	**Quand est-ce que les photos seront prêtes?** *kahng tess ker lay foto serawng prayt*
I'd like to pick up my photos.	**Je viens chercher mes photos.** *zher vyang shehrshay may foto*
Here's the receipt.	**Voilà le reçu.** *vwala ler rersew*

POLICE

Crime, theft, accidents or injuries should be reported to the **commissariat de police** in major cities or to the **gendarmerie nationale** in smaller towns.

To get the police in an emergency, ☎ 17 in France, ☎ 101 in Belgium, ☎ 117 in Switzerland.

Where's the nearest police station?	**Où est le commissariat le plus proche?** *oo eh ler komeessarya ler plew prosh*
Does anyone here speak English?	**Est-ce qu'il y a quelqu'un ici qui parle anglais?** *ess keel ee a kelkang eessee kee parl ahnggleh*
I want to report a(n) …	**Je veux signaler …** *zher vur seeñalay*
accident/attack	**un accident/une attaque** *ang nakseedahng/ewn atak*
mugging/rape	**une agression/un viol** *ewn agresyawng/ang vyol*
My child is missing.	**Mon enfant a disparu.** *Mawng nahngfahng a deesparew*
Here's a photo of him/her.	**Voilà sa photo.** *vwala sa foto*
I need an English-speaking lawyer.	**Il me faut un avocat qui parle anglais.** *eel mer foa ang navoka kee parl ahnggleh*
I need to make a phone call.	**Je dois téléphoner à quelqu'un.** *zher dwa taylayfonay a kelkang*
I need to contact the Consulate.	**Je dois contacter le consulat.** *zher dwa kawngtaktay ler kawngsewla*

YOU MAY HEAR

Pouvez-vous le/la décrire?	Can you describe him/her?
homme/femme	male/female
blond(e)/brun(e)/roux(-sse)/	blonde/brunette/red-headed/
aux cheveux gris	gray hair
aux cheveux longs/courts/	long/short hair/balding
un peu chauve	
qui mesure environ …	approximate height …
qui a environ … ans	aged (approximately) …
Il/Elle portait …	He/She was wearing …

Lost property/Theft

I want to report a theft/break-in.	**Je veux signaler un cambriolage.** *zher vur seeñalay ang kahngbreeolazh*
I've been robbed/mugged.	**J'ai été volé/agressé.** *zhay aytay volay/agressay*
I've lost my ...	**J'ai perdu ...** *zhay pehrdew*
My ... has been stolen.	**On m'a volé ...** *awng ma volay*
bicycle	**mon vélo** *mawng vaylo*
camera	**mon appareil photo** *mawng naparayy foto*
(rental) car	**ma voiture (de location)** *ma vwatewr (der lokasyawng)*
credit cards	**mes cartes de crédit** *may kart der kraydee*
handbag	**mon sac à main** *mawng sak a mang*
money	**mon argent** *mawng narzhahng*
passport	**mon passeport** *mawng passpor*
ticket	**mon billet** *mawng beeyeh*
wallet	**mon portefeuille** *mawng porterfuhy*
watch	**ma montre** *ma mawngtr*
I need a police report/form for my insurance claim.	**Il me faut un certificat de police pour ma compagnie d'assurances.** *eel mer foa ang sehrteefeeka der poleess poor ma kawngpañee dassewrahngss*

POST OFFICE

In addition to the normal range of services at French post offices – **La Poste**
– you can buy **Télécartes** (phonecards) and use a **Minitel terminal** (➤ 154)
for free services such as finding addresses and telephone numbers.

French post offices are recognized by the **PT** sign and Belgian by **Postes**
or **Posterijen**. Mailboxes (yellow in France and Switzerland, red in
Belgium) may have separate slots for postcards (**cartes postales**), letters
(**lettres**) and abroad (**l'étranger**).

General inquiries

Where is the post office?	**Où est le bureau de poste?** *oo eh ler bewroa der post*
the mailbox [postbox]	**la boîte aux lettres** *la bwa toa letr*
What time does the post office open/close?	**À quelle heure ouvre/ferme la poste?** *a kel urr oovr/fehrm la post*
Does it close for lunch?	**Est-elle fermée pour le déjeuner?** *eh tel fehrmay poor ler dayzhurnay*
Is there any mail for me?	**Est-ce qu'il y a du courrier pour moi?** *ess keel ee a dew kooryay poor mwa*

Buying stamps

A stamp for this postcard, please.	**Un timbre pour cette carte postale, s'il vous plaît.** *ang tangbr poor set kart postal seel voo pleh*
A ...-franc stamp, please.	**Un timbre à ... francs, s'il vous plaît.** *ang tangbr a ... frahng seel voo pleh*
What's the postage for a letter to ...?	**Quel est le tarif pour une lettre pour ...?** *kel eh ler tareef poor ewn letr poor*

IN A POST OFFICE

Des timbres pour ces cartes postales, s'il vous plaît.
day tangbr poor say kart postal seel voo pleh
(*Stamps for these postcards, please*)
Ça fait quinze francs. *sa feh kangz frahng* (*That's 15 francs.*)
Voilà. *vwala* (*Here you are.*)

Sending packages

I want to send this package [parcel] by … **Je voudrais envoyer ce paquet …** *zher voodray ahngvwahhay ser pakeh*

airmail **par avion** *par avyawng*

special delivery [express] **en exprès** *ahng express*

It contains … **Il contient …** *eel kawngtyang*

Telecommunications

I'd like a phonecard. **Je voudrais une Télécarte/carte de téléphone.** *zher voodray ewn taylaykart/kart der taylayfon*

Do you have a photocopier? **Est-ce qu'il y a un photocopieur?** *ess keel ee a ang fotokopyurr*

I'd like to send a message … **Je voudrais envoyer un message …** *zher voodray engvoiyay ang mesarj …*

by E-mail/fax **par e-mail/fax** *par eemail/fax*

What's your E-mail address? **Quelle est votre adresse e-mail?** *kel eh votrer adres eemail*

Can I access the Internet here? **Est-ce que je peux accéder à l'internet ici ?** *esker je pur aksedeh eesee a linternet*

What are the charges per hour? **C'est combien par heure?** *say combyang par hur*

How do I log on? **Comment est-ce que j'entre en communication?** *comong ess ker zhentr eng comunicasyon*

Minitel *meeneetel*
French telecommunications system with over 7,000 services (some in English). Terminals can be found in most public buildings, including the post office, for free services (including telephone directory). Access to a private terminal (charges go on the phone bill) allows booking tickets, home shopping, etc.

SOUVENIRS

Here are some suggestions for souvenirs from Belgium:

chocolate	**le chocolat**	*ler shokola*
crystal	**le cristal**	*ler kreestal*
glassware	**la verrerie**	*la vehrehree*
leather	**le cuir**	*ler kweer*
tapestry	**une tapisserie**	*ewn tapeessehree*

Popular souvenirs for visitors to Switzerland include chocolate, as well as:

cheese	**le fromage**	*ler fromazh*
cuckoo clocks	**les coucous**	*lay kookoo*
Swiss Army knives	**les couteaux suisses**	*lay kootoa swiss*
watches	**les montres**	*lay mawngtr*
wooden products	**les articles en bois**	*lay arteekl ahng bwa*
lace	**les dentelles**	*lay dahngtell*

Visitors to France may be attracted by cheeses, wines, liqueurs, as well as:

mustard	**la moutarde**	*la mootard*
perfume	**le parfum**	*ler parfahng*
porcelain	**la porcelaine**	*la poorserlehn*
pottery	**la poterie**	*la pottree*
(cast-iron) saucepans	**des casseroles (en fonte)**	*day cassrol (ahng font)*

Gifts

bottle of wine	**une bouteille de vin**	*ewn bootayy der vang*
box of chocolates	**une boîte de chocolats**	*ewn bwat der shokola*
calendar	**un calendrier**	*ang kalahngdreeay*
cloth (for drying dishes)	**un torchon**	*ang torshawng*
key ring	**un porte-clefs**	*ang porter klay*
postcard	**une carte postale**	*ewn kart postal*
souvenir guide	**un guide-souvenir**	*ang geed soovneer*
T-shirt	**un T-shirt**	*ang T-shirt*

Music

I'd like a … — **Je voudrais …** *zher voodray*

cassette — **une cassette** *ewn kassett*

compact disc — **un compact disc** *ang kawngpakt deesk*

record — **un disque** *ewn deesk*

videocassette — **une cassette vidéo** *ewn kassett veedayo*

Who are the popular French singers/bands? — **Quels sont les chanteurs/groupes français populaires?** *kel sawng lay shahngturr/groop frahngseh popewlehr*

Toys and games

I'd like a toy/game … — **Je voudrais un jouet/un jeu …** *zher voodray ang zhooeh/ang zhur*

for a boy — **pour un garçon** *poor ang garsawng*

for a 5-year-old girl — **pour une fille de cinq ans** *poor ewn fee der sangk ahng*

pail and shovel [bucket and spade] — **un seau et une pelle** *ang soa ay ewn pel*

chess set — **un jeu d'échecs** *ang zhur dayshek*

doll — **une poupée** *ewn poopay*

electronic game — **un jeu électronique** *ang zhur aylektroneek*

teddy bear — **un ours en peluche** *ang oorss ahng perlewsh*

Antiques

How old is this? — **Cela a quel âge?** *serla a kel azh*

Do you have anything from the … era? — **Avez-vous quelque chose de la période…?** *avay voo kelker shoaz der la payryod*

Can you send it to me? — **Pouvez-vous me l'envoyer?** *poovay voo mer lahngvwahyay*

Will I have problems with customs? — **Est-ce que je risque d'avoir des problèmes à la douane?** *ess ker zher reesk davwar day problem a la doowan*

Is there a certificate of authenticity? — **Y a-t-il un certificat d'authenticité?** *ee ateel ang sehrteefeeka doatahngteesseetay*

SUPERMARKET/CONVENIENCE STORE

Supermarkets such as **Monoprix**, **Prisunic** and **Casino** can be found in town centers; huge out-of-town hypermarkets such as **Carrefour**, **Leclerc**, **Mammouth** and **Auchan** encompass every shop you might find in the center. Convenience stores (**libres-services**) open until late, while **épiceries** – very small supermarkets – (including the **Casino** and **Franprix**) offer good products and service.

At the supermarket

Excuse me. Where do I find …?	**Excusez-moi. Où se trouve(nt) …?** *exkewzay mwa. oo ser troov*
Do I pay for this here or at the checkout?	**Je paye ça ici ou à la caisse?** *zher payy sa eessee oo a la kess*
Where are the baskets/ carts [trolleys]?	**Où sont les paniers/les chariots?** *oo sawng lay panyay/lay sharyoa*
Is there a … here?	**Y a-t-il … ici?** *ee ateel … eessee*
delicatessen	**un traiteur** *ang treturr*
pharmacy	**une pharmacie** *ewn farmassee*

YOU MAY SEE

EN ESPÈCES SEULEMENT	cash only
ARTICLES MÉNAGERS	household goods
BOUCHERIE	fresh meat
BOULANGERIE–PÂTISSERIE	bread and cakes
CONSERVES	canned fruit/vegetables
FRUITS ET LÉGUMES	fresh produce
POISSONNERIE	fresh fish
PRODUITS D'ENTRETIEN	cleaning products
PRODUITS LAITIERS/CRÉMERIE	dairy products
SURGELÉS	frozen foods
VINS ET SPIRITUEUX	wines and spirits
VOLAILLE	poultry

Food hygiene

AT THE CONVENIENCE STORE

I'd like some of that/these.	**Je voudrais de ça/ceci.** *zher voodray der sa/sersee*
I'd like …	**Je voudrais …** *zher voodray*
kilo of apples	**un kilo de pommes** *ang keelo der pom*
half-kilo of tomatoes	**une livre de tomates** *ewn leevr der tomat*
100 grams of cheese	**cent grammes de fromage** *sahng gram der fromazh*
liter of milk	**un litre de lait** *ang leetr der leh*
half-dozen eggs	**une demi-douzaine d'œufs** *ewn dermee doozayn dur*
… slices of ham	**… tranches de jambon** *trahngsh der zhahngbawng*
piece of cake	**un morceau de gâteau** *ang morsoa der gatoa*
bottle of wine	**une bouteille de vin** *ewn bootayy der vang*
carton of milk	**une brique de lait** *ewn breek der leh*
jar of jam	**un pot de confiture** *ang po dekawngfeetewr*
bag of chips [crisps]	**un paquet de chips** *ang pakeh desheeps*
can of coke	**une canette de coca cola** *ewn kaneht der koka kola*

Provisions/Picnic

beer	**de la bière**	*der la byehr*
butter	**du beurre**	*dew bur*
cheese	**du fromage**	*dew fromazh*
cookies [biscuits]	**des biscuits**	*day beeskwee*
eggs	**des œufs**	*day zur*
grapes	**du raisin**	*dew rezang*
instant coffee	**du café soluble**	*dew kafay solewbl*
loaf of bread	**du pain**	*dew pang*
margarine	**de la margarine**	*der la margareen*
milk	**du lait**	*dew leh*
rolls (bread)	**des petits pains**	*day pertee pang*
sausages	**des saucisses**	*day soasseess*
soft drinks/sodas	**des boissons gazeuses**	*day bwassawng gazurz*
tea bags	**des sachets de thé**	*day sasheh der tay*
wine	**du vin**	*dew vang*

une baguette *ewn baget*
bread: variations include **une demi-baguette** (half-size), **une ficelle** (a thinner version), **une couronne** (ring-shaped) and **un bâtard** (baton).

un gâteau *ang gatoa*
cake; for example **une tartelette aux fruits** (small fruit tart), **un mille-feuille** (napoleon/cream or vanilla slice), **un éclair** and **une religieuse** (frosted cream puff, shaped like a nun's habit).

un pain *ang pang*
loaf of bread, which may be **complet** (wholemeal/wheat), **de campagne** (white bread dusted with flour), **de mie** (sliced, sandwich loaf), **de seigle** (like rye bread), **au son** (with added bran) or **brioché** (sweet and rich).

CONVERSION CHARTS

The following conversion charts contain the most commonly used measures.

1 Gramme (g)	= 1000 milligrams	= 0.35 oz.
1 Livre (lb)	= 500 grams	= 1.1 lb
1 Kilogramme (kg)	= 1000 grams	= 2.2 lb
1 Litre (l)	= 1000 milliliters	= 1.06 U.S / 0.88 Brit. quarts
		= 2.11 /1.8 US /Brit. pints
		= 34 /35 US /Brit. fluid oz.
		= 0.26 /0.22 US /Brit. gallons
1 Centimètre (cm)	= 100 millimeter	= 0.4 inch
1 Mètre (m)	= 100 centimeters	= 39.37 inches/3.28 ft.
1 Kilomètre (km)	= 1000 meters	= 0.62 mile
1 Mètre carré (qm)	= 10.8 square feet	
1 Hectare (ha)	= 2.5 acres	
1 Kilomètre carré (km²)	= 247 acres	

Not sure whether to put on a bathing suit or a winter coat? Here is a comparison of Fahrenheit and and Celsius/Centigrade degrees..

				Oven Temperatures
-40°C – -40°F	5°C – 41°F			
-30°C – -22°F	10°C – 50°F			100°C – 212°F
-20°C – -4°F	15°C – 59°F			121°C – 250°F
-10°C – 14°F	20°C – 68°F			154°C – 300°F
-5°C – 23°F	25°C – 77°F			177°C – 350°F
-1°C – 30°F	30°C – 86°F			204°C – 400°F
0°C – 32°F	35°C – 95°F			260°C – 500°F

When you know	Multiply by	To find
ounces	28.3	grams
pounds	0.45	kilograms
inches	2.54	centimeters
feet	0.3	meters
miles	1.61	kilometers
square inches	6.45	sq. centimeters
square feet	0.09	sq. meters
square miles	2.59	sq. kilometers
pints (US/Brit)	0.47 / 0.56	liters
gallons (US/Brit)	3.8 / 4.5	liters
Fahrenheit	5/9, after subtracting 32	Centigrade
Centigrade	9/5, then add 32	Fahrenheit

HEALTH

Before you leave, make sure your health insurance policy covers any illness or accident while on vacation.

You'll be expected to pay doctors and dentists on the spot. EU citizens with a Form E111 should be able to obtain reimbursement (but not in Switzerland). But make sure the doctor you see is a **médecin conventionné**. These doctors charge the minimum and their fees are accepted by the social security system.

In an emergency, the doctor will come out to you: call **SOS Médecins**.

Ambulance: France ☎ 18, Belgium ☎ 100, Switzerland ☎ 114; **SAMU** (French emergency ambulance) ☎ 567 50 50.

DOCTOR/GENERAL

Where can I find a doctor/dentist [surgery]?	**Où est-ce que je peux trouver un médecin/dentiste?** *oo ess ker zher pur troovay ang maydsang/dahngteest*
Where's there a doctor who speaks English?	**Où y a-t-il un médecin qui parle anglais?** *oo ee a teel ang maydsang kee parl ahngleh*
What are the office hours?	**Quelles sont les heures de consultation au cabinet?** *kel sawng lay zurr der kawngsewltasyawng oa kabeeneh*
Could the doctor come to see me here?	**Est-ce que le médecin pourrait venir me voir?** *ess ker ler maydsang pooreh verneer mer vwar*
Can I make an appointment for …?	**Est-ce que je peux prendre rendez-vous pour …?** *ess ker zher pur prahngdr rahngdayvoo poor*
today/tomorrow	**aujourd'hui/demain** *oazhoordwee/dermang*
as soon as possible	**le plus tôt possible** *ler plew toa posseebl*
It's urgent.	**C'est urgent.** *seht ewrzhang*
I've got an appointment with Doctor …	**J'ai rendez-vous avec docteur …** *zhay rahngdayvoo avek dokturr*

Accident and injury

My … is hurt/injured.	**… s'est fait mal/est blessé(e).** *seh feh mal/eh blessay*
husband/wife	**Mon mari/Ma femme** *mawng maree/ma fam*
son/daughter	**Mon fils/Ma fille** *mawng feess/ma fee*
He/She is …	**Il/Elle est …** *eel/el eh*
unconscious	**sans connaissance** *sahng konessahngss*
(seriously) injured	**(gravement) blessé(e)** *(gravmahng) blessay*
He/She is bleeding. (heavily)	**Il/Elle saigne (beaucoup).** *eel/el señ (boakoo)*
I've got a/an …	**J'ai …** *zhay*
burn	**une brûlure** *ewn brewlewr*
cut	**une coupure** *ewn koopewr*
insect bite	**une piqûre d'insecte** *ewn peekewr dangsekt*
lump	**une boule/bosse** *ewn bool/boss*
rash	**une éruption cutanée** *ewn ayrewpsyawng kewtanay*
sprained muscle	**un muscle froissé** *ang mewskl frwassay*
swelling	**une enflure** *ewn ahngflewr*

Short-term symptoms

I've been feeling sick [ill] for … days.	**Je suis malade depuis … jours.** *zher swee malad derpwee … zhoor*
I feel faint.	**Je vais m'évanouir.** *zher vay mayvanooweer*
I feel feverish.	**J'ai de la fièvre.** *zhay der la fyehvr*
I've been vomiting.	**J'ai vomi.** *zhay vomee*
I've got diarrhea.	**J'ai la diarrhée.** *zhay la deearay*
I have (a/an) …	**J'ai …** *zhay*
cold	**un rhume** *ang rewm*
cramps	**des crampes** *day krangp*
headache	**mal à la tête** *mal a la tet*
sore throat	**mal à la gorge** *mal a la gorzh*
stiff neck	**un torticolis** *ang torteekolee*
stomachache	**mal à l'estomac** *mal a lestoma*

Health conditions

I have arthritis.	**J'ai de l'arthrite.**	*zhay der lartreet*
I have asthma.	**J'ai de l'asthme.**	*zhay der lasm*
I am …	**Je suis …**	*zher swee*
deaf	**sourd**	*soor*
diabetic	**diabétique**	*deeabayteek*
epileptic	**épileptique**	*aypeelepteek*
handicapped	**handicapé(e)**	*ahngdeekapay*
(… months) pregnant	**enceinte (de … mois)**	*ahngsangt (der … mwa)*
I have a heart condition.	**Je souffre du cœur.**	*zher soofrer dew kurr*
I have high blood pressure.	**J'ai de l'hypertension.** *zhay der leepehrtahngsyawng*	
I had a heart attack … years ago.	**J'ai eu une crise cardiaque il y a … ans.** *zhay ew ewn kreez kardyak eel ee a … ahng*	

Parts of the body

appendix	**l'appendice** *lapangdeess*		knee	**le genou** *ler zhernoo*	
arm	**le bras** *ler bra*		leg	**la jambe** *la zhangb*	
back	**le dos** *ler doh*		lip	**la lèvre** *la levr*	
bladder	**la vessie** *la vessee*		liver	**le foie** *ler fwa*	
bone	**l'os** *loss*		mouth	**la bouche** *la boosh*	
breast	**le sein** *ler sang*		muscle	**le muscle** *ler mewskl*	
chest	**la poitrine** *la pwatreen*		neck	**le cou** *ler koo*	
ear	**l'oreille** *lorayy*		nose	**le nez** *ler nay*	
eye	**l'œil** *loy*		rib	**la côte** *la koat*	
face	**le visage** *ler veezazh*		shoulder	**l'épaule** *laypoal*	
finger	**le doigt** *ler dwa*		skin	**la peau** *la poa*	
foot	**le pied** *ler pyay*		stomach	**l'estomac** *lestoma*	
gland	**la glande** *la glahngd*		thigh	**la cuisse** *la kweess*	
hand	**la main** *la mang*		throat	**la gorge** *la gorzh*	
head	**la tête** *la tet*		thumb	**le pouce** *le pooss*	
heart	**le cœur** *le kurr*		toe	**l'orteil** *lortayy*	
jaw	**la mâchoire** *la mashwar*		tongue	**la langue** *la lahngg*	
joint	**l'articulation** *larteekewlasyawng*		tonsils	**les amygdales** *lay zameegdal*	
kidney	**le rein** *ler rang*		vein	**la veine** *la ven*	

Doctor's inquiries

Depuis combien de temps vous sentez-vous comme ça?	How long have you been feeling like this?
Est-ce que c'est la première fois que vous avez ça?	Is this the first time you've had this?
Est-ce que vous prenez d'autres médicaments?	Are you taking any other medicines?
Est-ce que vous êtes allergique à quelque chose?	Are you allergic to anything?
Avez-vous perdu l'appétit?	Have you lost your appetite?

Examination

Remontez votre manche, s'il vous plaît.	Roll up your sleeve, please.
Déshabillez-vous jusqu'à la ceinture, s'il vous plaît.	Please undress to the waist.
Allongez-vous, s'il vous plaît.	Please lie down.
Ouvrez la bouche.	Open your mouth.
Respirez profondément.	Breathe deeply.
Toussez, s'il vous plaît.	Cough please.
Où est-ce que vous avez mal?	Where does it hurt?
Est-ce que ça vous fait mal ici?	Does it hurt here?

Diagnosis

Il faut vous faire une radio.	I want you to have an x-ray.
J'ordonne une prise de sang/ un examen des selles/ une analyse d'urine.	I want a specimen of your blood/stool/urine.
Je veux que vous alliez voir un spécialiste.	I want you to see a specialist.
Je veux vous hospitaliser.	I want you to go to the hospital.
C'est cassé/foulé.	It's broken/sprained.
C'est disloqué/déchiré.	It's dislocated/torn.
Vous avez ...	You have (a/an) ...
les amygdales	tonsillitis

l'appendicite	appendicitis
le cancer	cancer
une cystite	cystitis
une fracture	fracture
la grippe	flu
des hémorroïdes	hemorrhoids
une hernie	hernia
une inflammation de ...	inflammation of ...
une intoxication alimentaire	food poisoning
une maladie vénérienne	venereal disease
une pneumonie	pneumonia
la rougeole	measles
une sciatique	sciatica
une tumeur	tumor
C'est infecté.	It's infected.
C'est contagieux.	It's contagious.

Treatment

Je vais vous donner	I'll give you ...
un antiseptique	an antiseptic
un calmant/analgésique	a pain killer
Je vais vous prescrire ...	I'm going to prescribe ...
des antibiotiques	a course of antibiotics
des suppositoires	some suppositories
Est-ce que vous êtes allergique à certains médicaments?	Are you allergic to any medicines?
Prendre une pilule/un comprimé	Take one pill
toutes les ... heures	every ... hours
... fois par jour	... times a day
avant/après les repas	before/after each meal
en cas de douleurs	in case of pain
pendant ... jours	for ... days
Consultez un médecin à votre retour.	Consult a doctor when you get home.

GYNECOLOGIST

I have …	**J'ai …** *zhay*
abdominal pains	**des douleurs abdominales** *day doolurr abdomeenal*
period pains	**des règles douloureuses** *day regler dooloorurz*
a vaginal infection	**une infection vaginale** *ewn angfeksyawng vazheenal*
I haven't had my period for … months.	**Je n'ai pas eu mes règles depuis … mois.** *zher nay pa ew meh regl derpwee … mwa*
I'm on the Pill.	**Je prends la pilule.** *zher prahng la peelewl*

HOSPITAL

Please notify my family.	**Est-ce que vous pouvez prévenir ma famille?** *ess ker voo poovay prayvneer ma famee*
I'm in pain.	**J'ai mal./Je souffre.** *zhay mal/zher soofr*
I can't eat/sleep.	**Je ne peux pas manger/dormir.** *zher ner pur pa mahngzhay/dormeer*
When will the doctor come?	**Quand est-ce que le docteur passera?** *kahng ess ker ler dokturr passra*
Which section [ward] is … in?	**Dans quelle chambre est …?** *dahng kel shangbr eh*
I'm visiting …	**Je viens voir …** *zher vyang vwar*

OPTICIAN

I'm nearsighted/farsighted [shortsighted/longsighted]	**Je suis myope/hypermétrope.** *zher swee meeop/eepehrmaytrop*
I've lost …	**J'ai perdu …** *zhay pehrdew*
one of my contact lenses	**une de mes lentilles de contact** *ewn der meh lahngtee der kawngtakt*
my glasses	**mes lunettes** *meh lewnett*
a lens	**un verre** *ang vehr*
Could you give me a replacement?	**Est-ce que vous pourriez m'en donner un(e) de remplacement?** *ess ker voo pooryay mahng donnay ang (ewn) der rahngplassmahng*

DENTIST

I have a toothache.	**J'ai mal aux dents.** *zhay mal oa dahng*
This tooth hurts.	**Cette dent me fait mal.** *set dahng mer feh mal*
I've lost a filling/tooth.	**J'ai perdu un plombage/une dent.** *zhay pehrdew ang plawngbazh/ewn dahng*
Can you repair this denture?	**Est-ce que vous pouvez réparer ce dentier?** *ess ker voo poovay rayparay ser dahngtyay*
I don't want it extracted.	**Je ne veux pas que vous me l'arrachiez.** *zher ner vur pa ker voo mer larashyay*

YOU MAY HEAR

Je vais vous faire une piqûre/une anesthésie locale.	I'm going to give you an injection/a local anesthetic.
Il faut vous faire un plombage/vous mettre une couronne.	You need a filling/cap [crown].
Je dois l'arracher.	I'll have to take it out.
Je ne peux vous donner qu'un traitement provisoire.	I can only fix it temporarily.
Ne mangez rien pendant … heures.	Don't eat anything for … hours.

PAYMENT AND INSURANCE

How much do I owe you?	**Combien vous dois-je?** *kawnbyang voo dwazh*
I have insurance.	**J'ai une assurance.** *zhay ewn assewrahngss*
Can I have a receipt for my health insurance?	**Puis-je avoir un reçu pour mon assurance maladie?** *pweezh avwar ang rersew poor mawng nassewrahngss maladee*
Would you fill out this health insurance form, please?	**Pouvez-vous remplir cette feuille d'assurance maladie?** *poovay voo rahngpleer set fuhy dassewrahngss maladee*
Do you have …?	**Est-ce que vous avez …?** *ess ker voo zavay*
Form E111/health insurance	**un imprimé E111/une assurance maladie** *ang angpreemay er sang awngz/ewn assewrahngss maladee*

DICTIONARY ENGLISH-FRENCH

A

a few quelques-un(e)s
a little un peu
a lot beaucoup
a.m. du matin
able, to be *(also* ➤*can, could)* pouvoir
about *(approximately)* environ
above *(place)* au-dessus de
abroad à l'étranger m
abscess abcès m
abseiling descente f en rappel
accept, to accepter;
do you accept…? acceptez-vous?
access *(n)* accès m
accessories accessoires *mpl*
accident accident m; *(road)* accident
(de la route) m
accommodations logement m
accompany, to accompagner
accountant comptable m
ace *(cards)* as m
across de l'autre côté de, en face de
acrylic acrylique
action film film m d'aventure/d'action
activities activités fpl
actor/actress acteur m/actrice f
adapter adaptateur m
address adresse f,
adjoining room chambre f à côté
admission charge prix m d'entrée
adult adulte m,
advance, in à l'avance
aerial *(car/tv)* "antenne" f
after après; **aftershave** lotion f
après-rasage; **after-sun lotion** lotion f
après-soleil
afternoon, in the l'après-midi
age: what age? quel âge?
aged, to be avoir… ans
… ago il y a…
agree: I agree je suis d'accord

air air m; **~ conditioning** climatisation
f; **~ mattress** matelas m pneumatique;
~ pump compresseur m (pour l'air);
~ freshener désodorisant m
airline compagnie f aérienne
airmail par avion m
airport aéroport m
airplane avion m
air steward/hostess hôtesse f de l'air
aisle seat siège m côté couloir
alarm clock réveil m
alcoholic (drink) alcoolisé
all tous/toutes
all-night pharmacy
pharmacie f de garde
allergic, to be être allergique
allergy allergie f
allowance quantité f autorisée
allowed: is it allowed?
est-ce que c'est permis?
almost presque
alone seul(e)
already déjà
also aussi
alter, to faire des retouches
always toujours
am: I am je suis
ambassador ambassadeur m
ambulance ambulance f
American *(adj)* américain(e); *(n)*
américain; **~ football** football m
américain
amount somme f, montant m
amusement arcade salle f de jeux
anchor, to mouiller l'ancre
and et
anesthetic anesthésie f
angling pêche f (à la ligne)
animal animal m
anorak anorak m
another un(e) autre; **~ day** un
autre jour
antibiotics antibiotiques mpl
antifreeze antigel m
antiques antiquité f; **~ shop**
antiquaire m

antiseptic antiseptique; **~ cream** crème f antiseptique

any du, de l', de la

anyone quelqu'un; **~ else** quelqu'un d'autre m

anything cheaper quelque chose de moins cher

anything else? autre chose?

apartment appartement m

apologize: I apologize excusez-moi

apples pommes f/p

appointment rendez-vous m; **to make an ~** prendre rendez-vous

approximately environ

April avril m

archery tir m à l'arc

architect architecte

architecture architecture f

are you…? est-ce que vous êtes…?

area région f

area code code m

arm bras m

armbands *(swimming)* brassards mpl gonflables, flotteurs mpl

around *(place)* autour de; *(time)* vers

arrange: can you arrange it? pouvez-vous vous en occuper?

arrest, to be under être en état d'arrestation

arrive, to arriver; **to ~ in** arriver à

art art m; **~ gallery** galerie f d'art/ de peinture

artery artère f

arthritis, to have avoir de l'arthrose/arthrite

artificial sweetener édulcorant m

artist artiste

as soon as possible dès que possible

ashore, to go débarquer

ashtray cendrier m

ask, to demander; **I asked for…** j'ai demandé…

asleep, to be être endormi, dormir

aspirin aspirine f

asthma, to have avoir de l'asthme

at *(place)* à la, à l', au, aux; *(time)* à

at least au moins

attack attaque f; *(medical)* crise f, attaque f

attendant gardien(ne) m/f

attractive joli(e)

August août m

aunt tante

Australia Australie f

Australian *(adj)* australien(ne); *(n)* Australien(ne) m/f

authenticity authenticité f

automated teller/ATM distributeur m automatique

automatic *(car, camera)* automatique,

autumn automne m

avalanche avalanche f

away loin de

awful affreux(-se)

B

baby bébé m; **~ bottle** biberon m; **~ food** aliments mpl pour bébé; **~ seat** siège m pour bébé m; **~ sitter** baby-sitter f, garde f d'enfants; **~ wipes** lingettes fpl

back dos m

backache mal m au dos

backpacking faire du tourisme à pied

bad mauvais(e)

baggage bagages mpl; **~ allowance** poids m de bagages; **~ check** (**office**) consigne f; **~ reclaim** consigne f

bakery boulangerie f,

balance of account bilan m des comptes

balcony balcon m

ball ballon m, balle f

ballet ballet m,

band *(musical)* groupe m,

bandage bandage m

bank banque f; **~ account** compte m bancaire; **~ card** carte f bancaire; **~ loan** prêt m bancaire

bar bar m; *(hotel)* bar m

barbecue barbecue m

barber coiffeur m (pour hommes)

barge péniche m

basement sous-sol m

basin lavabo m
basket panier m
bath: to take a bath prendre un bain; **~ towel** serviette f de bain; **~ room** salle f de bains
bathrooms toilettes fpl; WC mpl
battery pile f; *(car)* batterie f
battleground champ m de bataille
be, to *(also ➤ am, are)* être; **I am** je suis; **we are** nous sommes
beach plage f
beard barbe f
beautiful beau (belle),
because parce que; **~ of** à cause de
bed lit m; **~ room** chambre f; **I'm going to ~** je vais au lit; **~ and breakfast** chambre f et petit déjeuner m
bedding literie f
bee abeille f
beer bière f,
before *(time)* avant,
begin, to *(also ➤ start)* commencer
beginner débutant(e) m/f
beginning commencement m, début m
beige beige
Belgian *(adj)* belge; *(n)* Belge m/f
Belgium Belgique f
below ... °C en-dessous de ... degrés
belt ceinture f
beneath sous
berth couchette f,
best meilleur(e)
better .mieux
between entre
bib bavoir m
bicycle vélo m; **~ hire/rental** location f de vélo; **~ parts**
bidet bidet m
big grand(e),
bikini bikini m
bill note f; billet m; addition f; **put it on the bill** mettez-le sur l'addition
bin liner sac m poubelle
binoculars jumelles fpl
bird oiseau m
birthday anniversaire m
biscuits *(cookies)* petits gâteaux mpl

bishop *(chess)* fou m
bite *(insect)* piqûre f (d'insecte)
bitten: I've been bitten by a dog j'ai été mordu par un chien
bitter amer(-ère)
black noir(e); **~ and white film** *(camera)* pellicule f noir et blanc
blanket couverture f
bleeding, to be saigner
bless you! à vos souhaits!
blind *(window)* store m
blister ampoule f
blocked, to be être bouché(e); **the road is ~** la route est barrée
blood sang m; **~ group** groupe m sanguin; **~ pressure** tension f (artérielle,
blouse chemisier m
blow-dry brushing
blue bleu(e)
blusher fard m à joues
boarding pass carte f d'embarquement
boat bateau m; **~ trip** voyage m en bateau
body: parts of the body; corps, m, parties du corps fpl
boil furoncle m
boiler chaudière f
bone os m
book livre m; **~ store** librairie f
booked up, to be être complet
book of tickets carnet de tickets m
boots bottes fpl; *(for sport)* chaussures fpl
border *(country)* frontière f
boring ennuyeux(se)
born: I was born in... je suis né(e) à *(place)*/en *(year)*
borrow: may I borrow...? est-ce que je peux emprunter...?
botanical garden jardin botanique m
bottle bouteille f; **~ bank** container à verre m; **~ opener** ouvre-bouteilles m
bow *(ship)* proue f
bowel intestins mpl
box boîte f; **~ of chocolates** boîte f de chocolats; **~ office** bureau de location m

boxing boxe f
boy garçon m,
boyfriend copain
bra soutien-gorge m
bracelet bracelet m
brand marque f
brass laiton m
bread pain m
break, to casser
breakage casse f, bris m
breakdown panne f; **to have a ~** tomber en panne
break-in cambriolage m
breakfast petit déjeuner m,
breast sein m
breathe, to respirer,
breathtaking époustouflant(e)
bridge pont m; *(cards)* bridge m
briefcase attaché-case, porte-document m
briefs culotte f
brilliant fantastique, superbe
bring, to apporter
Britain Grande-Bretagne f
British *(adj)* britannique
Briton *(n)* Britannique m/f
brochure dépliant m
broken, to be être cassé(e),
bronchitis bronchite f
bronze *(adj)* de bronze
brooch broche f
brother frère m
brown marron
browse, to regarder
bruise bleu m
brush brosse f
buffet car wagon-restaurant m
build, to construire
building bâtiment m
built construit(e)
bum-bag sac banane m
burger hamburger m; **~ stand** kiosque à hamburger m
burglary *(also* ►theft*)* cambriolage m
burn brûlure f
burnt, to be *(food)* être brûlé(e)
bus bus m; *(bus)* car m; **~ pass** carte f de bus; **~ route** itinéraire m des bus;

~ station gare f routière; **~ stop** arrêt m d'autobus; arrêt m de car
business affaires fpl; **~ class** classe f affaires; **~man** homme m d'affaires; **~ trip** voyage m d'affaires; **~ woman** femme f d'affaires; **on ~** pour affaires
busy, to be être occupé(e), avoir à faire
but mais
butane gas gaz butane m,
butcher shop la boucherie f
butter beurre m,
button bouton m
buy, to acheter,
buying tickets *(travel)* acheter des billets
by *(time)* avant *(at the latest)* pour; **~ car** en voiture f; **~ credit card** avec une carte de crédit f
bye! au revoir!, salut!
bypass route f de contournement

C

cabaret cabaret m
cabin cabine f
cable car téléphérique m
café café m,
cake gâteau m; **~ shop** pâtisserie f
calendar calendrier m
call, to *(phone)* téléphoner; appeler; **to ~ collect** appeler en P.C.V.; **call the police!** appelez la police!; **I'll call back** je rappellerai; **I'll call round** je passerai
camcorder caméscope m
camera appareil-photo m; **~ case** sac-photo m; **~ shop** magasin m de photos
campbed un lit de camp
camping camping m; **~ equipment** matériel m de camping
campsite terrain m de camping
can boîte f canette f
can I (have)…? est-ce que je peux (avoir)…?
can you help me? pouvez-vous m'aider?
can you recommend…? pouvez-vous recommander…?
can opener ouvre-boîte m
Canada Canada m

Canadian *(adj)* canadien(ne); *(n)* Canadien(ne) m/f
canal canal m
cancel, to annuler
cancer cancer m
candle bougie f
candy bonbons mpl
canoe canoë m
canoeing faire du canoë(-kayak)
cap casquette f; *(dental)* couronne f
capital city capitale f
captain *(boat)* capitaine m
car voiture f, –; **~ alarm** alarme de voiture m; **~ ferry** car-ferry m; **~ rental** location de voiture f; **~ parts; ~ pound** fourrière f; **~ repairs; ~ wash** laverie f automatique (de voiture); **by ~** en voiture; **rental ~** voiture f de location; *(train)* wagon m
carafe carafe f
caravan caravane f; **~ site/ park** terrain de camping/ caravaning m
card (➤ cash, credit, playing) carte f
careful: be careful! soyez prudent; *(urgent)* faites attention!
carpet *(fitted)* moquette f; *(rug)* tapis m
carrier bag sac (plastique) m
carry-cot lit-auto m (pour bébé)
cart chariot m
carton (of milk) brique f (de lait)
cash liquide m; **~ card** carte f bancaire; **~ desk** caisse f; **~ machine** distributeur automatique m
cash, to encaisser
cassette cassette f
castle château m
casualty dept. urgences fpl
cat chat(te) (m/f)
catch, to *(bus)* attraper
cathedral cathédrale f
cause, to causer
cave grotte f
CD CD m, disque compact m; **~ player** lecteur m de CD
cemetery cimetière m
central heating chauffage m central
center of town centre-ville m

ceramics céramique f
certificate certificat m,
chair chaise f; **~ lift** télésiège m
change *(coins)* monnaie f; **keep the change** gardez la monnaie
change, to *(buses)* changer; *(money); (reservation); (trains); (baby); (lanes); (clothes)* se changer
changing facilities salle f de change
changing rooms cabines fpl d'essayage
Channel (English) Manche f
chapel chapelle f
charge prix m; tarif m
charter flight vol m charter
cheap bon marché; f
cheaper moins cher(-ère)
check in, to *(plane)* faire enregistrer ses bagages
check out, to *(hotel)* partir
check note f; ticket de caisse *m*; addition f; **put it on the check** mettez-le sur l'addition
check: please check pouvez-vous vérifier
check-in desk bureau m d'enregistrement
checked *(patterned)* à carreaux
checkers dames fpl
checkout caisse f
cheers! santé!
cheese fromage m,
chemical toilet WC m chimique
cheque ➤ check
chess échecs mpl; **~ set** jeu m d'échecs
chest poitrine f
chickenpox varicelle f
child enfant m; **~ seat** *(car)* siège auto bébé/enfant; *(high chair)* chaise f haute (pour bébé)
children enfants mpl; *(reduction), (meals)*
children's meals repas mpl pour enfants

chips frites
choc-ice glace f au chocolat
chocolate chocolat m; **~ bar** tablette f de chocolat; **box of ~s** boîte f de chocolats; **hot ~** chocolat m chaud
Christian *(adj)* chrétien(ne); *(n)* Chrétien(ne) m/f
Christmas Noël m
church église f,
cigarette cigarette f; **~ machine** distributeur m de cigarettes
cigars cigares mpl
cinema cinéma m
circle *(balcony)* balcon m; *(U.S.) (road)* rond-point m
city wall rempart m
civil servant fonctionnaire m
claim ticket ticket de consigne m
clamp, to mettre un sabot
class: first class première classe f
clean *(adj)* propre; **to ~** nettoyer; **I'd like my shoes cleaned** je voudrais faire nettoyer mes chaussures
cleaner femme f de ménage
cleansing lotion lotion f démaquillante
cliff falaise f
cloakroom vestiaire m
clock pendule f
close *(near)* près
close, to fermer, *(shop)*
clothes vêtements mpl; **~ pins** épingles/pinces fpl à linge; **~ store/shop** magasin m de vêtements
cloudy: it's cloudy il y a des nuages
clubs *(golf)* clubs mpl
coast côte f
coat manteau m
coat hanger cintre m
coat room vestiaire m
cockroach cafard m
code *(area/dialling)* code m
coffee café m
coil *(contraceptive)* stérilet m
coin pièce f
cold *(adj)* froid(e); *(n)* rhume m,

collapse: he's collapsed il s'est effondré
collect, to venir chercher
college université f
color couleur f; **~ film** pellicule f couleur
comb peigne m
come back, to *(return)* revenir; **~ for** *(collection)* revenir chercher
commission commission f
communion communion f
compact disc/disk (disque) compact m
company *(business)* compagnie f; *(companionship)*
compartment *(train)* compartiment m
compass boussole f
complaint, to make a se plaindre
complaints *(restaurant)*; *(hotel)*
computer ordinateur m
concert concert m; **~ hall** salle de concert f
concussion, to have a avoir une commotion cérébrale/un traumatisme crânien
condoms préservatifs mpl
conference conférence f
confirm, to *(reservation)* confirmer
confirmation confirmation f
congratulations! félicitations! fpl
connection *(transport)* correspondance f
conscious, to be être conscient(e)
constipated, to be être constipé(e)
constipation constipation f
Consulate consulat m
consult, to consulter
consultant *(medical)* médecin m spécialiste
contact, to contacter
contact lens lentille f de contact; **~ fluid** liquide m pour lentilles de contact
contagious, to be être contagieux(-se)
contain, to contenir,
contemporary dance danse f contemporaine
contraceptive contraceptif m
convenience store mini marché m
convenient pratique

conversion chart table f de conversion
convertible (n) (car) voiture f décapotable
cook cuisinier(-ière) m/f
cook, to faire la cuisine
cookbook livre m de cuisine
cookies biscuits, petits gâteaux mpl
cooking (cuisine) cuisine f
coolbox glacière f
copper cuivre m
copy copie f
corduroy velours m côtelé
corkscrew tire-bouchon m
corner coin m
correct (► right) correct(e)
cosmetics produits mpl de beauté, cosmétiques mpl
cotton coton m
cotton wool coton m (hydrophile)
cough toux f; ~ **syrup** sirop m contre la toux; **to** ~ tousser
could I have...? est-ce que je peux avoir...?
counter caisse f, comptoir m
country (nation) pays m
countryside paysage m
course (meal) plat m
courthouse palais de justice m
cousin cousin(e) m/f
cover (lid) couvercle m
cover charge prix d'admission m
craft shop magasin m d'artisanat
cramps crampes fpl
crash: I've had a crash j'ai eu un accident
creak: the bed creaks le lit grince
creche crèche f
credit card carte f de crédit; ~ **number** numéro m de carte de crédit
credit status état m du crédit
credit, to be in avoir un compte approvisionné
apcrisps chips fpl
crib lit m d'enfant
crockery vaisselle f
cross (crucifix) croix f, crucifix m

cross, to (road) traverser
cross-country skiing track piste f de ski de fond
crossing (boat) traversée f
crossroads carrefour m
crowded encombré(e)
crown (dental) couronne f
cruise croisière f
crutches béquilles fpl
cup tasse f
cupboard placard m
curlers bigoudis mpl
currency devises fpl; monnaie f; ~ **exchange office** bureau m de change,
curtains rideaux mpl
cushion coussin m
customs douane f; ~ **declaration** déclaration f de douane
cut coupure f
cutlery couverts mpl,
cycle vélo m; ~ **helmet** casque m à vélo; ~ **path** piste f cyclable; ~ **route** circuit m cycliste; route f cycliste
cycling cyclisme m
cyclist cycliste m
cystitis cystite f

daily tous les jours, quotidiennement
damaged, to be être abîmé(e),
damp (n) humidité f; (adj) humide
dance spectacle m de danse
dancing, to go aller danser
dangerous dangereux(-se)
dark sombre; (color) foncé,
darts, to play jouer aux fléchettes
daughter fille f,
day jour m; ~ **ticket** ticket/billet m pour la journée; ~ **trip** excursion f d'une journée
dead mort(e); (battery) à plat
deaf, to be être sourd(e)
dear (greeting) cher (chère)
December décembre m
decide: we haven't decided yet nous n'avons pas encore décidé
deck chair chaise f longue

declare, to déclarer
deep profond
defrost, to décongeler
degrees (temperature) degrés mpl
delay retard m
delicate fragile
delicatessen charcutier m, traiteur m
delicious délicieux(-se)
deliver, to livrer
denim jean
dental floss fil m dentaire
dentist dentiste m,
dentures dentier m
deodorant déodorant m
depart, to (train, bus) (➤ leave) partir
department (in store) rayon m;
~ store grand magasin m
departure (train) départ m; ~ lounge
salle f de départ
depend: it depends on celà
dépend de f
deposit (hotel) arrhes fpl, (bicycle
rental); (car rental) caution f
describe, to décrire
design (dress) création f
designer dessinateur m, créateur m
destination destination f
details détails mpl
detergent détergent m
develop, to (photos) développer
diabetes diabète m
diabetic, to be être diabétique,
diagnosis diagnostic m
diamonds (cards) carreau m
diapers couches fpl
diarrhea diarrhée f
dice dés mpl
dictionary dictionnaire m
diesel diesel m
diet: I'm on a diet je suis au régime
difficult difficile
digital (watch) (montre) f à affichage
numérique
dinghy canot m pneumatique
dining car wagon-restaurant m,
dining room salle f à manger,
dinner jacket smoking m

dinner, to have dîner
direct direct(e)
direct, to indiquer
direct-dial telephone téléphone m à
ligne directe
direction direction f; in the ~ of en
direction de
director (film) réalisateur m; (of
company) directeur m, PDG m
directory (telephone) annuaire m
directory Enquiries
Renseignements mpl
dirty sale,
disabled (n) handicapés mpl,
disco discothèque f
discount réduction f,
discount: can you offer me a
discount? pouvez-vous me faire une
remise?
disgusting dégoûtant(e)
dish (meal) plat m
dish cloth lavette f
dish washing detergent poudre pour
lave-vaisselle f
disk film pellicule f disque
dislocated, to be être disloqué(e)
display cabinet vitrine f
display case vitrine f
disposable camera appareil-photo m
jetable
distilled water eau f distillée
district région f, quartier m
disturb: don't disturb ne pas déranger
dive, to plonger
diversion déviation f
divorced, to be être divorcé(e)
DIY (Do It Yourself) store magasin m
de bricolage
dizzy, to feel avoir le vertige
do: things to do choses à faire
doctor médecin m; docteur m
doctor's office cabinet m médical
does anyone here speak English? y
a-t-il quelqu'un ici qui parle anglais?
dog chien m
doll poupée f
dollar dollar m

door porte f,

dosage posologie f

double *(room)* (chambre f) pour deux personnes; **~ bed** grand lit m

downstairs en bas

downtown area centre-ville m

dozen douzaine f,

drain tuyau m (d'écoulement)

drama drame m

draught *(wind)* courant m d'air

dress robe f

drink boisson f; quelque chose à boire; verre m

drinking water eau f potable

drive, to conduire

driver *(bus, etc.)* conducteur m

driver's license [licence] permis m de conduire

drop off, to déposer; amener

drowning: someone is drowning quelqu'un se noie

drugstore droguerie f; pharmacie f

drunk ivre

dry cleaner's pressing m, nettoyage m à sec

dry cut coupe f sur cheveux secs

dry-clean, to nettoyer à sec

dual carriageway route f à quatre voies

dubbed, to be être doublé(e) (film)

due, to be *(payment)* être dû (due)

during pendant

dusty poussiéreux(-se)

duty-free hors-taxe; **~ goods** marchandises fpl hors-taxe; **~ shop** magasin m hors-taxe; **~ shopping** duty: **to pay duty** payer une taxe

duvet couette f

E

each: how much each? combien chacun?

ear oreille f

earache mal m à l'oreille

earlier plus tôt,

early tôt,

earrings boucles fpl d'oreilles

east est m

Easter Pâques fpl

easy facile

eat, to manger; **places to eat** endroits où manger

eaten: have you eaten? avez-vous mangé?

we've already eaten nous avons déjà mangé

economical économique

economy class classe f économique

eight huit

either... or soit... soit; ou... ou

elastic *(adj)* élastique

electric blanket couverture f chauffante

electric meter compteur m électrique

electric shaver rasoir m électrique

electrical appliance store magasin m d'électroménager

electrician électricien m

electricity électricité f

elevator ascenseur m,

eleven onze

else: something else quelque chose d'autre

E-mail courrier m électronique, e-mail

embark, to *(boat)* embarquer

embassy ambassade f

emergency urgence f; **~ exit** sortie f de secours; **~ room** urgences fpl; **it's an emergency** c'est urgent

empty vide

end, to finir

end: at the end au bout m

engaged, to be être fiancé(e)

engine moteur m

engineer ingénieur m

England Angleterre f

English *(language)* anglais m; **in ~** en anglais; **~-speaking** qui parle anglais

English person Anglais(e) m/f

enjoy, to aimer

enlarge, to *(photos)* agrandir

enough assez,

entertainment guide guide m des spectacles

entrance fee prix m d'entrée

entry visa visa m d'entrée
envelope enveloppe f
epileptic, to be être épileptique
equipment *(sports)* équipement m
error erreur f
escalator escalier m roulant
essential essentiel(le)
estate agent agent m immobilier
EU UE f
Eurocheque eurochèque m
evening dress tenue f de soirée
evening, in the le soir; dans la soirée
events spectacles mpl
every day tous les jours
every week chaque semaine
examination *(medical)* examen m
example, for par exemple
except sauf
excess luggage bagages *(mpl)* trop lourds
exchange, to changer
exchange rate taux m de change
excursion excursion f
excuse me *(getting attention)* excusez-moi,
exhausted, to be être épuisé(e)
exhibition exposition f
exit sortie f; **at the ~** à la sortie
expected: it's expected il faut s'y attendre
expensive cher (chère),
expire: when does it expire? quelle est la date de péremption?
expiration date date d'expiration f
expressway autoroute f
extension *(telephone)* poste f
extension cord rallonge (électrique) f
extra *(additional)* supplémentaire,
extracted, to be *(tooth)* arracher
extremely extrêmement
eye œil m *(pl* yeux)
eyeliner crayon pour les yeux m
eyeshadow ombre f/fard m à paupières

fabric *(material)* tissu m
face visage m

facilities équipement m; aménagements mpl
factor *(sun cream)* facteur
faint, to feel être prêt(e) à s'évanouir
fairground fête f foraine
fall *(autumn)* automne m
fall: he's had a fall il a fait une chute
family famille f,
famous célèbre
fan *(air)* ventilateur m
fan: I'm a fan of je suis un fan/passionné(e) de
far loin; **is it far?** c'est loin?
farce farce f
fare prix m
farm ferme f
farsighted hypermétrope
fashionable, to be être à la mode
fast vite; **~ food** fast food m
fast, to be *(clock)* avancer
fat gras m
father père m
faucet *(tap)* robinet m
fault, it's my/your ~ c'est ma/ votre faute
faulty, to be avoir un défaut m
favorite préféré(e), favori(te)
fax fax m; télécopieur m; **~ office** bureau m de fax/de télécopie; **~ machine** fax m
February février m
feed, to allaiter
feeding bottle biberon m
feel ill, to se sentir malade
feel sick, to se sentir malade
feel nauseous, to avoir envie de vomir
female femme f; *(adj)* femelle
ferry ferry m
festival festival m
fetch help! allez chercher de l'aide!
feverish, to feel se sentir fiévreux(-se)
few quelques
fiancé(e) fiancé(e) m/f
field champ m
fifth cinquième
fight *(brawl)* bagarre f
fill out, to remplir

filling *(dental)* plombage m; *(in sandwich)* garniture f
filling station station-service f
film *(movie)* film m; *(camera)* pellicule f; **~ speed** vitesse f de pellicule
filter filtre m; **~ paper** *(for coffee)* filtre m en papier
fine *(penalty)* amende f; *(well)* très bien
finger doigt m
fire: there's a fire! il y a le feu!; **~ alarm** alarme f d'incendie; **~ escape** escalier m de secours; **~ extinguisher** extincteur m; **~ department** pompiers mpl; **~lighters** allume-feu mpl; **~place** cheminée f; **~wood** bois m de chauffage
first premier(-ière); **~ class** première classe f; **~ floor** *(U.K.)* premier étage m; *(U.S.)* rez-de-chaussée m
first-aid kit trousse f de secours
fish store poissonnerie f
fishing rod canne f à pêche
fishing, to go aller à la pêche
fit: it fits *(clothes)* ça va
fitting room cabine f d'essayage
five cinq
fix: can you fix it? pouvez-vous le réparer?
flag drapeau m
flannel *(fabric)* flanelle f; *(face-cloth)* gant m de toilette
flash *(photo)* flash m
flashlight lampe de poche f
flat, have a être crevé f, être à plat
flea puce f; **~ market** marché m aux puces
flight vol m; **~ number** numéro m de vol; **~ attendant** hôtesse f de l'air
flip-flops tongs fpl
flood inondation f
floor *(storey)* étage m; **~ mop** balai m laveur; **~ show** spectacle m de cabaret
florist fleuriste m
flower fleur f

flu grippe f
fluent: to speak fluent French parler français couramment
fly *(insect)* mouche f
foggy: it's foggy il y a du brouillard
folding chair/table chaise/table f pliante
follow, to *(signs)* suivre; *(pursue)* suivre
food plats; nourriture f; cuisine; **~ poisoning** intoxication f alimentaire
foot pied m
footpath sentier m, chemin m
for a day pour une journée
for a week pour une semaine
forecast prévisions fpl météo
foreign étranger(-ère); **~ currency** devises fpl étrangères
forest forêt f
forget, to oublier
for hire libre
fork fourchette f; *(in the road)* embranchement m
form fiche f; formulaire m; feuille f
formal dress tenue f de soirée
fortnight quinzaine f
fortunately heureusement
forwarding address adresse f pour faire suivre le courrier
foundation *(make-up)* fond m de teint
fountain fontaine f
four quatre
four-door car voiture f quatre portes
four-wheel drive à quatre roues f motrices
fourteen quatorze
fourth quatrième
foyer *(hotel/theater)* hall m d'entrée
frame *(glasses)* monture f
France France f
Francs francs mpl
free *(of charge)* gratuit; *(available/vacant)* libre,
freezer congélateur m
French *(language)* français m,
French person Français(e) m/f
frequently souvent

fresh frais (fraîche)
Friday vendredi m
fridge réfrigérateur m, frigo m
friend ami(e) m/f
friendly aimable
fries frites fpl,
fringe frange f
from *(place)* de; *(time)*
front door porte f d'entrée;
~ key clé f de la porte d'entrée
frozen surgelé(e)
fruit juice jus m de fruit
frying pan poêle f
fuel *(gasoline)* carburant m
full plein(e)
full board pension f complète
full insurance assurance f tous risques
fun, to have s'amuser
funny *(amusing)* amusant(e); *(odd)* drôle
furniture mobilier m, meubles mpl
fuse fusible m; **~ box** boîte f à fusibles; **~ wire** plomb m (à fusible)

G

gallon gallon m (, litres)
gamble, to jouer pour de l'argent
game *(toy)* jeu m
garage garage m
garbage bag sac m poubelle
garden jardin m
gardener jardinier m
gardening jardinage m
gas: I smell gas! ça sent le gaz!;
~ bottle bouteille f de gaz
gasoline essence f;
~ can bidon m d'essence
gastritis gastrite f
gate *(airport)* porte f
gauze bandage
gay club club m gay
general delivery poste f restante
generous généreux (-euse)
genuine authentique; original(e)
Germany Allemagne f
get by: may I get by? est-ce que je peux passer?

get off, to *(transport)* descendre
get to, to arriver à; *(find)* se rendre à, aller à; **how do I get to...?** pour aller à...?,
gift cadeau m; **~ shop** magasin m de cadeaux
girl fille f,
girlfriend copine
give, to donner
glass verre m,
glasses *(spectacles)* lunettes fpl
gliding vol m plané
glossy finish *(photos)* brillant(e)
glove gant m
go, to aller; **to ~ back** *(turn around)* retourner; **to ~ for a walk** aller se promener; **to ~ out** *(in evening)* sortir; **to ~ shopping** aller faire des courses fpl; **where does this bus go?** où va ce bus?;
go away! allez-vous en!
goggles lunettes fpl de protection
gold or m
gold plate plaqué-or m
golf golf m; **~ course** terrain m de golf
good *(adj)* bon(ne); **~ afternoon** bonjour; **~ evening** bonsoir; **~ morning** bonjour; **~ night** bonne nuit
good-bye au revoir
got: have you got...? avez-vous...?
grade *(fuel)* qualité f
gram [gramme] gramme m
grandparents grands-parents mpl
grass herbe f; *(lawn)* pelouse f
gratuity pourboire m
gray [grey] gris(e)
graze égratignure f
greasy *(hair)* gras
great fun très amusant
green vert(e)
greengrocer marchand m de fruits et légumes
grocery store/grocer épicerie f
ground *(camping)* terrain m (de camping)
ground floor rez-de-chaussée m
group groupe m

guarantee garantie f; **is it guaranteed?** est-ce sous garantie?
guide *(tour)* guide m; **~book** guide m
guided tour visite f guidée
guitar guitare f
gynecologist gynécologue m

H

hair cheveux mpl; **~ brush** brosse f à cheveux; **~ dryer** sèche-cheveux m; **~ gel** gel m pour cheveux; **~ mousse** mousse f pour cheveux; **~ spray** laque f
haircare soin des cheveux m
haircut coupe f de cheveux
hairdresser coiffeur m
hairstylist coiffeur m styliste
half board demi-pension f
half fare demi-tarif m
half past … et demie
half, a moitié f, demi m
hammer marteau m
hand main f; **~ cream** crème f pour les mains; **~ luggage** bagages mpl à main; **~ towel** torchon m/serviette f pour les mains; **~ washable** lavable à la main
handbag sac m à main,
handicapped, to be être handicapé(e)
handicrafts artisanat m
handkerchief mouchoir m
handle poignée f
hang-gliding vol m libre
hanger cintre m
hangover *(n)* gueule f de bois
happen: what happened? qu'est-ce qui s'est passé?
happy: I'm not happy with the service je ne suis pas content(e) du service
harbor/harbour port m
hard shoulder *(road)* bande f d'arrêt d'urgence
hardware store quincaillerie f
hat chapeau m
hatchback coupé m avec hayon arrière
have to, to *(must)* devoir

have, to (➤); **I have** j'ai; **we have** nous avons
hay fever rhume m des foins
head tête f
head waiter maître m d'hôtel
headache mal m à la tête
health food store/shop magasin m de diététique
health insurance assurance f maladie
hear, to entendre
hearing aid appareil m de surdité
heart cœur m; **~ attack** crise f cardiaque; **~ condition** problèmes mpl cardiaques
hearts *(cards)* cœur m
heater radiateur m
heating chauffage m
heavy lourd(e)
height taille f; hauteur f
helicopter hélicoptère m
hello bonjour,
help aide f
help, to aider; **could you help me?** pourriez-vous m'aider?
hemorrhoids hémorroïdes fpl
her la; *(to her)* à elle; *(possessive)* son/sa/ses
here ici,
hers: it's hers c'est le sien/la sienne
hi! salut!
high haut; **~ tide** marée f haute
highlight, to *(hair)* faire des mèches
highway autoroute f
hike *(walk)* randonnée f
hill colline f
him le; *(to him)* à lui
his à lui; *(possessive)* son/sa/ses; **it's his** c'est le sien/la sienne
history histoire f
hitchhike, to faire de l'auto-stop
hitchhiking auto-stop m
HIV-positive séropositif(-ive)
hobby hobby m, passe-temps m
hockey *(field)* hockey m
hold, to *(contain)* contenir; **to ~ on** *(phone)* patienter; **~ on** ne raccrochez pas

hole *(in clothes)* trou m
holiday resort station f de vacances
home, to go rentrer chez soi
homosexual *(adj)* homosexuel(le)
honeymoon, to be on être en lune de miel
horse cheval m
horseracing courses fpl de chevaux
horseback trip promenade f à cheval
hospital hôpital m,
hot *(warm)* chaud(e); *(weather)* très chaud; ~ **dog** hot dog m; ~ **water** eau f chaude; ~ **water bottle** bouillotte f
hotel hôtel m; ~ **reservation**
hour heure f; **in an ~** dans une heure
house maison f, villa f
housewife femme f au foyer
hovercraft hovercraft m
how? comment?; ~ **are you?** comment allez-vous?
how far? à combien de km?; à quelle distance?
how long? combien de temps?,
how many? combien?,
how much? combien?,
how often? combien de fois?
how old? quel âge?
however toutefois
hundred cent
hungry, to be avoir faim
hurry, to be in a être pressé(e)
hurt: it hurts j'ai mal; **to be ~** être blessé(e)
husband mari m,
hypermarket hypermarché m

I

I'd like... je voudrais...,
ice glaçons mpl; ~ **dispenser** distributeur m de glace; ~ **hockey** hockey m sur glace; ~ **pack** pack m de glace; ~ **rink** patinoire f
ice cream glace f; ~ **cone** cornet m de glace
identification pièce f d'identité
ill, to be être malade
illegal, to be être illégal(e)
illness maladie f

immediately tout de suite
impressive impressionnant(e)
in *(place)* à, en; *(time)* dans
in-law: mother~ belle-mère f;
father~ beau-père f;
included: is... included? est-ce que... est compris?,
indicate, to *(car)* mettre son clignotant
indigestion indigestion f
indoor pool piscine f couverte
indoors à l'intérieur
inexpensive bon marché
infected, to be être infecté(e)
infection infection f
inflammation inflammation f
informal *(dress)* tenue f de ville
information renseignements mpl; ~ **desk** bureau m des renseignements; ~ **office** office m du tourisme
injection piqûre f
injured, to be être blessé(e),
innocent innocent(e)
insect insecte m; ~ **bite** piqûre f d'insecte; ~ **repellent** crème/lotion f contre les insectes
inside à l'intérieur
insist: I insist j'insiste
insomnia insomnie f
instead of au lieu de
instructions instructions fpl
instructor moniteur m
insulin insuline f
insurance assurance f; ~ **certificate** certificat m d'assurance; ~ **claim** demande f d'indemnité; ~ **company** compagnie f d'assurance
interest *(hobby)* intérêt m, hobby m
interest rate taux m d'intérêt
interesting intéressant(e)
international international(e)
International Student Card carte f d'étudiant internationale
Internet Internet m
interpreter interprète m,
intersection croisement m
interval intervalle m
into dans
introduce oneself, to se présenter

invitation invitation f
invite, to inviter
involved, to be être impliqué(e)
Ireland Irlande f
Irish irlandais(e)
Irish person Irlandais(e) m/f
iron *(for clothing)* fer m à repasser
iron, to repasser
is there...? y a-t-il...?
island île f
it is... c'est...
Italian *(adj)* italien(ne)
Italy Italie f
itemized bill note f détaillée

J

jack/knave *(cards)* valet m
jacket veste f
jammed, to be être coincé(e)
January janvier m
jar pot m
jaw mâchoire f
jeans jean m/*sing*
jet lag décalage m horaire
jet ski scooter m de mer
Jew *(n)* Juif(-ve) m/f
jeweler bijoutier m
jewelry store bijouterie f
Jewish *(adj)* juif(-ve)
job: what's your job?
quelle est votre profession?
joint passport passeport m joint
joke plaisanterie f
joker *(cards)* joker m
journalist journaliste m/f
jug (of water) pichet m/pot m (d'eau)
July juillet m
jumper cables [jump leads] câbles
mpl de secours (pour batterie)
junction *(exit)* sortie f (d'autoroute);
(intersection) bretelle f, intersection f
June juin m

K

keep the change gardez la monnaie
ketchup ketchup m

kettle bouilloire f
key clé f; **~ ring** porte-clé m
kidney rein m
kilo(gram) kilo(gramme) m
kilometer kilomètre m
kind *(pleasant)* gentil(le)
kind: what kind of...? quelle sorte
de...?, quel genre de...?
king *(cards/chess)* roi
kiosk kiosque m
kiss, to embrasser
kitchen cuisine f; **~ paper** papier m
absorbant
knapsack sac m à dos,
knave *(cards)* valet m
knee genou m
knife couteau m,
knight *(chess)* cavalier m
knocked down, to be être renversé(e)
know: I don't know je ne sais pas
kosher kascher

L

label étiquette f
lace dentelle f
ladder échelle f
ladies *(toilet)* femmes/dames fpl
lake lac m
lamp lampe f; *(oil)* lampe à pétrole
land, to atterrir
landing *(house)* palier m
landlord/landlady propriétaire m/f
lane voie f
language course cours m de langue
large *(adj)* gros(se); *(drink)* grand(e);
(clothing) grand
last *(final/previous)* dernier(-ière); **to**
last *(time)* durer
late tard; *(delayed)* en retard
later plus tard,
laugh, to rire
laundromat laverie f automatique
laundry service service m de
nettoyage
lavatory toilettes fpl, WC mpl
lawn pelouse f
lawyer avocat(e) m/f

laxative laxatif m
lead-free *(gas)* sans plomb m
leader *(of group)* chef m
leaflet dépliant m
leak: it leaks *(car, roof, pipe)* il fuit
learn, to *(language/sport)* apprendre
learner étudiant(e) m/f
leather cuir m
leave, to *(depart)* partir; *(leave behind: car)* laisser; *(luggage)* laisser; **to ~ from** *(transport)* partir de; **leave me alone!** laissez-moi tranquille!
left, on the à gauche
left-hand side gauche
left-handed gaucher(-ère)
left: are there any left? est-ce qu'il en reste?
leg jambe f
legal, to be être légal(e)
leggings legging m/sing
lemon citron m
lemonade limonade f
lend: could you lend me…? pourriez-vous me prêter…?
length longueur f
lens *(camera)* objectif m; *(optical)* verre m
lesbian club club m pour lesbiennes
less moins
lesson leçon f
let: please let me know pourriez-vous me faire savoir
letter lettre f; **~ box** boîte f aux lettres
library bibliothèque f
license plate number numéro m d'immatriculation,
lie down, to s'allonger, se coucher
lifebelt bouée f de sauvetage
lifeboat canot m de sauvetage
lifeguard maître-nageur m
lifejacket gilet m de sauvetage
lift *(hitchhiking)* trajet m; **~ pass** forfait m
light *(adj)* *(color)* clair(e); *(weight)* léger(-ère); *(n)* *(bicycle)* phare m, feu m; *(cigarette)* feu m; *(electric)* lumière f; **~ bulb** ampoule f

lighter *(cigarette)* briquet m
lightning foudre f
like: I'd like… je voudrais…; j'aimerais; **like this** *(in this way)* comme ça
line *(subway)* ligne f; *(profession)* branche f; queue f, file f *(d'attente)*; **to stand in line** faire la queue; *(phone)* **an outside line, please** je voudrais appeler à l'extérieur
linen lin m
lip lèvre f
lipbalm stick-lèvres m
lipstick rouge m à lèvres
liqueur liqueur f
liter litre m,
little petit(e)
live, to vivre; **~ together** vivre ensemble
liver foie m
living room salon m, salle f de séjour
lobby *(theatre/hotel)* hall m d'entrée
local local(e); **~ anesthetic** anesthésie f locale; **~ road** route f locale/départementale
lock *(canal)* écluse f
locked, to be fermé (à clé);
it's locked c'est fermé à clé
locker casier m
lock-up coffre-fort m
London Londres
long long(ue) *(clothing)*; *(time)* longtemps; **how ~?** combien de temps?
long-distance bus *(auto)*car m
long-distance call appel m à longue distance
longer: how much longer? encore pour combien de temps?
look for, to chercher
look like, to ressembler à
look, to have a *(check)* vérifier
look: I'm just looking je jette *(juste)* un coup d'œil
loose ample; *(clothing)* large
lorry camion m
lose, to perdre; **I've lost…** j'ai perdu…
loss perte f
lost, to be être perdu(e)

lost-and-found bureau m des objets trouvés
lots beaucoup de
loud: it's too loud c'est trop fort
love, to aimer, adorer; **I love you** je t'aime
low-fat allégé(e), à teneur peu élevée en matière grasse
lower *(berth)* inférieur(e)
luck: good luck! bonne chance!
luggage bagages mpl; **~ allowance** poids m de bagages autorisé; **~ carts** chariots mpl à bagages **~ locker** consigne f automatique; **~ tag** étiquette f pour bagages; **~ ticket** ticket m de consigne
lump boule f, bosse f
lumpy *(mattress)* défoncé(e)
lunch déjeuner m
lung poumon m
Luxembourg Luxembourg m

M

machine washable lavable en machine
(dear) madam (chère) madame
made of, what is it en quoi est-ce (fait)?
magazine magazine m
magnificent magnifique
maid femme f de chambre
maiden name nom m de jeune fille
mail *(post)* courrier m; **~ box** boîte f aux lettres; **by ~** par lettre; **~ office** (bureau de) poste f
mail, to poster
main principal(e); **~ course** plat m principal; **~ railway station** gare f principale; **~ street** rue f principale,
make *(brand)* marque f
make, to faire; **~ tea/coffee** faire du thé/café; **~ an appointment** prendre rendez-vous
make-up maquillage m
male *(n)* homme m; *(adj)* mâle
man homme m
manager directeur m; patron m
manicure manucure f

many beaucoup
map carte f; *(road)* carte f routière
March mars m
margarine margarine f
market marché m; **~ day** jour m de marché
married, to be être marié(e)
mascara mascara m
mass messe f
massage massage
match *(game)* match m
matches allumettes fpl,
material tissu m
matinée matinée f
matte finish *(photos)* mat m
matter: it doesn't matter ça ne fait rien; **what's the matter?** que se passe-t-il?
mattress matelas m
May mai m
may I? puis-je?
maybe peut-être
me me; *(to me)* à moi
meal repas m; *(dish)* plat m
mean, to signifier
measure, to mesurer
measurement mesures fpl
meat viande f
medical certificate certificat m médical
medicine *(medication)* médicament m
medium *(adj)* moyen(ne); *(steak)* à point
meet, to se retrouver; **pleased to meet you** enchanté(e)
meeting place point m de rendez-vous
member *(of club)* membre m,
memorial monument m (aux morts)
men *(toilets)* messieurs/hommes mpl
mend, to réparer
mention: don't mention it je vous en prie, il n'y a pas de quoi; de rien
menu menu m
message message m
metal métal m
meter *(taxi)* compteur m
methylated spirits alcool m à brûler
microwave oven four m à micro-ondes

midday midi m
midnight minuit m
migraine migraine f
mileage kilométrage m
milk lait m; **with ~** au lait; **~ of magnesia** magnésie f (hydratée)
million million m
mind: do you mind? est-ce que ça vous dérange?; **I've changed my mind** j'ai changé d'avis
mine à moi; **it's mine** c'est le mien/la mienne
mineral water eau f minérale
minibar mini-bar m
minibus minibus m
minimum *(n)* minimum m
minister pasteur m
minute minute f
mirror miroir m, glace f; *(car)* rétroviseur m
miss, to manquer
missing, to be *(lacking)* manquer; *(person)* avoir disparu; **there is...** **missing** il manque…
mistake erreur f
misunderstanding, there's been a il y a eu un malentendu m
mittens mouffles fpl
mobile home camping car m
modern moderne; **~ art** art m moderne
Monday lundi m
money argent m; **~ belt** ceinture f pour transporter de l'argent; **~ order** mandat m
month mois m
monument monument m
moor, to amarrer
mooring amarrage m
moped mobylette f
more plus; d'autre; **I'd like some more** j'en voudrais un peu plus
morning, in the le matin,
morning-after pill pilule du lendemain f
Moslem *(adj)* musulman(e);*(n)* Musulman(e) m/f
mosque mosquée f

mosquito moustique m; **~ bite** piqûre f de moustique
mother mère f
motorboat canot m automobile
motorcycle moto f; **~ parts**
mountain montagne f; **~ bike** VTT (vélo m tout terrain); **~ pass** col m (de montagne); **~ range** chaîne f de montagnes
mountaineering alpinisme m
moustache moustache f
mouth bouche f; **~ ulcer** aphte m
move, to *(house)* déménager; *(rooms)* changer de; **don't move him!** ne le déplacez pas!
movie film m; **~ theater** cinéma m,
Mr. M. (monsieur)
Mrs. Mme (madame)
much beaucoup
mugged, to be être agressé
mugging agression f
multiplex cinema cinéma m multiplex
mumps oreillons mpl
muscle muscle m
museum musée m
music musique f; **~ box** boîte f à musique
musician musicien(ne) m/f
my mon, ma, mes

N

nail polish vernis m à ongles
nail scissors ciseaux mpl à ongles
name nom m,
name: my name is je m'appelle; **what's your name?** comment vous appelez-vous
nappies/diapers couches fpl
narrow étroit(e)
national national(e)
nationality nationalité f
nature reserve parc naturel m
nature trail circuit forestier éducatif m
nausea nausée f
navy blue bleu marine m
near près
nearby près d'ici

nearest le/la plus proche
nearsighted myope
necessary nécessaire
neck cou m; *(clothes)* encolure f
necklace collier m
need: I need to je dois +inf.
needle aiguille f
negative *(photo)* négatif m
neighbor voisin(e) m/f
nephew neveu m
Netherlands Pays-Bas mpl
never jamais
new neuf (neuve)
New Year Nouvel An m
New Zealand Nouvelle Zélande f
newsdealer/newsagent marchand m de journaux
newspaper journal m
newsstand kiosque m à journaux
next prochain(e); suivant(e); **next stop!** prochain arrêt!
next to à côté de,
niece nièce f
night porter gardien de nuit m
night/at night la nuit; **per night** par nuit f
nightclub nightclub m
nightdress chemise de nuit f
nine neuf
nipple *(for baby)* tétine f
no non
no one personne,
noisy bruyant(e),
non-alcoholic non alcoolisé(e)
non-smoking *(adj)* non-fumeur; ~ **area** zone f non-fumeur
none aucun(e),
noon midi m
normal normal(e)
north nord m
North Africa Afrique f du Nord
Northern Ireland Irlande f du Nord
nose nez m
nosebleed saignement m de nez
not that one pas celui-ci (celle-ci)
not yet pas encore
notebook cahier m, carnet m

nothing else rien d'autre
nothing for me rien pour moi
nothing to declare rien à déclarer
notice board tableau m d'affichage
notify, to informer, prévenir
November novembre m
now maintenant,
nudist beach plage f pour nudistes
number *(telephone)* numéro m; **sorry, wrong number** désolé, faux numéro
number plate plaque f d'immatriculation
nurse infirmière f
nursery slope *(skiing)* piste f pour débutants
nylon nylon m

O

o'clock, it's... il est... heures
observatory observatoire m
occupied occupé(e)
October octobre m
odds *(betting)* cote f
of de
of course bien sûr
off-peak hors saison
off-road (multipurpose) vehicle véhicule m tout-terrain, quatre-quatre m
office bureau m
often souvent
oil huile f
oily *(hair)* gras
okay d'accord
old vieux (vieille)
old-fashioned démodé(e)
on *(day, date)* le...; *(position)* sur
on, to be *(showing)* passer
on/off switch interrupteur m
on board *(ship)* à bord; *(train)* dans le train
on foot à pied,
on the left à gauche
on the other side of... de l'autre côté de...,
on the right à droite
once une fois f; **once a week** une fois par semaine

one un(e);
one like that un(e) comme ceci
one-way ticket aller-simple m ticket/billet aller m
open ouvert(e); ~ **to the public** ouvert(e) au public
open, to ouvrir; *(shop)*
opening hours heures fpl d'ouverture,
opera opéra m; ~ **house** opéra m,
operation opération f
operator *(tel.)* conducteur m
opposite en face de
optician opticien m,
or ou
orange *(color)* orange; *(fruit)* orange f
orchestra orchestre m
order, to commander; *(taxi)* appeler
organized organisé(e)
others autres
our notre, nos; **ours** à nous
out: he's out il est sorti
outdoor(s) à l'extérieur
outdoor pool piscine f en plein air
outside dehors,
oven four m
over there là-bas,
overcharged: I've been overcharged on m'a fait payer trop cher
overdone *(food)* trop cuit(e)
overdraft découvert m
overdrawn à découvert
overheat, to surchauffer
overnight service *(photo)* développement en 24h
owe: how much do I owe you? combien vous dois-je?
own: on my own tout(e) seul(e)
owner propriétaire m

P

p.m. de l'après-midi m
pacifier sucette f, tétine f
pack paquet m; ~ **of cigarettes** paquet m de cigarettes
pack of cards jeu m de cartes
pack, to faire les valises
package colis m

---

packed lunch panier m repas m, repas m froid
paddling pool petit bassin m
padlock cadenas m
pail seau m
pain, to be in avoir mal, souffrir
pain killer analgésique m; calmant m
paint, to peindre
painter peintre m
painting tableau m
pair of, a une paire, deux
pajamas pyjama m/sing.
palace palais m
panorama panorama m
panties culotte f
pantomime pantomime f
pants pantalon m
paper papier m; ~ **napkin** serviette f en papier
paraffin pétrole m
paralysis paralysie f
parcel *(package)* paquet m
pardon? pardon?
parents parents mpl
park parc m,
park, to se garer
parking stationnement m; ~ **disc** disque m de stationnement; ~ **lot** parking m; ~ **meter** parcmètre m; ~ **space** emplacement m de parking
parliament building parlement m
partner partenaire m/f
parts *(components)* pièces fpl
party *(social)* soirée f, réception f; *(celebration)* fête f
pass col m
pass, to passer
pass through, to être en transit
passenger passager(-ère) m/f
passport passeport m; ~ **control**
pastry shop pâtisserie f
patch, to raccommoder
path sentier m, chemin m
patient patient m
pavement trottoir m

pay, to payer; **~ a fine** payer une amende; **~ by credit card** payer avec une carte de crédit

pay phone téléphone public m

paying (*hotel*); (*restaurant*); (*shopping*)

peak pic m, sommet m

pebbly beach plage f de galets

pedalo pédalo m

pedestrian crossing passage m piétons

pedestrian zone zone f piétonnière

pen stylo m

pencil crayon m de papier

penicillin pénicilline f

penknife canif m

penpal correspondant(e) m/f

pensioner retraité(e) m

people gens mpl; **~ carrier** (*minivan*) monospace m

pepper poivre m

per: per day par jour m; **per hour** par heure f; **per night** par nuit f; **per week** par semaine f,

performance représentation f

perhaps peut-être

period période f; (*menstrual*) règles fpl; **~ pains** règles fpl douloureuses

perm permanente f

permit permis m

personal stereo baladeur m, walkman® m

pet (*n*) animal m de compagnie

petrol essence f; **~ can** bidon m d'essence

pharmacy pharmacie f; droguerie f

phone téléphone m; **~ call** appel m téléphonique; **~ card** télécarte f; carte f de téléphone (➤ telephone)

photo, to take a prendre une photo

photo (passport-size) photo f d'identité f

photocopier photocopieur m

photographer photographe m

photography photographie f

phrase expression f; **~ book** guide m de conversation

piano piano m

pick up, to aller chercher

picnic pique-nique m

picnic area aire f de pique-nique

piece morceau m; **a ~ of** un morceau de

Pill (contraceptive) pilule f

pillow oreiller m; **~ case** taie m d'oreiller

pilot light veilleuse f

pink rose

pint (= . *liter*) pinte f

pipe pipe f; **~ cleaners** cure-pipe m; **~ tobacco** tabac m à pipe

piste map plan m des pistes

pitch (*for camping*) emplacement m; **~ charge** prix m de l'emplacement

pity: it's a pity c'est dommage

place (*area*) endroit m; (*space*) place f

place a bet, to faire un pari

plain (*not patterned*) uni(e)

plane avion m

plans projets mpl

plant plante f

plastic bag sac m plastique

plate assiette f,

platform quai m,

play, to jouer; (*drama*) jouer; **~ an instrument** jouer (d'un instrument); **~ music** jouer (de la musique)

playground cour f de récréation

playgroup garderie f

playing cards cartes fpl à jouer

playwright auteur m

pleasant (*nice*) agréable

please s'il vous plaît

pliers pinces fpl, tenailles fpl

plug (*socket*) prise f; (*on flex*) fiche f

plumber plombier m

point to, to montrer

poison poison m

poisonous toxique

police police f; **~ report [certificate]** certificat de police; **~ station** commissariat m (de police),

pollen count taux m de pollen

pond étang m

pony ride promenade f sur un poney

pop music musique f pop
popular populaire
port *(harbor)* port m
porter *(hotel)* porteur m; *(station)* portier m
portion portion f
possible, as soon as dès que possible
possibly peut-être
post *(mail)* courrier m
post office (bureau m de) poste f
post, to poster
postbox boîte f aux lettres
postcard carte f postale,
poste restante poste f restante
poster affiche f, poster m
postman facteur m
pottery poterie f
pound *(sterling)* livre f (sterling)
power failure [cut] coupure f de courant
power point prise f électrique
practice: to practice speaking French s'entraîner à parler français
pregnant, to be être enceinte
prescribe, to prescrire
prescription ordonnance f,
present *(gift)* cadeau m
press, to *(iron)* repasser
pretty joli(e)
priest prêtre m
primus stove réchaud m (de camping)
prison prison f
private bathroom salle f de bains particulière
probably probablement
program programme m; ~ **of events** programme m des spectacles
prohibited interdit(e)
promenade deck pont m promenade
pronounce, to prononcer
properly correctement
Protestant protestant(e)
public building bâtiment m public
public holiday jour m férié
pullover pullover m, pull m
pump pompe f; *(gas)* pompe f à essence

puppet show spectacle m de marionettes
pure *(fabric)* pur(e)
purple violet(tte)
purse porte-monnaie m
push-chair poussette f
put aside [by], to *(in shop)* mettre de côté
put up: can you put me up for the night? pouvez-vous m'héberger pour la nuit?
put: where can I put…? où puis-je mettre…?
pyjamas pyjama m/sing.

Q

quality qualité f
quantity quantité f
quarantine quarantaine f
quarter past/after et quart
quarter to/before moins le quart
quarter, a un quart
quarter-deck *(ship)* gaillard m d'arrière
quartz à quartz
quay quai m
Quebec Québec m
Quebecois Québécois m/f
queen *(cards)* reine f; *(chess)* reine f
question question f
quick rapide
quickest: what's the quickest way to…? quel est le chemin le plus court pour…?
quickly vite
quiet silencieux(-ieuse)
quieter plus calme,
quoits jeu m de palet

R

rabbi rabbin m
race *(cars/horses)* course f; ~ **track [course]** *(track)* hippodrome m
racing bike vélo m de course
racket *(tennis, squash)* raquette f
radiator radiateur m électrique

radio radio f
railroad/railway voie ferrée f
rain, to pleuvoir
raincoat imperméable m
rape viol m
rappeling descente f en rappel
rare *(steak)* saignant; *(unusual)* rare
rarely rarement
rash éruption f cutanée
razor rasoir m; **~ blades** lames fpl de rasoir
re-enter, to entrer à nouveau
reading *(interest)* lecture f;
~ glasses lunettes fpl de vue
ready, to be être prêt(e),
real *(genuine)* véritable
real estate agent agent m immobilier
receipt reçu m; ticket de caisse m,
reception (desk) accueil m; réception f
receptionist réceptioniste m/f
reclaim, to réclamer
reclining seat siège inclinable m
recommend, to recommander; **can you ~...?** pouvez-vous recommander...?,
record *(lp)* disque m
red rouge; **~ wine** vin m rouge
refreshments boissons fpl
refrigerator réfrigérateur m, frigo m
refund remboursement m
regards to amitiés à
region région f
register receipt ticket m de caisse
registered mail courrier m en recommandé
registration form fiche f d'inscription
registration number numéro m d'immatriculation
regular *(gas)* ordinaire; *(size of drink)* moyen(ne)
religion religion f
remember: I don't remember je ne me souviens pas
rent, to louer;
to rent out louer; **for ~** à louer
repair, to réparer,

repairs réparations fpl; *(car)*
repeat, to répéter; **please repeat that** pouvez-vous répéter ça?
replacement remplacement m;
~ part pièce de rechange f
report, to signaler
representative représentant m
required, to be il faut +inf.
reservation *(table)* réservation f; *(hotel)*; *(train)*; *(restaurant)*; *(plane)*; **~ desk** bureau m des réservations
reserve, to *(tickets)* réserver; *(table)*
rest, to se reposer
restaurant restaurant m,
restrooms toilettes fpl; WC mpl
retired, to be être retraité(e)
return ticket (ticket/billet) m aller-retour
return, to *(give back)* rapporter; *(come back)* revenir
reverse the charges, to appeler en P.C.V.
revolting dégoûtant(e)
rheumatism rhumatisme m
rib côte f
right juste; *(correct)* bon(ne); **that's ~** c'est vrai; **on the ~** à droite,
right of way priorité f; droit de passage m
right-hand drive volant m à droite
right-handed droitier(-ière)
ring bague f
rip-off: it's a rip-off c'est du vol
river rivière f; **~ cruise** croisière f sur la rivière
road route f; **~ accident** accident m de la route; **~ assistance** assistance f routière; **~ map** carte f routière; **~ signs** pancartes fpl (routières)
robbed, to be être volé
robbery cambriolage m
rock climbing escalade f
rocks rochers mpl
roller blades patins mpl à roulettes
romantic romantique
roof *(house/car)* toit m
roof-rack fixe-au-toit m
rook *(chess)* tour f

room chambre f; **~ with a bath** chambre f avec bain; **~ service** service m de chambre
rope corde f
rouge fard m à joues
round *(adj)* rond(e); *(of golf)* partie f; **it's my round** c'est ma tournée
roundabout rond-point m
round-trip ticket (ticket/billet) m aller et retour,
route chemin m; route f; itinéraire m
row boat canot m (à rames)
rubbish *(trash)* ordures fpl
rude, to be être impoli(e)/ grossier(-ière)
rugby rugby m
ruins ruines fpl
run into, to *(crash)* rentrer dans
run out: I've run out of gas je suis en panne d'essence
rush hour heure f de pointe

S

safe coffre-fort m; *(not dangerous)* sans danger
safe, to feel se sentir en sécurité
safety sécurité f
safety pins épingles fpl de sûreté
sag: the bed sags le lit s'affaisse
sailboat bateau à voiles, voilier m
sailboard planche f à voile
sailboarding faire de la planche à voile
salad salade f
sales tax TVA f; **~ receipt** reçu m pour la TVA
salt sel m
same le/la même; **the same again please** la même chose, s'il vous plaît
sand sable m
sandals sandales fpl
sandwich sandwich m
sandy beach plage f de sable
sanitary napkins serviettes fpl hygiéniques
satellite TV télévision f par câble

satisfied: I'm not satisfied with it je n'en suis pas satisfait(e)
Saturday samedi m
sauna sauna m
saw *(tool)* scie f
say: how do you say…? comment dites-vous…?; **what did he say?** qu'a-t-il dit?
scarf écharpe f
scenic route route f touristique
scheduled flight vol m normal
school école f
scientist scientifique m/f
scissors ciseaux mpl
scooter scooter m
Scotland Écosse f
Scottish écossais(e)
scouring pad tampon à récurer
screw vis f
screwdriver tournevis m
scrubbing brush brosse f dure
sculptor sculpteur
sea mer f
seasick, I feel j'ai le mal de mer
season ticket carte f d'abonnement
seasoning assaisonnement m
seat siège m; *(place)* place f,
second second(e), deuxième; **~ class** deuxième classe f; **~ floor** *(UK)* deuxième étage m; *(US)* premier étage
second-hand d'occasion
secretary secrétaire f/m
security guard garde m chargé de la sécurité
sedative sédatif m
see, to voir; *(inspect)*; *(witness)*
see s.o. again, to revoir quelqu'un
self-employed, to be être à son compte
self-service self-service m
sell, to vendre
send, to envoyer; *(help)*
senior citizen personne f âgée
separated, to be être séparé(e)
separately séparément
September septembre m

serious grave
served, to be *(meal)* être servi
service (charge) service m; **is service included?** le service est-il compris?
service station *(gas)* station f service services
set menu menu m à prix fixe
seven sept
sex *(gender)* sexe m; *(act)* rapports mpl sexuels
shady ombragé(e)
shallow peu profond(e)
shampoo shampooing m;
~ for dry/oily hair shampooing m pour cheveux secs/gras
shape forme f
share, to partager
sharp pointu(e)
shatter, to *(windshield/windscreen)* casser
shaver rasoir m (électrique);
~ socket prise f pour rasoir
shaving brush blaireau m (à raser)
shaving cream crème f à raser
she elle
sheet *(bed)* drap m
shelf rayon m, étagère f
sherbet sorbet m
ship bateau m; navire m
shirt chemise f
shivery, to feel avoir des frissons
(electric) shock choc (électrique) m
shoelaces lacets mpl
shoepolish cirage m
shoe repair ressemelage m
shoemaker cordonnier m
shoes chaussures fpl
shop magasin m
shop assistant vendeur(-euse) m/f
shopkeeper commerçant(e) m/f
shopping: ~ area rues fpl commerçantes; **~ basket** panier m; **~ cart** chariot m **~ mall** centre m commercial; **~ list** liste f de commissions **shopping, to go** aller faire les courses
shore *(sea/lake)* rivage m

short court(e)
shorts short m
shoulder épaule f
shovel pelle f
show, to montrer; **can you show me?** pouvez-vous me montrer?,
shower douche f;
~ gel gel m pour la douche
shrunk: they've shrunk ils ont rétréci
shut fermé(e)
shutter volet m
shy timide
sick: to feel ~ être malade
I'm going to be ~ je vais vomir
sickbay *(ship)* infirmerie f
side *(of road)* côté m
side street rue f transversale
sidewalk, on the sur le trottoir
sights panorama m
sightseeing tour visite f touristique
sightseeing, to go faire du tourisme; *(in town)* visiter la ville
sign *(road)* panneau f,
signpost pancarte f
silk soie f
silver argent m
silverplate plaqué-argent m
similar, to be ressembler à
since *(time)* depuis
singer chanteur m
single room chambre f à un lit
single, to be être célibataire
sink évier m
sister sœur f
sit, to s'asseoir,
sit down, please asseyez-vous, s'il vous plaît
six six
size taille f; *(shoes)* pointure f
skates patins mpl
skating rink patinoire f
ski: ~ bindings fixations fpl; **~ boots** chaussures fpl de ski; **~ instructor** moniteur m de ski; **~ poles** bâtons mpl; **~ suit** combinaison f de ski; **~ trousers** pantalon m de ski
ski lift remonte-pente m

ski school école f de ski
skid: we skidded nous avons glissé
skiing ski m
skin peau f
skirt jupe f
skis skis mpl
slalom slalom m
sledge luge m
sledge run piste f de luge
sleep, to dormir
sleeping bag sac m de couchage
sleeping car wagon-lit m
sleeping pill somnifère m
sleeve manche f
slice tranche f
slide film pellicule f pour diapositives
slip *(undergarment)* combinaison f
slippers pantoufles fpl
slope *(ski)* piste f, pente f
slot machine machine f à sous
slow lent(e)
slow down! ralentissez!
slow, to be *(clock)* retarder
slowly lentement; *(speak)*,
SLR camera appareil-photo m
reflex
small petit(e); *(drink)*
small change (petite) monnaie f
smoke, to fumer; **I don't smoke** je ne
fume pas
smoking *(adj)* fumeur,
smoky: it's too smoky c'est trop
enfumé
snack bar snack bar m, buffet m
snacks casse-croûte m
sneakers (chaussures fpl de) tennis
snorkel tuba m (plongée)
snow neige f
snow, to neiger
snowed in, to be être bloqué par
la neige
snowplow chasse-neige m
soap savon m
soap powder lessive f
soccer football m
socket prise f électrique
socks chaussettes fpl

sofa canapé m
sofabed canapé-lit m
soft drink *(soda)* boisson f gazeuse
solarium solarium m
sold out *(concert)* complet
sole *(shoes)* semelle f
some du/de la/de l'/des
someone quelqu'un
something quelque chose
sometimes quelquefois
son fils m,
soon bientôt
soon: as soon as possible dès que
possible
sore throat mal m de gorge;
mal m a la gorge
sore: it's sore ça fait mal
sorry! désolé(e)!
sort sorte f; **a ~ of** une sorte de
sour acide
south sud m
South Africa Afrique f du Sud
South African *(n)* Sud-africain(e) m/f
souvenir souvenir m,
spa ville f thermale
space place f
Spain Espagne f
spare *(extra)* supplémentaire
speak, to parler; **do you speak
English?** parlez-vous anglais?
special requirements régimes mpl
spéciaux
specialist spécialiste m
specimen prise f, analyse f
spectacles lunettes fpl
speed limit limite f de vitesse
speed, to aller trop vite
spell, to épeler
spend, to *(money)* dépenser;
(time) passer
spin-dryer essoreuse f
spine colonne f vertébrale
spoon cuillère f,
sport sport m
sports club club m sportif
sprained, to be être foulé(e)

spring *(season)* printemps m; *(water)* source f

square *(adj)* carré(e)

squash *(sport)* squash m

stadium stade m

stain tache f

stainless steel acier m inoxydable

stairs escalier m/sing.

stale rassis(e)

stall: the engine stalls le moteur cale

stalls *(orchestra)* parterre m

stamp timbre m,

stamp machine distributeur m (automatique) de timbres

stand in line, to faire la queue

standby ticket billet m sans garantie

start *(n)* début m

start, to *(begin)* commencer; *(car)* démarrer

starter entrée f

statement déclaration f; *(police)* déposition f

station gare f,

station wagon (voiture f) break m

statue statue f

stay *(n)* séjour m

stay, to *(lodge)* rester; loger; *(remain)* rester

steak house (restaurant)-gril m

stereo stéréo f

stern *(ship)* poupe f

stiff neck torticolis m

still: I'm still waiting j'attends encore

sting piqûre f

stocking bas mpl

stolen, to be être volé(e)

stomach estomac m;
~ ache mal m à l'estomac

stool *(feces)* selles fpl

stop *(bus/tram)* arrêt m; *(metro)* station f

stop, to s'arrêter; **~ here** arrêtez-vous ici; **I'll stop by** je passerai

stopover halte f

store magasin m

store detective agent m de surveillance

store guide plan du magasin m

storekeeper commerçant(e) m/f

stove cuisinière f,

straight ahead tout droit

strained muscle muscle m froissé

strange étrange

straw *(drinking)* paille f

stream ruisseau m

string ficelle f

striped *(patterned)* à rayures

stoller poussette f

strong fort

student étudiant(e) m/f,

study, to étudier

stunning stupéfiant(e)

stupid: that was stupid! c'était bête!

sturdy solide

style style m

styling mousse mousse f coiffante

subtitled, to be être sous-titré

subway métro m; **~ station** station de métro m,

suede daim m

suggest, to suggérer

suit costume m

suitable for, to be convenir à

summer été m

sun block écran m total

sun lounger chaise f longue

sunbathe, to prendre un bain de soleil

sunburn coup m de soleil

Sunday dimanche m

sunglasses lunettes fpl de soleil

sunstroke insolation f

suntan lotion crème f solaire

super *(gas)* super

superb superbe

supermarket supermarché m

supplement supplément m,

suppositories suppositoires mpl

sure: are you sure? êtes-vous sûr(e)?

surfboard planche f de surf

surname nom m de famille

suspicious suspect(e)

swallow, to avaler

sweater pullover m, pull m

sweatshirt sweatshirt m
sweet *(taste)* sucré(e)
sweets bonbons mpl
swelling enflure f
swim, to nager, se baigner
swimming natation f;
~ pool piscine f;
~ trunks slip de bain m
swimsuit maillot de bain m
Swiss *(person)* Suisse m/f
switch *(electric)* interrupteur m
switch on, to allumer
switch off, to éteindre
Switzerland Suisse f
swollen, to be être enflé(e)
symptoms symptômes mpl
synagogue synagogue f
synthetic synthétique

T

T-shirt T-shirt m
table table f
table cloth nappe f
table tennis tennis m de table
tablet comprimé m
take away, to à emporter
take photographs, to prendre des photos,
take someone home, to raccompagner
take, to *(bus)* prendre; *(carry)* emporter; *(medicine)* prendre; *(last)* durer; *(to a place)* emmener;
I'll take it *(purchase)* je le/la prends; *(room)*
takeaway *(takeout)* plats mpl à emporter
taken *(occupied)* occupé(e), pris(e)
talcum powder talc m
talk, to parler
tall grand(e)
tampons tampons mpl
tan bronzage m
tarpaulin tapis de sol
taste goût m
taxi taxi m,
taxi driver chauffeur m de taxi

taxi stand station f de taxi
tea thé m
tea bags sachets mpl de thé
teacher instituteur m, professeur m
team équipe f
teaspoon cuillère f à café,
teenager adolescent(e) m/f
telephone téléphone m;
~ bill note f de téléphone; **~ booth** cabine f téléphonique; **~ calls** coups mpl de téléphone; **~ directory** annuaire m; **~ kiosk** cabine f téléphonique; **~ number** numéro m de téléphone
(➤ phone)
telephone, to téléphoner
television télévision f
tell, to dire; **tell me** dites-moi
temperature *(water)* température f; *(body)*
temporary temporaire
ten dix
tendon tendon m
tennis tennis m;
~ ball balle m de tennis; **~ court** court m de tennis
tent tente f; **~ pegs** piquets mpl de tente; **~ pole** montant m de tente; grand piquet de tente
terrible terrible
tetanus tétanos m
thank you merci,
that cela; **~ one** celui-là (celle-là); **that's all** c'est tout
thawing snow neige f fondue
theater théâtre m,
theft vol m; cambriolage m
their leur
theirs à eux (à elles)
it's ~ c'est le/la/les leur(s)
them les; *(to them)* à eux (à elles); **for ~** pour eux/elles
theme park parc m d'attraction
then *(time)* alors, ensuite
there là
there is... il y a...
thermometer thermomètre m
thermos flask bouteille f thermos

these ceux-ci, celles-ci
they eux (elles)
thick épais(se)
thief voleur m
thigh cuisse f
thin mince
think: I think je pense
third troisième; a ~ un tiers
third party insurance assurance f au tiers
thirsty assoiffé(e)
this one celui-ci (celle-ci)
those ceux-là (celles-là)
thousand mille
thread fil m
three trois
throat gorge f; ~ lozenges pastilles fpl pour la gorge
thrombosis thrombose f
through à travers
thumb pouce m
Thursday jeudi m
ticket billet m; ticket m; ~ agency agence f de spectacles; ~ office guichet m
tie cravate f
tie pin épingle f à cravate
tight (clothing) serré(e)
tights collant m
time heure f; free ~ temps m libre; on ~ à l'heure
timetable horaire m
tin (can) boîte f; ~ opener ouvre-boîte m
tin foil papier m d'aluminium
tinted (glass/lens) teinté(e)
tip pourboire m
tire (auto) pneu m
tired, to be être fatigué(e)
tissues mouchoirs mpl en papier
to (place) jusqu'à
toaster grille-pain m
tobacco tabac m
tobogganing, to go faire de la luge
today aujourd'hui
toe orteil m
together ensemble

toilet paper papier m toilette
toiletries
tomorrow demain,
tongs pinces fpl
tonight ce soir; for tonight pour ce soir
tonsillitis angine f
tonsils amygdales fpl
too (also) aussi; (extreme) trop; ~ much trop
tooth dent f
toothache mal m de dent
toothbrush brosse f à dents
toothpaste dentifrice m
top sommet m, bouchon m
top floor étage m supérieur
torch lampe f de poche/électrique
torn, to be (muscle) être déchiré(e)
tote pari mutuel m
tough (food) dur(e)
tour tour m; visite f
tour guide guide m touristique
tour operator organisateur m de voyages
tour representative représentant m de vacances
tourist touriste m
tourist information office office m de tourisme
tow rope corde f de remorquage
tow, to remorquer
towards vers, en direction de
towel serviette f
tower tour f
town ville f
toy jouet m
track piste f, sentier m
tracksuit jogging m, survêtement m
traditional traditionnel(le)
traffic circulation f
traffic jam embouteillage m, bouchon m
traffic violation/offence infraction f au code de la route
trail chemin m, sentier m
trailer caravane f

trailer park terrain m de camping caravaning
train train m; *(subway)* rame f
train station gare f
train times horaires mpl des trains
trainers chaussures fpl de sport
tram tram m,
translate, to traduire
translation traduction f
translator traducteur(-trice) m/f
trash ordures fpl
trash can poubelle f
travel agency agence f de voyages
travel sickness mal m des transports
travel, to voyager
traveler's check chèque m de voyage
tray plateau m
tree arbre m
tremendous formidable
trip voyage m; promenade f
truck camion m
true north plein nord m
true: that's not true ce n'est pas vrai
try on, to essayer
Tuesday mardi m
tunnel tunnel m
turn, to tourner; **~ down** *(volume, heat)* baisser; **~ off** arrêter, éteindre; **~ on** mettre en marche, allumer; **~ up** *(volume, heat)* monter, augmenter
turning intersection f
TV télévision f; **~ room** salle f de télévision; **~-listings magazine** magazine m de télévision
tweezers pince f à épiler
twelve douze
twice deux fois
twin beds lits mpl jumeaux
two deux
two-door car voiture f deux portes
type type m; **what ~?** quel genre?
typical typique

U

ugly laid(e)

U.K. Royaume-Uni
ulcer ulcère m
umbrella parapluie m; **beach ~** parasol
uncle oncle m
unconscious, to be avoir perdu connaissance; être sans connaissance
under *(place)* sous
underdone *(food)* pas assez cuit(e)
underpants slip m/sing.
underpass passage m sous-terrain
understand, to comprendre;
do you understand? vous comprenez?
I don't understand je ne comprends pas
undress, to se déshabiller
unfortunately malheureusement
uniform uniforme m
unit unité f
university université f
unleaded gas essence f sans plomb
unlock, to ouvrir
unpleasant désagréable
unscrew, to dévisser
until jusqu'à
upper *(berth)* supérieur(e)
upset stomach mal m de ventre
upstairs en haut
up to jusqu'à
urgent urgent
us: for/with us pour/avec nous
U.S. Etats-Unis mpl
use, to utiliser
use: for my personal use pour mon usage personnel
useful utile

V

vacancy chambre f libre
vacant libre
vacate, to libérer
vacation, on en vacances fpl,
vaccinated against, to be être vacciné(e) contre
vaccination vaccin m, vaccination f
valet service service m de nettoyage complet
valid valable

validate, to *(ticket)* composter
valley vallée f
valuable de (grande) valeur
value valeur f
vegetables légumes mpl
vegetarian *(adj/n)* végétarien(ne) m/f; **to be vegetarian** être végétarien(ne)
vehicle véhicule m; **~ registration document** carte f grise
vein veine f
velvet velours m
venereal disease maladie f vénérienne
very très
vest maillot m de corps
vet(erinarian) vétérinaire m
video cassette vidéo f; **~ game** jeu vidéo m; **~ recorder** magnétoscope m
view: with a view of the sea avec vue sur la mer
viewpoint belvédère m; point m de vue
village village m
vineyard vigne f
visa visa m
visit visite f
visit, to *(sights)* visiter; *(person in hospital)* venir voir
visiting hours heures fpl de visite
visitor center centre m pour visiteurs
vitamin pills vitamines fpl
voice voix f
voltage voltage m
vomit, to vomir

W

waist taille f
wait, to attendre; **~ for** attendre
wait! attendez!
Waiter! garçon! m
waiting room salle f d'attente
Waitress! mademoiselle! f
wake, to *(self)* se réveiller; *(s.o. else)* réveiller
wake-up call appel m de réveil
Wales Pays de Galles m

walk promenade f; **to go for a ~** aller faire une promenade
walk home, to rentrer chez soi à pied
walking marche f; **~ boots** chaussures fpl de marche; **~ route** circuit m de randonnée; **~ (hiking) gear** équipement m pour la marche
wall mur m
wallet portefeuille m
want, to vouloir
ward *(hospital)* chambre f
warm *(weather)* chaud
warm, to réchauffer
warmer plus chaud(e)
wash, to laver
washbasin lavabo m
washer *(for faucet)* joint m
washing: ~ instructions conseils mpl de lavage; **~ machine** machine f à laver; **~ powder** lessive f
washing, to do faire la vaisselle
washing-up liquid liquide m vaisselle m
wasp guêpe f
watch montre f
watch band bracelet m de montre m
watch TV, to regarder la télé(vision)
watchmaker horloger m
water eau f; **~ bottle** bouillote m; **~ heater** chauffe-eau m
water skis skis mpl nautiques
waterfall cascade f
waterproof imperméable, étanche; **~ jacket** blouson m imperméable
waterskiing ski m nautique
wave vague f
waxing épilation f à la cire
way: I've lost my ~ je me suis perdu(e); **on the ~** sur la route
we nous
weak *(coffee)* clair
I feel ~ je me sens faible
wear, to porter
weather temps m
weather forecast météo f
wedding mariage m; **~ ring** alliance f

Wednesday mercredi m
week semaine f
weekend weekend m; **on [at] the weekend** le weekend; **weekend rate** tarif m de week-end
weekly ticket ticket m/billet m pour la semaine
weight: my weight is... je pèse...
welcome to... bienvenue à...
Welsh (adj) gallois(e)
Welsh person Gallois(e) m/f
west ouest m
wetsuit combinaison f de plongée
what? qu'est-ce que?
what sort of? quel genre de?
what time...? à quelle heure...?
what's the time? quelle heure est-il?
when? quand?, à quelle heure?
where? où; **~ are you from?** d'où êtes-vous?; **~ can we...?** où pouvons-nous...?
which quel(le)
~ one? lequel (laquelle)?
while pendant que
white blanc(he); **~ wine** vin m blanc
who? qui?
whole: the whole day toute la journée
whose? à qui?
why? pourquoi
wide large
wife femme f
wildlife faune f et flore f
windbreaker coupe-vent
window fenêtre f; (shop) vitrine f; **~ seat** siège m côté hublot
windshield [windscreen] pare-brise m
windsurfer planche f à voile
windy, it's il y a du vent m
wine vin m; **~box** caisse de vins; **~ list** carte f des vins
winery vignoble m
winter hiver m
wishes: best wishes to... meilleurs vœux à...
with avec
withdraw, to (money) retirer
without sans

witness témoin m
wood (forest, material) bois m
wool laine
work, to (job) travailler; (function) marcher; fonctionner
worry: I'm worried je me fais du souci
worse pire
it's become worse ça a empiré
worst le/la/les pire(s)
worth: is it worth seeing? est-ce que ça vaut la peine d'être vu?
wound blessure f
wrap up, to faire un paquet-cadeau
write down, to écrire
write soon! écrivez [écris] vite!
writing pad papier m à lettres
wrong faux (fausse); mauvais(e)
~ number (phone) faux numéro m

XYZ

x-ray radio f
yacht yacht m
year année f
yellow jaune
yes oui
yesterday hier
yogurt yaourt m
you (sing/pl) vous, tu
to ~ à vous; à toi
young jeune
your votre/vos; ton/ta/tes
yours à vous, à toi; **it's ~** c'est le/la vôtre/les vôtres; c'est le tien/la tienne/les tien(ne)s
youth hostel auberge f de jeunesse
zebra crossing passage m piéton
zero zéro m
zip(per) fermeture f éclair
zone zone f
zoo zoo m
zoology zoologie f

DICTIONARY FRENCH-ENGLISH

This French-English dictionary concentrates on all the areas where you may need to de-code written French: hotels, public buildings, restaurants, shops, ticket offices and transportation. It will also help with understanding forms, maps, product labels, road signs and operating instuctions (for telephones, parking meters, etc.).

If you can't locate the exact sign, you may find key words or terms listed separately.

[Note: entries are not listed under the particles: **à**, **au**, **aux**, **d'**, **de**, **des**, **le**, **l'**, **la**, or **les**.]

A

à la ... … style
abonnement season ticket
abribus bus shelter
l'accès aux véhicules est interdit pendant la traversée no access to car decks during crossing
accès réservé aux voyageurs munis de billets ticket holders only
accôtements non stabilisés soft edges
ACF French automobile association
acier steel
ACS Swiss Automobile Association
administration public building
adresse domicile home address
adressez-vous à la réception ask at reception
aérogare airport, air terminal
affranchissement stamps
agence de spectacles ticket agency
agence de voyage travel agent
agence immobilière real estate agent
agent de la RATP subway ticket inspector
aire de croisement passing area
aire de pique-nique picnic area
aire de repos/de stationnement rest area
aller-retour round-trip

aller-simple one-way trip
allumez vos feux de route/croisement/phares switch on/use headlights
alpinisme mountaineering
altitude par rapport au niveau de la mer height above sea level
ambassade embassy
amélioré improved
ameublement furniture
ampoules auto-cassables easy-to-open capsules [ampules]
anglais English
annuaire téléphonique directory
annulé cancelled
août August
appareils photo interdits no photography
appuyer pour ouvrir press to open
après-demain the day after tomorrow
l'après-midi p.m.
argent money; silver
arrêt de bus bus stop
arrêt facultatif request stop
arrêt interdit no stopping
arrêtez votre moteur turn off your engine
arrivées arrivals
arrondissement administrative district
articles vendus avec défaut damaged goods
ascenseur elevator
atelier d'artiste studio
attachez vos ceintures (de sécurité) fasten your seat belt
attendez votre billet wait for your ticket
attendre la tonalité wait for tone
attente d'environ ... mn wait approx … mins.
attention caution, warning
attention à la fermeture automatique des portières warning! automatic doors!
attention à la marche mind the step
attention bétail warning! cattle!
attention station en courbe mind the gap (subway)
auberge de jeunesse youth hostel
aujourd'hui today
autocar coach
automne fall/autumn
autoroute highway

autoroute à péage toll route
autres directions other directions
avant … before …
avant les repas before meals
avec douche with shower
avec nos remerciements
with thanks
avec plomb leaded
avec salle de bains with bathroom
avec vue sur mer with sea view
avion plane
avis de coup de vent gale warning
avril April

B

baie bay
baignade surveillée supervised swimming
bains publics baths
bande d'arrêt d'urgence hard-shoulder
banlieue suburbs, outskirts
banque bank
bassin pond
bassin d'alimentation reservoir
bateau ship
bateau à vapeur steamer
bateaux-mouches river boats
bazar general store
bd boulevard
berge river bank
bibliothèque library
bienvenue! welcome!
bière beer
bijoutier jeweler's
billet ticket
billet Section Urbaine ticket valid for
métro, RER and suburban train
billets périmés used tickets
"le blanc" household linen
blanchisserie laundry
bois wood
boissons drinks
bonnes affaires bargains
bonnets de bain obligatoires
bathing caps must be worn
boucherie butcher
bouchons traffic jams: delays likely
boulangerie bakery/baker's
boules French game of bowls

bourse stock exchange
bouteille consignée returnable bottle
boutique hors-taxes duty-free shop
BP P.O. Box
braderie discount store, clearance sale
bricolage et jardinage
hardware and garden store
brocante(ur) secondhand shop
brouillard fréquent risk of fog
bureau d'accueil reception center
bureau d'information information desk
bureau de change currency exchange
office
bureau de vente (des billets) ticket office
bureau des objets trouvés lost and found

C

cabine d'essayage fitting room
cabine de bain bathing cabana/hut
cabine de téléphérique cable car cabin
cabinet médical/dentaire
doctor's/dentist's office [surgery]
cachets pills, tablets
cadeau gratuit free gift
cadeaux gifts
caisse checkout, please pay here
caisse 5 articles 5 items or less
caisse d'épargne savings bank
caisse livraison à domicile
checkout for home delivery
caisse rapide/éclair express checkout
caissiers cashiers
camion truck
canne à pêche fishing rod
canton administrative district
caravane trailer
carnet book (of tickets)
carrosserie repair garage
carte d'abonnement season ticket
carte d'assuré social national
insurance card
carte d'embarquement boarding card
carte d'identité ID card
carte orange pass for Paris metro/bus
carte routière road map
carte verte green (insurance) card
carte téléphonique phonecard

les cartes de crédit ne sont pas acceptées credit cards not accepted

caserne de pompiers fire station

casque crash helmet

casser la vitre en cas d'urgence break glass in case of emergency

ce bus dessert … this bus is going to …

ce matin this morning

ce soir this evening

ce train desservira les gares de … this train stops at …

cet appareil rend la monnaie this machine gives change

cédez le passage give way (yield)

ceinture circle (ramparts or mountains)

ceinture de sauvetage lifebelt

centre commercial shopping mall

centre médico-social health clinic

centre ville downtown area

cet après-midi this afternoon

cette machine ne rend pas la monnaie this machine does not give change

CH Switzerland

chaise longue deck chair

chambre d'hôte bed & breakfast

la chambre a besoin d'être faite this room needs making up

chambres à louer rooms to let

chambres libres vacancies

champ field

change currency exchange

changer à change at …

charcuterie delicatessen

charge maximum load limit

chariots carts

chasse hunting

château castle, stately home

chaud hot

chaussée déformée poor/uneven road surface

chaussée glissante/verglacée icy road

chaussures shoes

chemin walk(way), path

les chèques ne sont pas acceptés checks not accepted

chez at (the home/place of)

chien méchant beware of the dog

choisir la destination/la zone select destination/zone

au choix of your choice

Chronopost® express mail

chutes de pierres falling rocks

cimetière cemetery

cinéma permanent continuous performance

cinq ampères 5 amp

circulation interdite closed to traffic

circulation opposée traffic from the opposite direction

circulation ralentie slow traffic

citoyens (non-)européens (non-)EU citizens

classé monument historique listed building

clé minute keys while you wait

climatisé air conditioned

club de voile sailing club

coiffeur hairdresser

coiffeur pour hommes barber

coiffeur-visagiste stylist

col (mountain) pass

Colissimo express parcel post

collège secondary (U.S. middle) school

colline hill

commence à … begins at …

commissariat (de police) police station

complet full, sold out

complexe industriel industrial estate

composez votre code confidentiel dial your PIN

composez votre numéro dial number

compostez votre billet validate/punch your ticket

compris included (in the price)

compteur électrique electric meter

comptoir d'enregistrement check-in counter

concierge caretaker

concours contest

conducteur/conductrice driver

confiseur confectioner's

confiture jam

congelé frozen

conseillé recommended

conseils de préparation cooking recommendations

conservateurs preservatives

à conserver au congélateur/réfrigérateur keep frozen/refrigerated

à conserver au frais keep in a cool place

conservez votre ticket de caisse/titre de transport keep your receipt/ticket

consigné returnable

consigne automatique luggage lockers

consigne manuelle baggage check

consommation au comptoir drink at the bar

à consommer de préférence avant fin ... best before end ...

consultations consulting room, outpatients

conteneur papier newspapers only

conteneur verre bottle bank

contre-allée service road

contrôle des douanes customs control

convient aux végétariens/végétaliens suitable for vegetarians/vegans

convoi exceptionnel long vehicle

cordonnier cobbler's

correspondance connection

côte coast

couloir d'autobus bus lane

cour yard

cours du change exchange rate

cousu main hand-sewn

crème peaux grasses/sèches moisturizer for oily/dry skin

crème solaire (indice 8) (factor 8) sun cream

crémerie dairy

croisement crossing, intersection

croisières cruises, river trips

à croquer chewable

CRS French riot police

c centime (1/100 of a franc)

cuir leather

cuisine kitchen

cuisson sans décongélation cook without defrosting

CV horsepower

D

dames ladies (toilets)

danger de mort danger of death

date d'expiration expiration date

date de fraîcheur best before (date)

date de naissance date of birth

date de péremption use-by date

date limite de vente sell by date

de ... à ... from ... to ...

débranché disconnected

début d'autoroute expressway entrance

déchetterie waste point

déchirer ici tear here

décoration home furnishings

décrochez lift receiver

défense d'entrer keep out

dégustation de vins wine tasting

demain tomorrow

demander un vendeur please ask for assistance

demi-pension half board

déposer vos clés à la réception leave keys at reception

dépôt d'ordures interdit don't dump trash

dépôts et retraits deposits and withdrawals

dernière entrée à ... latest entry at ... p.m.

dernière station essence avant l'autoroute/la voie rapide last gas station before the expressway

descente en rappel abseiling

deuxième étage second (U.S. third) floor

déviation obligatoire pour véhicules lourds diversion for trucks, truck route

devises étrangères foreign currency

dimanche Sunday

Dimanche de Pâques Easter Sunday

directeur manager

disquaire record dealer

dissoudre dans un peu d'eau dissolve in water

distribanque/distributeur automatique ATM/cash-dispenser

dons donations

dos d'âne (en voie de formation) ramps

douanes customs

doublé dubbed (film)

douches showers

eau courante running water
eau (non) potable (non) drinking water
échange exchange
échangeur (d'autoroute) freeway interchange/junction
échelle scale
école school
écran total sun block cream
effets indésirables side effects
église church
électro-ménager electrical goods
embarquement en cours boarding now
embarquement immédiat last call
emplacement gravier/herbeux/sableux stone/grass/sand (camping site)
empruntez le passage souterrain use the underpass
en bas downstairs
en cas d'accident, prière de téléphoner à.../de contacter.. in case of breakdown, phone/contact …
en cas d'incendie in the event of fire
en chantier under construction/proposed
en dehors des repas without food
en haut upstairs
en plein air open air
en (projet de) construction under construction/proposed
en retard delayed
… en vente ici … on sale here
enceinte city wall
enfants children
entre … et … between … and … (time)
entrée entrance, way in
entrée gratuite admission free
entrée interdite no entry
entrée – ne pas stationner do not block entrance
entrer par la porte arrière/avant enter by the rear/front door
enregistrement check in
envois en nombre bulk mailing
épicerie grocer's
épicerie fine delicatessen
équitation horseback riding
escalade rock climbing

escalier de service back stairs/service stairs
espèces cash
essence (sans plomb) (unleaded) gas
essorage dry spin
(d')est east(ern)
étang pond
été summer
éteignez/éteindre switch off
étranger foreign
étudiant student
EU (États-Unis) United States
événement event
évêque bishop
excédent de bagages excess baggage
exigez votre reçu ask for a receipt
exp./expéditeur sender
extincteur fire extinguisher

F(F) French franc
fabriqué en … made in …
faille fault (geol.)
faire la queue derrière la barrière please wait behind barrier
fait main handmade
fait maison homemade
fait sur mesure made to measure
falaise cliff
farine flour
fauteuil (près du) hublot window seat
FB Belgian franc
femmes women (toilets); ladies wear
fer iron
ferme farm
fermé closed
fermé pendant les travaux closed for renovations
fermer la porte close the door
fermeture annuelle closed for vacation [holiday]
fermeture automatique des portières automatic doors
fête nationale National holiday
feux d'artifice fireworks
feux interdits no fires/barbeques
février February
film en version française/originale film in French/original version

fin d'autoroute freeway exit
fin d'interdiction de stationner end of no parking zone
fin de BAU end of hard shoulder
fin de travaux end of construction (*road*)
fleuriste florist
foire fair
... fois par jour ... times a day
forêt forest
frais fresh
frais d'opérations bank charges
français French
frapper knock
frère brother
froid cold
fromage cheese
fumeurs smoking

G

galerie viewing gallery; arcade
garage en sous-sol underground garage
gardien caretaker
gare (ferroviaire/SNCF) railroad station
gare routière haulage depot
gas-oil fuel; diesel
gélules capsules, gel caps
gendarmerie nationale highway police
généraliste general practitioner
gilets de sauvetage lifejackets
gîte d'étape self-catering cottage, B&B
gîte rural self-catering cottage
gouttes drops
gradin tier
grand large
grand bassin deep end
grand magasin department store
grand teint colorfast
grande surface department store
grandes lignes intercity trains
gratuit free
gravillons loose stones (*road*)
grotte cave
groupes acceptés parties welcome
groupe sanguin blood group
guichet box office, ticket office

H

h. hour, o'clock

habit de rigueur formal wear
habitation à loyer modéré (H.L.M) low rent apartment
halle covered market; hall
hammam Turkish bath
haut-lieu historique important historical feature
haute tension high voltage
hauteur limitée à ... m headroom/height restriction: ...
hebdomadaire weekly
heures d'ouverture business hours/opening
heure hour
heures de levée times of collection
hippodrome racetrack
hiver winter
hommes menswear; men (toilets)
hôpital hospital
horaires (d'été/ d'hiver) (summer/ winter) timetable
horaires d'ouverture visiting hours
horaires de vacances holiday timetable
horloger watchmaker
horodateur parking meter
hors service out of order
hôtel de ville town hall
hôtesse de l'air flight attendant
huile oil
hydroptère jetfoil

I

ici here
ici on brade tout prices slashed
ici on vous sert service
immeuble apartment building
impasse dead end
indéformable will not lose its shape
infirmerie infirmary
infirmières nurses
information clientèle customer information
informations de vol flight information
insérez pièce insert coin
insérez votre billet insert ticket
insérez votre carte insert credit card
interactions médicamenteuses interference with other drugs

interdiction de déposer des ordures no littering, no dumping
... interdit (de) … forbidden
interdit à toute circulation traffic-free zone
interdit aux deux roues no access for cyclists and motorcyclists
interdit aux enfants de moins de .... no children under …
interdit aux mineurs non accompagnés no unaccompanied children
interdit sauf aux riverains residents only
intérieur indoor
introduire carte/ les pièces insert card/coins
issue de secours fire exit
itinéraire bis alternative route
itinéraire de déviation diversion, detour
itinéraire obligatoire pour véhicules lourds truck route

<h2>J</h2>

janvier January
jardin public public gardens/park
jardinerie garden center
jeudi Thursday
à jeun on an empty stomach
jeunesse young adult/youth
jeux de ballon interdits no ball games
jouets toys
jour de fermeture: day off/closed
jour férié Bank/National Holiday
le jour de l'An New Year's Day
journal féminin women's magazine
jours de semaine weekdays
jours pairs/impairs (parking allowed on) even/odd days
juillet July
juin June
jus de fruits fruit juices
jusqu'à until

<h2>L</h2>

lac lake
laine wool
laisser descendre les passagers let passengers off first

laisser fondre dans l'eau/la bouche dissolve in water/suck
laisser vos sacs à l'entrée du magasin leave your bags here
langues étrangères foreign languages
lavable en machine machine washable
lavabos wash bowl
lavage à la main hand wash only
laver séparément wash separately
layette baby wear
légumes vegetables
lettre recommandée registered letter
lever de rideau curtain up
libérer votre chambre avant ... vacate your room by …
librairie bookstore
libre vacant, for hire
libre-service bancaire ATM/cashpoint
lieu de bataille battle site
lieu de naissance place of birth
lieu touristique tourist spot
ligne de bus bus route
ligne directe direct service
ligne réservée reserved lane
limitation de vitesse speed limit
lin linen
linge de maison household linen
liquidation clearance
liquide cash
livraisons uniquement deliveries only
livre sterling pound sterling
livres de poche paperbacks
location de voitures car rental
locations accommodations for rent
logement accommodations
loisirs hobbies and interests
lot multi pack
lotion après-soleil after sun lotion
lotissement housing area [estate]
loto lottery
à louer for hire/for rent
lundi Monday
Lundi de Pâques Easter Monday
lunettes de soleil sunglasses
lycée secondary (U.S. high) school

<h2>M</h2>

M. (Monsieur) Mr.

magasin d'antiquités antiques store
magasin de diététique health-food store
magasin de jouets toy store
magasin d'usine factory outlet
mai May
maigre fat-free
mairie town hall
la maison house and home
maison de la presse newsstand
maison de village terraced house
maison à louer house to rent
mandats postaux money orders, postal orders
manoir manor house
manette du signal d'alarme pull for alarm
marais swamp, marsh
marchand de légumes greengrocer's
marchandises hors-taxes duty-free goods
marche walking, hiking
marché market
marché aux puces flea market
mardi Tuesday
mare pond
mars March
match aller first leg
match retour second leg
matière grasse fat content
mazout fuel oil
le matin a.m.
Me (Maître) lawyer (title)
médecin doctor
meilleur au monde world leader
mensuel monthly
menu fixe/à … F set menu/for … francs
menu minceur dieter's menu
mer sea
merci pour vos dons thank you for your contribution
mercredi Wednesday
mère mother
messieurs gentlemen (toilets)
météo weather forecast
métro subway
mettez vos chaînes use chains or snow tires

mettre la pièce et prendre le ticket insert money in machine and remove ticket
meublé self-catering; furnished accommodations
meubles furniture
midi noon
(du) midi south(ern)
minuit midnight
mise en fourrière immédiate unauthorized vehicles will be towed away
Mlle (Mademoiselle) Miss
Mme (Madame) Mrs.
mode d'emploi instructions for use
au moins at least
à moitié prix half price
moniteur (de voile) (sailing) instructor
montagne mountain
montant exact exact change
monument aux morts war memorial
monument classé listed historic building
mosquée mosque
mouillage interdit no anchorage
moulin à vent windmill
mur wall
musée museum

N

natation swimming
navette shuttle service
ne circule pas le dimanche doesn't run on Sundays
ne contient pas de … contains no …
ne laissez pas vos bagages sans surveillance do not leave baggage unattended
ne pas affranchir free post
ne pas avaler not to be taken orally
ne pas brûler do not burn
ne pas consommer sans avis médical consult your doctor before use
ne pas courir no running
ne pas déranger do not disturb
ne pas doubler no passing
ne pas exposer à la lumière do not expose to sunlight
ne pas fumer dans le pont des véhicules no smoking on car decks

ne pas klaxonner use of horn prohibited

ne pas laisser à la portée des enfants keep out of reach of children

ne pas laisser d'objets de valeur dans les voitures do not leave valuables in your car

ne pas marcher sur les pelouses keep off the grass

ne pas parler au conducteur do not talk to the driver

ne pas repasser do not iron

ne pas se pencher hors des fenêtres do not lean out of windows

ne pas traverser les voies do not cross

neige glacée icy (snow)

neige lourde/mouillée/poudreuse heavy/wet/powdery (snow)

nettoyage à sec dry-cleaning

ni repris, ni échange goods cannot be refunded or exchanged

nids de poules potholes

niveau intermédiaire intermediate level

niveau de la mer sea level

Noël Christmas

nom de famille surname, last name

nom de jeune fille maiden name

nom de l'époux/l'épouse name of spouse

non compris not included (in the price), exclusive

non consigné non-returnable

non-fumeurs non-smoking

(du) nord north(ern)

normal two-star/regular gas

normes de qualité quality standard

nos suggestions serving suggestions

notez le numéro de votre emplacement note your parking space number

n'oubliez pas de … don't forget to …

n'oubliez pas de composter votre billet don't forget to validate your ticket

n'oubliez pas le guide remember to tip your guide

nous acceptons les cartes de crédit we accept credit cards

nous achetons et revendons … we buy and sell …

nous déclinons toute responsabilité en cas de dommage ou vol the owners can accept no responsibility for any damage or theft.

nouveau brand-new

nouveautés new titles, new releases

Nouvel an New Year

nouvelle signalisation new traffic system in operation

nouvelles news

nuit night

numéro d'immatriculation car license plate number

numéro de secours emergency number

numéro de siège seat number

numéro de vol flight number

numéro vert toll-free number

numérotez dial

O

objets perdus/trouvés lost property, lost and found

oblitérez votre billet punch your ticket

occasions opportunity, second-hand

(d')occident west(ern)

office du matin morning mass

office du soir evening service

l'office est commencé service in progress

on achète à … currency bought at …

on demande des … … required

on n'accepte pas les cartes de crédit no credit cards

on parle anglais English spoken

on vend à … currency sold at …

opticien/optique optician's

or gold

ordinaire regular (gas)

ordinateurs computers

ordonnance prescription

(de l')orient east(ern)

orientations directions; plan

(de l')ouest west(ern)

ouvert open

ouvert 24 heures sur 24 24-hour service

ouvert le/les … open until/on …

ouvert(ure) open

ouvrir ici open here

pages jaunes yellow pages
pain bread
palais de justice courthouse
palais des congrès convention hall
panier shopping basket
papiers trash
papeterie stationer's
Pâques Easter
paquets packages
par jour/semaine per day/week
parapente parasailing
parc d'attractions amusement park
parcmètre parking meter
parcotrain parking for train users
parfum flavoring, perfume
parking à étages
multi-story parking lot
parking clients/clientèle
customer parking lot
parking longue/courte durée
long-/short-term parking
parking payant pay parking lot
paroisse parish
parterre orchestra [stalls]
à partir de... commencing …
passage à niveau
automatique/manuel railroad crossing
passage clouté pedestrian crossing
passage interdit no access
passage piétons pedestrian crossing
passage sous-terrain underground
passage
passe au lave-vaisselle dishwasher-
proof
passe au micro-ondes microwaveable
pâtes pasta
patientez please wait
patinage ice skating
patins à glaces skates
pâtisserie pastry shop
pavillon pavilion; ward (separate building)
pavillon de banlieue bungalow
payez à l'horodateur pay at the meter
payez à l'ordre de ... payable to …
payer au guichet pay at counter
payez avant de vous servir
pay for gas before filling car

payer comptant pay cash
payez en entrant pay on entry
PCV collect call/reverse-charge
péage toll
pêche à la ligne angling
pêche interdite no fishing
peinture fraîche wet paint
pendant ... jours for … days
pendant le service during services
pendant les repas with food/meals
péniches barges, river boats
péninsule peninsula
pension complète full board
pension de famille guest house
pente incline
Père/père fr. (Father) (rel.)/father
périphérique (extérieur/intérieur)
(outer/inner) ring-road
permis de conduire driver's license
permis obligatoire permit-holders only
pétanque bowls/boules
petit small
petit bassin shallow end
petit déjeuner breakfast
p.ex. e.g.
phare lighthouse; headlight
pharmacie (de garde) (all-night/duty)
drugstore
pièce coin; play
piétons pedestrians
piscine (dé)couverte indoor (outdoor)
swimming pool
piste (skiing) trail
piste bleue ski trail for intermediates
piste cyclable cycle lane/path
piste de cours racing track
piste rouge/noire for advanced skiers
piste verte beginner slope
PJ criminal investigation dept.
place square
placer le ticket derrière le pare-brise
place ticket on windshield
places assises seulement no standing
plage (nudiste) (nudist) beach
plan du magasin store guide
planche à voile windsurf, sailboard;
windsurfing
planche de surf surfboard

plaque minéralogique license plate
plongée interdite no diving
plat du jour dish of the day
plats à emporter take-away
plongeoir diving board
poids de bagages autorisé luggage allowance
poids lourd heavy goods vehicle
poids maximum autorisé en charge load limit
poids net net weight
point d'eau water tap
point de rassemblement meeting place
point de rendez-vous/rencontre meeting point
point de vue view point
point noir blackspot
point téléphone pay phone
poisson fish
poissonnerie fish stall
police (de la route) (traffic) police
pompe à essence pump
pompiers firefighters
pont bridge; deck
pont basculant drawbridge
pont cabines cabin decks
pont des véhicules car deck
pont promenade sun deck
port port, harbor
port du casque obligatoire crash helmets obligatory
porte (d'embarquement) (boarding) gate , door
porte anti-incendie fire door
porte de secours fire (protection) door
les portes seront fermées ... minutes après le début de la représentation doors close ... minutes after performance begins
portier de nuit night porter
posologie dosage
poste post office
poulailler gallery
pour cheveux gras/normaux/secs for oily/normal/dry hair
pour débutants for beginners
pour deux personnes for two

pour obtenir la réception, composez le ... dial ... for reception
pour obtenir un numéro à l'extérieur, composez le ... dial ... for an outside line
pour tout échange, conservez votre ticket de caisse keep your receipt for exchange or refund
pour tous renseignements, s'adresser à for inquiries, see ...
pour usage externe not to be taken internally
2 pour le prix d'1 buy 2 get 1 free
pourboire tip
pousser push
précautions d'emploi instructions for use
premier balcon dress circle
premier étage first (U.S. second) floor
première classe first class
premiers secours first aid
prendre/prenez le ticket take ticket
à prendre après les repas/à la fin des repas take after meals
prenez un jeton à la caisse buy a token at cash desk
préparation rapide easy-cook
présentez vos papiers show your registration documents
présenter vos sacs ouverts à la sortie du magasin show your bags before leaving the store
pressing dry-cleaner's
prière de ... please ...
prière de présenter la somme exacte exact fare, no change given
prière de s'essuyer les pieds avant d'entrer please wipe your feet
prières prayers
primeur greengrocer's
printemps spring
priorité à droite right of way
prise en charge minimum (standard) charge
prise pour rasoirs seulement shavers only
privé private
prix au litre price per liter
prix cassés reduced prices, sale prices

prix des chambres room rate
prix nets no discounts
prochain arrêt bus stopping
prochaine levée à ... h
next collection at …
prochaine séance/visite à ...
next performance/tour at …
proche des commerces/plages
within easy reach of shops/beaches
produits congelés frozen foods
produits diététiques health foods
produits laitiers dairy products
propriété privée private property
P&T Post & telecommunications
PTT Post, Telegraph, Telephone (Bel., Sw.)
puits well
PV parking ticket

Q

quai platform; docks
quartier d'affaires business district
quincaillerie hardware store

R

rabais discount
radeaux de sauvetage lifeboats
rafraîchissements refreshments available
ralentir slow down
ralentissement slowdown [tailback]
ralentisseurs speed bumps
Rameaux Palm Sunday
rangée row, tier
RATP Parisian transport authority
rayon department
réactualisé updated
réduction money off
refermer la barrière keep gate shut
régime diet
remboursement refund
remis à jour updated
renseignements information desk
réparations repairs
représentation performance
RER Paris suburban subway
réseau network
réservations faites à l'avance
advance bookings

**réservations pour la représentation
de ce soir** tickets for tonight
réservé reserved
réservé au fret freight only
réservé aux riverains
access (to residents) only
réservés aux abonnés
season ticket holders only
résidence apartment building
résiste aux chocs shockproof
restez en première
leave your car in first gear
retard de ... mn/h … minutes/hours
delay
retardé delayed
retirez votre argent/carte
take your money/card
retrait des bagages baggage claim
retraits withdrawals
revue magazine, periodical
revue de bandes dessinées comics
rez-de-chaussée ground floor
rez-de-jardin garden apartment
RF French Republic
rien à déclarer nothing to declare
risque d'orages storm warning
riverains autorisés residents only
rivière river
RN national highway
rocade bypass
romans fiction/novels
rond-point circle/roundabout
roulez à droite drive on the right
roulez au pas dead slow
route road
route à péage toll road
route à quatre voies two-lane highway
route départementale secondary road
route en travaux road under
construction
route étroite narrow road
route fermée road closed
route nationale main road
route verglacée icy road
RU (Royaume-Uni) UK
rue street
rue à double sens two-way street
rue à sens unique one-way street

ruelle lane, alley
ruisseau stream

s/ on, at
SA Ltd., Inc.
sables mouvants quicksand
la Saint-Sylvestre New Year's Eve
salle hall; ward
salle à manger dining room
salle d'attente waiting room
salle de bains bathroom
salle de jeux game room
salle de petit déjeuner
breakfast room
salle de réunion conference room
salle en étage seats upstairs
salon lounge
samedi Saturday
SAMU emergency medical service
sanisette automated public toilet
sans arrêt jusqu'à ... non-stop to …
sans entracte no intermission
sans issue dead-end
sans plomb unleaded
sans sucre sugar-free
sauf le ... except on …
saut à l'élastique bungee-jumping
scooter de mer jet ski
sèche-cheveux hairdryer
secours emergency
sel salt
self self-service restaurant
selon arrivage/disponibilité
subject to availability
selon saison according to season
(à la) semaine (per) week
la semaine seulement weekdays only
sens interdit no entry
sens unique one-way street
sentier (balisé) (marked) path, footpath
serrez à droite keep to the right
serrez à gauche keep to the left
service service charge; department
service clientèle customer service
service compris service included
service des chambres room service
service non-compris service not included

service omnibus local [stopping] service
le service n'est pas compris
service charge not included
services de secours emergency services
SI tourist office
servir froid best served chilled
seulement only
siège (près de l')allée aisle seat
**siège réservé aux personnes ayant
des difficultés à se tenir debout** please
give up this seat to the old or infirm
signal d'alarme emergency brake
ski de descente downhill skiing
ski de fond/de randonnée
cross-country skiing
ski hors-piste interdit
no skiing off the trail [off-piste]
ski nautique waterskiing
société de dépannage emergency road
[breakdown] service
soie silk
soins de beauté beauty care
soins intensifs intensive care
soldes (clearance) sale
soldes avant changement d'activités
closing down sale
les soldes ne seront pas échangés
sale goods cannot be exchanged
sommet peak
sonner, SVP please ring the bell
sonnette de nuit night bell
sortie exit, way out
sortie de poids lourds/de camions
truck exit
sortie de secours emergency exit
sortie interdite no exit
sortir par la porte arrière/avant
exit by the rear/front door
SOS amitié helpline
... sous peine d'amende/de poursuites
… under penalty of a fine/prosecution
sous-titré subtitled
sous-vêtements lingerie, underwear
soyez prudent drive carefully
spectacle show
stade stadium
standardiste operator
station de gonflage air pump
station de péage toll booth

station de taxis taxi stand
stationnement autorisé parking permitted
stationnement gênant keep clear
stationnement interdit no parking
station essence/service service/filling station
sucre sugar
(du) sud south(ern)
suivre le mode d'emploi
follow usage instructions
super four-star/super gasoline
sur on, at
sur commande made to order
surf des neiges snowboard
surveillée supervised
SVP (s'il vous plaît) please
syndicat d'initiative tourist office

T

taille économique economy size
taille unique one size fits all
tarif de jour/nuit day/night rate
tarif des consommations price list
tarif normal/réduit first-/second-class
mail
tarif postaux intérieurs/pour
l'étranger inland/overseas postage
tarif réduit/spécial reduced/special fare
tarifs rates
taux d'achat buying rate
taux de change exchange rate
taux de vente selling rate
télécarte phonecard
télécopie faxes sent
téléphérique cable car, gondola
téléphone à cartes card telephone
téléphone bureau work phone number
téléphone de secours emergency
telephone
téléphone domicile home phone number
télévision dans toutes les chambres
TV in every room
tenez votre droite keep to the right
tenir au frais et au sec keep cool and
dry
tenue de ville informal wear
tergal® terylene®
terminer le traitement finish the treatment

terrain d'aviation airfield
terrain vague vacant lot
tête de station taxi stand
TGV (train à grande vitesse)
extra-high-speed train
théâtre de boulevard farce
timbres stamps
tir à l'arc archery
tire-fesses ski tow
tirer pull
tissus fabrics
tissus d'ameublement soft furnishings
titre de transport ticket
tour de hanches/poitrine/taille
hip/chest/waist measurement
tour tower
tous les jours sauf ... every day except ...
tous les plats ci-dessus sont servis
accompagnés de ... all the above
served with ...
tout article cassé doit être payé
all breakages must be paid for
tout compris all inclusive
tout contrevenant sera puni
penalty for traveling without ticket
tout public universal (movie)
toutes directions all directions
toutes les ... heures every ... hours
toutes opérations all transactions
train à supplément supplement to pay
on this train
train auto-couchettes motorail train
train corail local train
train de nuit sleeper (train)
train grandes lignes intercity train
train omnibus local train
tranchée cutting
travaux construction [roadworks] ahead
tribunal courthouse
trousse de secours first-aid kit
TTC inclusive of tax
TVA comprise VAT/sales tax included

U

UE European Union
un train peut en cacher un autre
one train may hide another

213

une collation vous sera servie a snack will be served
une pièce d'identité sera exigée proof of identity required
uniquement only
… unités disponibles … units remaining
utiliser avant … use before …
urgences emergency
usage externe for external use only
usine factory

V

vacances vacation [holiday]
valable jusqu'au valid until …
valeur nutritionnelle nutritional information
valide jusqu'au … valid until …
validez validate
variétés popular music
véhicules lents slow vehicles
véhicules lourds heavy vehicles
veilleuses sidelights, parking lights
vélo bicycle
vélomoteur moped
à vendre for sale
vendredi Friday
verglas black ice
vérifier votre monnaie check your change
vernissage preview, opening
verre glass
vestiaires changing rooms
vêtements pour femmes/hommes ladies wear/menswear
veuillez … please …
veuillez attendre votre tour please wait your turn
veuillez composter votre titre de transport please validate your ticket
veuillez laisser descendre les passagers let passengers off first
veuillez payer avant de vous servir please pay for gas before filling car
veuillez respecter ce lieu de culte please respect this place of worship
viande meat
vidange graissage oil change
vignes vineyard
vignoble winery

villa individuelle detached house
village de vacances holiday village
ville city/town
vin wine
virage dangereux dangerous bend
viseur viewfinder
vitesse limitée à … speed limit …
vitesse maximum maximum speed
VO in original language (movie)
voie lane; platform
voie à double sens two-way traffic
voie ferrée railroad/railway
voie rapide expressway
voie sans issue no through road
voile sailing
voir date fond de la boîte see date on bottom of can/box
voiture car, automobile
vols intérieurs domestic flights
vous êtes ici you are here
voyages travel
vu à … as seen on …

WXYZ

wagon-lit sleeping car
zone à stationnement limité limited parking zone
zone bleue restricted parking zone
zone commerciale shopping area
zone de déchargement loading bay
zone piétonne pedestrian zone

REFERENCE

GRAMMAR

Verbs and their tenses

There are three verb types which follow a regular pattern, their infinitives ending in **-er**, **-ir**, and **-re**, e.g. *to speak* **parler**, *to finish* **finir**, *to return* **rendre**. Here are the most commonly used present, past and future forms.

	PRESENT	PAST	FUTURE
je / j' *I*	parle	ai parlé	parlerai
tu *you* (informal)	parles	as parlé	parleras
il/elle *he/she*	parle	a parlé	parlera
nous *we*	parlons	avons parlé	parlerons
vous *you*	parlez	avez parlé	parlerez
ils/elles *they*	parlent	ont parlé	parleront
je / j' *I*	finis	ai fini	finirai
tu *you* (informal)	finis	as fini	finiras
il/elle *he/she*	finit	a fini	finira
nous *we*	finissons	avons fini	finirons
vous *you*	finissez	avez fini	finirez
ils/elles *they*	finissent	ont fini	finiront
je / j' *I*	rends	ai rendu	rendrai
tu *you* (informal)	rends	as rendu	rendras
il/elle *he/she*	rend	a rendu	rendra
nous *we*	rendons	avons rendu	rendrons
vous *you*	rendez	avez rendu	rendrez
ils/elles *they*	rendent	ont rendu	rendront

Examples: **J'aime la musique.** *I like music.*
Parlez-vous anglais? *Do you speak English?*

There are many irregular verbs whose forms differ considerably.

The most common way to express the past is by using the conjugated form of *to have* **avoir** and the past participle of the verb as demonstrated above. Many verbs, especially verbs related to movement are conjugated with *to be* **être**. In that case the participle agrees with number and gender of the subject.

AVOIR TO HAVE	ÊTRE TO BE
j'ai *I have*	**je suis** *I am*
tu as *you have*	**tu es** *you are*
il/elle a *he/she has*	**il/elle est** *he/she is*
nous avons *we have*	**nous sommes** *we are*
vous avez *you have*	**vous êtes** *you are*
ils/elles ont *they have*	**ils/elles sont** *they are*

Examples:

Nous avons visité Paris. *We visited Paris.*

Elle est arrivée en retard. *She arrived late.*

Elles sont allées au cinéma. *They (fem.) went to the movies.*

Nouns and their determiners

In French, nouns are either masculine or feminine. Generally, nouns ending in **-e**, **-té**, and **–tion** are feminine. There are no other rules that define gender. The definite articles are **le** (mas.) and **la** (fem.). In the plural (**les**) the endings are **-s**, or **-x** but the final **s** or **x** is not pronounced.

Examples: Singular **le train** *the train* Plural **les trains** *the trains*

la table *the table* **les tables** *the tables*

The indefinite articles also indicate gender: **un** (masculine), **une** (feminine), **des** (plural masculine).

Examples: Singular **un livre** *a book* Plural **des livres** *books*

une porte *a door* **des portes** *doors*

Possessive adjectives agree in gender and number with their noun:

	MASCULINE	FEMININE	PLURAL
my	**mon**	**ma**	**mes**
your	**ton**	**ta**	**tes**
his/her/its	**son**	**sa**	**ses**
our	**notre**	**notre**	**nos**
your	**votre**	**votre**	**vos**
their	**leur**	**leur**	**leurs**

Examples:

Je cherche leurs clés. *I'm looking for their keys.*

Où est votre billet? *Where is your ticket?*

C'est ma place. *That's my seat.*

Word order

The conjugated verb comes after the subject.

Example: **Nous habitons à Lyon.** *We live in Lyon.*

Questions are formed by simply raising your voice at the end of the sentence, by adding **Est-ce que** before the sentence or by reversing the order of subject and verb. Subject and verb must be reversed when using key question words like *where* **où**.

Examples:
Vous avez des cartes?	*Do you have maps?*
Est-ce que tu es en vacances?	*Are you on vacation?*
Où est la banque?	*Where is the bank?*

Negations

Negative sentences are generally formed by adding **ne** before the verb and **pas** after it.

Examples:
Nous <u>ne</u> fumons <u>pas</u>.	*We don't smoke.*
Ce <u>n'</u>est <u>pas</u> neuf.	*It's not new.*
Tu <u>n'</u>as <u>pas</u> acheté ça?	*You didn't buy that?*

Imperatives (command form)

Imperative sentences are formed by using the stem of the verb with the appropriate ending.

tu *you* (informal)	**Parle!**	*Speak!*
nous *we*	**Parlons!**	*Let's speak!*
vous *you*	**Parlez!**	*Speak!*
tu *you* (informal)	**Finis!**	*Finish!*
nous *we*	**Finissons!**	*Let's finish!*
vous *you*	**Finissez!**	*Finish!*

Comparatives and superlatives

Comparatives and superlatives are formed by adding *more* **plus** or *less* **moins, le/la plus, le/la moins** before the adjective.

ADJECTIVE	COMPARATIVE	SUPERLATIVE
grand	**plus grand/e**	**le/la/les plus grand/e**
big	*bigger*	*the biggest*
cher	**moins cher**	**le/la/les moins cher**
cheap	*cheaper*	*cheapest*

Example: **Où est la pharmacie <u>la plus</u> proche?**
Where is the nearest pharmacy?

Possessive pronouns

Pronouns serve as substitutes and relate to number and gender.

	SINGULAR	PLURAL
mine	**le mien/la mienne**	**les miens/les miennes**
yours (inf.)	**le tien/la tienne**	**les tiens/les tiennes**
his/her/its	**le sien/la sienne**	**les siens/les siennes**
ours	**le/la nôtre**	**les nôtres**
yours	**le/la vôtre**	**les vôtres**
theirs	**le/la leur**	**les leurs**

Examples: **Nos passeports? <u>Le mien</u> est dans mon sac et <u>le tien</u> est dans la valise.**
Our passports? Mine is in my bag and yours is in the suitcase.

Demonstrative pronouns

The following are used to differentiate <u>this</u> and <u>that</u>:

this one	**celui-ci** (sing. masc.)	**celle-ci** (sing. fem.)
that one	**celui-là** (sing. masc.)	**celle-là** (sing. fem.)
these	**ceux-ci** (pl. masc.)	**celles-ci** (pl. fem.)
those	**ceux-là** (pl. masc.)	**celles-là** (pl. fem.)

Examples: **<u>Celui-ci</u> coûte moins cher.** *This one costs less.*
Je préfère <u>celle-là</u>. *I prefer that one.*

Adjectives

Adjectives describe nouns. They agree with the noun in gender and number. Most of them form the feminine by adding **-e** to the masculine unless the word already ends in **-e**. For the plural, add **-s**. Most adjectives follow the noun.

Examples: **J'ai une auto américain<u>e</u>.** *I have an American car.*
Mon patron est agréab<u>le</u>. *My boss is nice.*

Adverbs and adverbial expressions

Adverbs describe verbs. They are often formed by adding **-ment** to the feminine form of the adjective.

Examples: **Jean conduit lente<u>ment</u>.** *Jean drives slowly.*
Robert conduit rapide<u>ment</u>. *Robert drives fast.*

Some common adverbial time expressions:

tout de suite *immediately* **pas encore** *not yet* **encore** *still*
avant *before* **déjà** *already* **ne ... jamais** *never*

NUMBERS

Note that the French use a comma for a decimal point and a period or space to indicate '000s; e.g. 4.575.000; 265.932; 4,95 FF

0	**zéro** *zayroa*	81	**quatre-vingt-un** *katrer vang ang*
1	**un** *ang*	90	**quatre-vingt-dix**
2	**deux** *dur*		*katrer vang deess*
3	**trois** *trwa*	100	**cent** *sahng*
4	**quatre** *katr*	101	**cent un** *sahng ang*
5	**cinq** *sangk*	102	**cent deux** *sahng dur*
6	**six** *seess*	200	**deux cents** *dur sahng*
7	**sept** *set*	1 000	**mille** *meel*
8	**huit** *weet*	10 000	**dix mille** *dee meel*
9	**neuf** *nurf*	1 000 000	**un million**
10	**dix** *deess*		*ang meelyawng*
11	**onze** *awngz*	2001	**deux mille un**
12	**douze** *dooz*		*dur meel ang*
13	**treize** *trez*	first	**premier(-ière)**
14	**quatorze** *katorz*		*prermyay(-yehr)*
15	**quinze** *kangz*	second	**second/deuxième**
16	**seize** *sez*		*sergawng/durzyem*
17	**dix-sept** *deesset*	third	**troisième** *trwazyem*
18	**dix-huit** *deezweet*	fourth	**quatrième** *katryem*
20	**vingt** *vang*	fifth	**cinquième** *sangkyem*
21	**vingt et un** *vangt ay ang*	once	**une fois** *ewn fwa*
22	**vingt-deux** *vangt dur*	twice	**deux fois** *dur fwa*
30	**trente** *trahngt*	a half	**une moitié**
31	**trente et un** *trahngt ay ang*		*ewn mwatyay*
32	**trente-deux** *trahngt dur*	half a	**un demi réservoir**
40	**quarante** *karahngt*	tank	*ang dermee rayzehrvwar*
50	**cinquante** *sangkahngt*	a quarter	**un quart** *ang kar*
60	**soixante** *swassahngt*	a third	**un tiers** *ang tyehr*
70	**soixante-dix** *swassahngt deess*	a pair of	**deux/une paire de**
71	**soixante et onze** *swassahngt ay awngz*		*dur/ewn pehr der*
80	**quatre-vingts** *katrrevang*	a dozen	**une douzaine de**
			ewn doozayn der

DAYS

Monday	**lundi** *langdee*
Tuesday	**mardi** *mardee*
Wednesday	**mercredi** *mehrkrerdee*
Thursday	**jeudi** *zhurdee*
Friday	**vendredi** *vahngdrerdee*
Saturday	**samedi** *samdee*
Sunday	**dimanche** *deemahngsh*

MONTHS

January	**janvier** *zhahngvyay*
February	**février** *fayvryay*
March	**mars** *marss*
April	**avril** *avreel*
May	**mai** *may*
June	**juin** *zhwang*
July	**juillet** *zhweeyeh*
August	**août** *oot*
September	**septembre** *septahngbr*
October	**octobre** *oktobr*
November	**novembre** *novahngbr*
December	**décembre** *daysahngbr*

DATES

It's …	**Nous sommes …** *noo som*
July 10	**le dix juillet** *ler dee zhweeyeh*
Tuesday, March 1	**mardi premier mars** *mardee prermyay marss*
yesterday	**hier** *yehr*
today	**aujourd'hui** *oazhoordwee*
tomorrow	**demain** *dermang*
this …/last …	**ce …/… dernier** *ser/dehrnyay*
next week	**la semaine prochaine** *la sermayn proshayn*
every month/year	**tous les mois/ans** *too lay mwa/zahng*
on [at] the weekend	**(pendant) le weekend** *(pahngdahng) ler weekend*

SEASONS

spring	**le printemps**	*ler prangtahng*
summer	**l'été**	*laytay*
fall [autumn]	**l'automne**	*loatonn*
winter	**l'hiver**	*leevehr*
in spring	**au printemps**	*oa prangtahng*
during the summer	**pendant l'été**	*pahngdahng laytay*

GREETINGS

Happy birthday!	**Bon anniversaire!**	*bo naneevehrsehr*
Merry Christmas!	**Joyeux Noël!**	*zhwahyur nowell*
Happy New Year!	**Bonne année!**	*bo nannay*
Best wishes!	**Meilleurs vœux!**	*mayurr vur*
Congratulations!	**Félicitations!**	*fayleesseetasyawng*
Good luck!	**Bonne chance!**	*bon shahngss*
Have a good trip!	**Bon voyage!**	*bawng vwahyazh*

PUBLIC HOLIDAYS

National holidays in France (F), Belgium (B) and Switzerland (CH):

January 1	**Nouvel An**	New Year's Day	F	CH	B
January 2				CH	
May 1	**Fête du Travail**	Labor Day	F		
May 8	**Fête de la Libération**	Victory Day (1945)	F		
July 14	**Fête Nationale**	Bastille Day	F		
July 21	**Fête Nationale**	National Holiday			B
August 1	**Fête Nationale**	National Holiday		CH	
August 15	**Assomption**	Assumption Day	F		B
November 1	**Toussaint**	All Saints Day	F		B
November 11	**Armistice**	Armistice Day	F		B
December 25	**Noël**	Christmas	F	CH	B
December 26	**Saint-Etienne**	St Stephen's Day		CH	

Movable dates:

Vendredi-Saint	Good Friday		CH	
Lundi de Pâques	Easter Monday	F	CH	B
Ascension	Ascension	F	CH	B
Lundi de Pentecôte	Pentecost Monday	F	CH	B

The official time system uses the 24-hour clock. However, in ordinary conversation, time is generally expressed as shown below, often with the addition of **du matin** (morning), **de l'après-midi** (afternoon) or **du soir** (evening).

Excuse me. Can you tell me the time?	**Pardon. Pouvez-vous me dire l'heure?** *pardawng poovay voo mer deer lurr*
It's …	**Il est …** *eel eh*
five past one	**une heure cinq** *ewn urr sangk*
ten past two	**deux heures dix** *dur zurr deess*
a quarter past three	**trois heures et quart** *trwa zurr ay kar*
twenty past four	**quatre heures vingt** *katr urr vangt*
twenty-five past five	**cinq heures vingt-cinq** *sangk urr vangt sangk*
half past six	**six heures et demie** *see zurr ay dermee*
twenty-five to seven	**sept heures moins vingt-cinq** *set urr mwang vangt sangk*
twenty to eight	**huit heures moins vingt** *weet urr mwang vang*
a quarter to nine	**neuf heures moins le quart** *nurf urr mwang ler kar*
ten to ten	**dix heures moins dix** *dee zurr mwang deess*
five to eleven	**onze heures moins cinq** *awngz urr mwang sangk*

twelve o'clock (noon/midnight)	**midi/minuit** *meedee/meenwee*
at dawn	**à l'aube** *a loab*
in the morning	**le matin** *ler matang*
during the day	**pendant la journée** *pahngdahng la zhoornay*
before lunch	**avant le repas** *avahng ler rerpa*
after lunch	**après le repas** *apreh ler rerpa*
in the afternoon	**dans l'après-midi** *dahng lapreh-meedee*
in the evening	**dans la soirée** *dahng la swaray*
at night	**la nuit** *la nwee*
I'll be ready in five minutes.	**Je serai prêt(e) dans cinq minutes.** *zher serray preh(t) dahng sang meenewt*
He'll be back in a quarter of an hour.	**Il sera de retour dans un quart d'heure.** *eel serra der rertoor dahng zang kar durr*
She arrived an hour ago.	**Elle est arrivée il y a une heure.** *el eh tareevay eel ee a ewn urr*
The train leaves at …	**Le train part à …** *ler trang par a*
13:04	**treize heures quatre** *trez urr katr*
0:40	**zéro heures quarante** *zayroa urr karahngt*
10 minutes late/early	**dix minutes en retard/en avance** *dee meenewt ahng rertar/ahng navahngss*
5 seconds fast/slow	**cinq secondes d'avance/de retard** *sangk sergawngd davahngss/der rertar*
from 9am to 5pm	**de neuf heures à cinq/dix-sept heures** *der nurf urr a sangk/deesset urr*
between 8am and 2pm	**entre huit heures et deux/quatorze heures** *ahngtr weet urr ay dur/katorz urr*
I'll be leaving by …	**Je partirai avant …** *zher parteeray avahng*
Will you be back before …?	**Est-ce que vous serez revenu(e)/ de retour avant …?** *ess ker voo serray rervernew/der rertoor avahng*
We'll be here until …	**Nous serons ici jusqu'à …** *noo serrawngeesee zhewska*